T0305081

A Research Agenda for Global Rural Development

**Elgar Research Agendas** outline the future of research in a given area. Leading scholars are given the space to explore their subject in provocative ways, and map out the potential directions of travel. They are relevant but also visionary.

Forward-looking and innovative, Elgar Research Agendas are an essential resource for PhD students, scholars and anybody who wants to be at the forefront of research.

Titles in the series include:

A Research Agenda for Climate Justice
*Edited by Paul G. Harris*

A Research Agenda for Federalism Studies
*Edited by John Kincaid*

A Research Agenda for Media Economics
*Edited by Alan B. Albarran*

A Research Agenda for Environmental Geopolitics
*Edited by Shannon O'Lear*

A Research Agenda for Studies of Corruption
*Edited by Alina Mungiu-Pippidi and Paul M. Heywood*

A Research Agenda for Digital Politics
*Edited by William H. Dutton*

A Research Agenda for Environmental Economics
*Edited by Matthias Ruth*

A Research Agenda for Academic Integrity
*Edited by Tracey Bretag*

A Research Agenda for Entrepreneurship Policy
*Edited by David Smallbone and Friederike Welter*

A Research Agenda for Global Rural Development
*Terry Marsden, Claire Lamine and Sergio Schneider*

A Research Agenda for Social Wellbeing
*Neil Thin*

A Research Agenda for Territory and Territoriality
*Edited by David Storey*

A Research Agenda for Human Rights
*Edited by Michael Stohl and Alison Brysk*

A Research Agenda for Knowledge Management and Analytics
*Edited by Jay Liebowitz*

A Research Agenda for Heritage Tourism
*Edited by Maria Gravari-Barbas*

A Research Agenda for Border Studies
*James W. Scott*

A Research Agenda for Sales
*Edited by Fernando Jaramillo and Jay Prakash Mulki*

# A Research Agenda for Global Rural Development

TERRY MARSDEN
*Sustainable Places Research Institute, Cardiff University, UK*

CLAIRE LAMINE
*INRAE-Ecodéveloppement, France*

SERGIO SCHNEIDER
*Department of Sociology and the Graduate Programs of Sociology and Rural Development, Federal University of Rio Grande do Sul, Brazil*

**Elgar Research Agendas**

Edward Elgar
PUBLISHING

Cheltenham, UK • Northampton, MA, USA

Published by
Edward Elgar Publishing Limited
The Lypiatts
15 Lansdown Road
Cheltenham
Glos GL50 2JA
UK

Edward Elgar Publishing, Inc.
William Pratt House
9 Dewey Court
Northampton
Massachusetts 01060
USA

A catalogue record for this book
is available from the British Library

Library of Congress Control Number: 2020944222

This book is available electronically in the **Elgar**online
Social and Political Science subject collection
http://dx.doi.org/10.4337/9781788974196

ISBN 978 1 78897 418 9 (cased)
ISBN 978 1 78897 419 6 (eBook)

Printed and bound by CPI Group (UK) Ltd, Croydon, CR0 4YY

*Dedication*

*Philip Lowe, Larry Busch and Teodor Shanin were inspirational thinkers and writers on many of the themes that emerge in this book. Sadly, as we were composing it, all three passed away; and so we would like to dedicate this work to their long-lasting contributions, in so many ways, to the field.*

*Not least they all shared an unusual breadth as well as depth of knowledge and insight into the intellectual development of the field of rural development as an interdisciplinary activity. They all authoritatively strode across the disciplinary boundaries of rural sociology, peasant studies, geography, politics, and the sociology of science and environment, and indeed dedicated their professional lives to these very transgressions and international comparative researches. We hope this book augments their legacies.*

# Contents

# Acknowledgements

It is something unusual, even extraordinary, that the three of us managed to complete this book precisely in the midst of the coronavirus (Covid-19) pandemic crisis.

This was largely possible thanks to our working conditions, especially the 'home office'. In a sense, it made us more productive and improved our interaction over the internet, which has become, at the time of writing, the new normal in our lives.

For that, we have to thank our universities and our colleagues at work – thank you very much.

However, the understanding and collaboration of our family members, spouses, children, companions were also decisive. To all of them, our deepest thanks for their patience and understanding.

The authors particularly wish to thank Steven Goundrey (Sustainable Places Research Institute at Cardiff University) for his help with various aspects of the manuscript, as well as Matthew Pitman, Stephanie Hartley and colleagues at Edward Elgar, both for first suggesting this venture, and for their support and patience.

Thanks also to the Marsden (expanding) family of Mary Anne, Joseph, Tilly and Bobby, Hannah, Tom and Timmy, for their constant interest in the venture. Terry would also like to acknowledge the very valuable and continuing discussions and related collaborations with Tim Lang, Erik Millstone and Paul Hebinck.

Claire Lamine wants to thank her colleagues and students, especially in France and in Brazil, for the discussions held together on many issues tackled in this book, and particularly Sibylle Bui, Floriane Derbez, Lucile Garçon, Nassima

Hakimi, Morgan Jenatton, Pedro Lopez Merino, Juliano Palm, Terena Peres, Florette Rengard and Martina Tuscano for the work carried out during their PhDs and Masters. The research carried out in France and Brazil benefited from the support of the Franco–Brazilian CAPES-COFECUB Programme, the *Fondation de France* foundation and the INRAE.

Sergio Schneider would also like to thank his students and colleagues at the GEPAD (Study and Research Group on Agriculture, Food and Development), as well as Jan Douwe van der Ploeg, Paul Hebinck, on nested markets, and Alexander Nikulin, Alexander Kurakin, Ye Jingzhong, He Congzhi, Wu Huifang, Ben Cousins, Ruth Hall, Sergio Sauer and Paulo Niederle for the rich discussions on BRICS agrarian studies. Sergio is grateful also for the inspiring exchanges with Tim Lang, Henry Bernstein, Leandro Vergara-Camus and Ian Scoones during a period living in England in 2015 and 2016. Special thanks go to Moisés Balestro, Abel Cassol, Natália Brasil and Potira Preiss, with whom he has been working in Brazil. He also appreciates the support of CNPq in the form of a Scientific Research Grant and FAPERGS for supporting his research projects.

# Introduction to *A Research Agenda for Global Rural Development*

## 1. Setting some seeds for the research agenda in rural social science

For our contribution to the Elgar Research Agendas series, we three long-standing rural and environmental researchers have come together to begin to answer the timely and creative question of, *what is the current research agenda for rural development studies?* This is clearly an ambitious and challenging question too. As authors, we have been pursuing internationally comparative research over most of our long careers, as well as being based deeply within our own national research cultures in France, the UK and Brazil. We have also increasingly evolved as interdisciplinary rural researchers, as indeed the sub-disciplines of rural sociology, geography and development, and rural social science have merged not least as a result of the wider challenges of the environmentalization of social science (see Marsden (ed) 2018). Moreover, this is not unrelated to the radical questions being posed about global rural development in a post-colonial, increasingly globalized and 'underdeveloping' as well as 'developing' world. There are clearly many routes to rural 'development' and clearly competing ideas and theorizations of modernities.

Indeed, the whole question of rural 'development', it can be argued, is now in need of critical 'surgery' in a non-deterministic, open-ended and post-disciplinary way. As authors, we are strongly rooted in and associated with the traditional disciplines of rural sociology and rural geography, but this book, in both its critical reviews of the 'state of the art' and its suggestions for the future research agenda, adopts a wider canvas. This is to contribute to how research *both on and with* rural peoples in their places and spaces needs to be directed and practiced in (as we start in Chapter 1) an increasingly urban, resource intensive and cosmopolitan world; where mobilities, sustainabilities and a host of vulnerabilities continue to collide. Without doubt, the study of the rural can no longer be seen as the study of stable, traditional communities, if it ever could. Rather, we propose to apply a critical conceptual mirror to the rural, examining its re-location and re-positioning at the heart of global problems and increasingly cosmopolitan cultures. Ruralities and the rural experience become more significant in a globalized and cosmopolitan world. This necessitates a post-disciplinary approach, one that, for instance, blends disciplines like anthropology, environmental politics, heterodox economics and environmental philosophy into its vectors of scholarly endeavour and investigation.

## 2.   A working conceptual model for global rural development: the emerging rural development agenda

This volume explores and develops key areas and themes of the rural development research agenda by focussing upon eight key dimensions (see Figure 0.1): *new ruralities, governance, power and transformation, financialization, land and bio-sphere rights, agroecology, family farming,* and *markets and exchange.* We have prioritized these areas for several reasons. First, and overall, they clearly exemplify and analytically and conceptually develop all eight of the more generic and cross-cutting themes outlined below. Second, we argue that in a contemporary sense the eight key dimensions represent critical areas for the research agenda for the increasingly interdisciplinary and transdisciplinary areas of rural development. And third, the chapters all combine a retrospective, contemporary and prospective lens to different bodies of international research and research practice, which are of critical concern. In each of the chapters we also attempt to provide an internationally comparative perspective, by citing empirical work from our own both individual and collaborative research ventures over the past decades. We confess that these examples are related most notably to our varied but long-running empirical experiences in the UK, France, and Brazil, and more widely in Latin America, Europe and Southeast Asia. In all of the chapters, however, we also cite the international work of many other rural scholars. We will come back to critically consider and reflect on the progress we have made in developing the eight meta-themes outlined above in the conclusion to the volume.

As we envisage in Figure 0.1, the proceeding eight research agenda chapters are both interlinked by a set of wider transversal dimensions that stem broader social science questions, the contribution of rural studies to these, and the ways in which interdisciplinary and transdisciplinary research may proceed. We outline these here at the start of the volume, almost as a set of questions and postulates. They are then taken up in varying degrees in the eight substantive chapters. Then, in conclusion, and as a way of creating some critical and prospective synthesis, we will re-address these cross-cutting themes. We recognize, thus, that our *eight-by-eight* approach here is not exhaustive of the themes and topics that could be included in such an ambitious agenda. However, we believe that this framing of the rural research agenda does act as a significant and creative 'conceptual and empirical compass', which can direct and stimulate rural researchers and scholars over the coming decades.

So let us now outline the wider transversal themes here by way of concluding this introduction to the volume. These are framed largely as a set of critical questions. There are some that we will return to in the conclusion to the book, while others are embedded in varying degrees in the eight succeeding substantive chapters. They are thus a conceptual framing device in which to embed the substantive chapters and indeed to encourage readers to make links between the chapters (as suggested in Figure 0.1). They are also, more pragmatically, a way of containing the substantially wide and diverse focus on the overall question (see above) that we have set ourselves: *what is the current research agenda for rural development studies?*

## 3.    The transversal themes and the framing of meta-research questions

1. **Socio-political dynamics:** This concerns the power and politics involved in contestations between hierarchical/distributed control and governance, and the question of the re-democratization and empowerment of power relations over space and through institutions (see Chapter 2 on governance, 3 on power and 5 on land). What are the different power geometries and geographies that are unfolding in rural areas and in urban–rural relations? Will the post-carbon transition lead to just a continuation of centralized systems of control by the public, community and private actors, and public institutions? And/or can we see new experimental associational and institutional arrangements being developed that are emerging in the interstices of established systems of governance and governance practices? Indeed this is inherently a dialectical process, including both conventional forms of domesticated governance and politics (chapters 1 and 2), and wider, more empowering systems of association that re-energize rural

and urban relations (e.g. in the form of new solidarity movements, new digital-based inter-communication, climate change emergence, extinction movements, etc.). On the other hand, as we shall see in Chapter 2, the rise of counter-nationalist and populist movements, not least drawing upon traditional rural values and property rights, are creating opposite tendencies towards what we term 'disruptive governance'. Are we moving away from a 'post-political' stance in rural research? How do we develop explicit political and ecological integrations?

As many cities and towns cope with combinations of the ecological and neo-liberal crisis that is engulfing them – not least in higher levels of in-migration on continental scales, the social and political reactions to this crisis is to 'blame the other' – often those indeed who have been most dispossessed from the crisis in the first instance. Part of the unintended consequences of the ecological and neo-liberal crisis of reducing resources and choices for many urban residents and dispossessed migrants to cities, is then a political shift towards new authoritarian 'solutions' that express themselves as disruptive forms of governance. We see this in Brazil and the UK and many parts of Europe at the moment. The agri-food and rural sectors become caught up in these geopolitical shifts either directly or indirectly.

2. **Socio-economic dynamics:** There are concentrated processes of financialization and profit abstraction versus re-territorialized spaces for new and reproduced 'petty capitals', small businesses and profit sharing (see Chapter 4 on financialization). Here we see growing social inequalities leading to new politics and new social movements, and the growth of alternative financing arrangements outwith the dominant financialized frameworks. A key question here is, what are going to be the features of the post-carbonized economy? What degrees of partial, radical decoupling with prevailing industrialized and intensive systems of production and circulation will emerge? And to what extent will rural areas become sites for the 're-coupling' and reconnecting of new, more sustainable forms of (more distributed?) production and circulation? What will be the nature of rural work in this transformation?

3. **Socio-natural dynamics:** Are new dualisms emerging *within nation states* rather than just between them? We see the rise of concentrated land and bio-sphere rights and enclosures versus multispecies rights, and 'extinction' movements that stress the re-attribution of new common pool resources and sustainable place making. What moves are there towards new, more nexus-based eco-system matrices of rural relations? There is a potential broadening of the scope of agri-food dynamics to wider nexus and circular economy concerns on the one hand, and linking to wider

social and urban movements on the other. A deeper understanding of what 'market relations' now mean in this more diversified rural context is necessary (see Chapter 8 on markets and exchange). The role of the social relations underpinning property rights (Chapter 5) is critical here; are they still based upon class lines, or other criteria?

4. **Transformational ontologies:** The chapters will be contributions to co-produced and pragmatist, multi-perspective approaches to enacting agrarian transformations; and thus of relevance in the practice of rural development research as well as the theory. This involves questions such as: Who are the key actors and assemblages in creating transformations in rural processes and practices? How and by what means are they enacted and mobilized? How much institutional support can and should they expect? How can we build new and adapted rural transformational theory that builds upon earlier transition management models (see chapters 3 and 6)? How do we build the ecological and the bio-physical into these models? How is power assembled and then mobilized? How can knowledge be enacted effectively?

5. **Epistemological theories of rural development in post-colonial contexts:** We realize the significance of the fact that 'development' is different in different contexts, but that does not deny the significance of real place-based sustainable rural development in its proper and sensitized context. This requires new epistemologies that are sensitized to place-based agency and endogenous and indigenous forms of rural development. What do we mean by sustainable rural development 'in context'; can and should it be generalized or generalizable?

6. **Towards pragmatic pathways of rural development at multi-scale levels:** How do we bring together more structuralist and more constructivist approaches, given that both are needed in order to foster real sustainable transformations? What examples do we have; is this lacking in the literature?

7. **The contested nature of the post-carbon transition**, the politics (and economics of denial) versus new sustainable organizations, social innovations and institutional innovations; also the tyranny of short-term thinking and short-term politics – how do we overcome these obstacles; what sorts of political projects do we need to support? How will agro-ecological processes and practices develop in the post-carbon transition (Chapter 6), and what will be the role of transdisciplinary research in progressing these transformations?

8. Finally, there are **the social and political dilemmas surrounding new rural development pathways**, and in rural society more generally, demographic and consumer-based threats and challenges to the authenticity

of rural life and society. At the heart of rural development should come understandings of how rural (and urban) people comprehend the dilemmas and contradictions that confront them. Here lies a tension between managing and surviving in their own daily and family/domestic practices, but coping with changes that may for at least a time make them more vulnerable. Why should we expect already vulnerable people to endure the costs of change and transition when it does not seem to be in their short- or medium-term interests? How important are effective forms of community leadership in this regard? Can we expect community leaders to emerge automatically and autonomously, or do they need to be fosters – but by what means can this be achieved? What will be the effects of continued demographic shifts on the politics and economies of rural places? These represent significant and often contradictory dilemmas for rural people and rural researchers. What are the implications for how we go about our research evolving effective co-production methods and practices?

**Figure 0.1**     Agenda: global rural development flow chart

# 1. New ruralities and centralities for rural development

## 1. Introduction: rural enclosures and urban domestications

It is common to assume that in the second demographic transition, argued to have begun around 1950, the world is becoming less rural. By 2007 more than 50 per cent of the world's population was urban, even though the developing world still remains more rural than urban. Countries like the US, Canada, Sweden, Australia, China and Japan have experienced or are experiencing a severe decline, with 'attractive' urban living standards being seen as the major cause. The majority of countries in the world experienced rapid decreases in rural populations between 1981 and 2016. This was especially the trend in newly industrializing and urbanizing countries in East and South Asia, Latin America and parts of Africa. The rural population of China has decreased by 45.9 per cent during the past 35 years, whilst the figure in Brazil has almost reached 60 per cent (Li et al., 2019).

Increasingly it would seem that the burgeoning numbers living in urban areas, and indeed many of these in the intermediate suburban areas surrounding these expanding city regions, are experiencing, we can argue, a new process of *cosmopolitan domestication*. This has of course been a feature since early industrialization in 19th-century Europe, but by the middle of the 20th century it had become a dominant and mass demographic shift. By the start of the 21st century the world had witnessed a scale of con-urbanization that was unprecedented, with urban population densities increasing whilst becoming, at the same time, more dependent upon distanced rural resources (such as foods, energy and minerals). People are continuing to lose their rural roots, identities and ways of living as they become re-domesticated in urban – 'post-natural' – environments that make them, somewhat paradoxically, even more dependent upon complex supply chains and services in order for them to survive (see Scott, 2017).

In turn, and importantly, many new urban dwellers lose the wherewithal and the skills to self-procure as they become increasingly reliant on purchasing commodified and manipulated goods and services. Urban domestication is often taken for granted as a sign of 'progress', and indeed progressive modernization, part of the 'knowledge economy' and successful economic growth. It historically and in a contemporary sense of course tends to demand more commoditization of life, as opposed to self-provisioning and self-sufficiency. Naturally this is a highly variegated process and certainly hides high levels of differentiated urban–rural relations.

We want to suggest here that this massive and historically unique process currently underway places rural development in a significantly re-located and critical position. The highly conglomerated and interconnected cities of China, for example, become increasingly dependent upon rural-based resources, not least rocks and minerals. A hundred miles west of Shanghai, one can witness the devastation of rural hills and mountains, quarried for their urban building materials. Around many more established cities (like London or Sao Paulo) vastly extended food supply chains spread not only to their geographically close rural hinterlands, but also to internationalized importing platforms for fresh fruits and vegetables (such as the Sao Francisco valley in North East Brazil, or the rural heartlands of Ghana). Rural people not only move temporarily or permanently to these cities, but even if they stay on in their rural heartlands many become affected by the urban and cosmopolitan insatiable demands for rural-based resources. Thus we have to recognize that the age of urban cosmopolitanism comes with new human and cultural processes of rural development, urban re-domestication and, indeed, rural enclosure. These twin processes become a major feature of global rural development, as we shall see.

As Li et al., 2019 (p140) comment:

> Rural decline is an inevitable process associated with the transformation from an agrarian to the urban-industrialized economy, and further on to the knowledge economy. However, rural decline is not pre-destined. It is by the interactions between rural areas and the external environment that rural communities either grow, decline or even vanish. How rural evolution proceeds depends upon the capacity of the rural communities, which respond to external changes through adjusting their internal components and structure. In this process, rural communities of different geographical conditions, natural resource endowments and social relationships, as well as people's values, attitudes and institutions will make different responses, which finally lead to different evolution patterns and outcomes.

Given then an ongoing process of what we might term 'urban domestication', it now seems that significant differences may be occurring between the expanding and densely living urban and the more sparsely populated rural peoples. For instance:

- Mortality in the South at least tends to be higher in rural areas than in urban areas, largely owing to higher mortality of children under the age of five. This stems from many rural areas having lower incomes, poorer nutrition, less clean water and sanitation, and fewer medical services than their urban counterparts. But this is a mean observation, and as we know urban domestication is recreating many health disadvantages (higher obesity, higher vulnerability to non-communicable diseases like diabetes, high rates of water and air contamination, and higher rates of anti-microbial vulnerability) (ODI, 2016).

- Fertility in rural areas also tends to be higher than in urban areas. That may also be a function of lower incomes, but may be associated with agriculture too, since it is easier for mothers to combine child raising and farm work compared with working in a factory – and the children tend to help on the farm from an earlier age.

- The combination of higher mortality and fertility can delay the process of urban domestication so that rates of natural population growth can be higher in rural areas, although most rural areas in the South experience out-migration to the cities, such that these grow proportionately faster.

- Without migration out of rural areas, the higher natural rates of population growth in rural areas would tend to ruralize rather than urbanize countries. Migration is thus essential for continuing and fuelling the process of urban domestication; and it seems that at least under current carbonized systems of economic growth, without urbanization, economic 'growth' would be severely impaired.

- Urban domestication can, especially for women and girls, bring improved living and reproductive standards, and is leading to higher levels of aggregate carbonized energy use, creating far larger ecological 'footprints' in the all-consuming cities. As urban domestication implies far higher levels of consumption, and correspondingly lower levels of direct participation in production (e.g. of energy and foods, etc.), surrounding rural hinterlands become critical for supply and equating this spatial and ecological dependency.

- If more and more of us are to varying degrees effectively 'domesticated urbanists', i.e. we are locked into path-dependent lifestyles and consumption patterns not of our own making, what effects does this have: (i) on existing rural areas and peoples; (ii) on urban people's resilience or vulnerability; and (iii) on creating opportunities or obstacles for post-carbonized forms of transformation? In short, how will the current demographic fix play out once it is realized that the agglomerative economic and cultural advantages of the city no longer apply? And what does this suggest to us about the re-calibration of rural and urban livelihoods? Is not the triumphalist 21st-century city not fit for purpose as the world strives towards post-carbonism? Should we not at the very least seriously question the extreme processes of urban domestication that have been unleashed (especially since 1950), and indeed the profound spatial fixes upon which this process has depended?

- Of course experiences of social inequality, poverty and social exclusion are now rife in both urban and rural settings. But it remains a stark fact that migrations to the city are often an expression of desperation and distress in rural living standards, whilst return migration (especially in the North) is often associated with a quest to retain non-urban domesticated ways of living for the urban relatively rich and successful.

- Today rural–urban relations are at something of a turning point: will the urbanization trend that has risen from 20 per cent in 1960 to 46 per cent in 2014 continue in the face of wholesale transformations in our use of energy, material resources, and food supplies? What will be the main pathways towards more sustainable forms of rural development given that, more than ever, they will have to be the bases for producing and generating these forms of renewable and bio-spherical natural resources? Will we undergo a 'third demographic transition' with huge dispersals of now urban-domesticated populations re-occupying rural hinterlands? Will rural areas face new forms of 'urban-based enclosure' where their resources are appropriated under conditions of more extreme resource depletion for the purposes of satisfying stronger states and hegemons?

## 2.   Urban domestication, rural enclosure and pathways to empowerment

Now we can begin to draw what some might regard as a new societal and cultural dichotomy between the urban and the rural in the context of our current global and indeed globalizing ecological and economic crisis. This does not of course suggest that the rural and the urban are disconnected. They are quite the opposite, in that they increasingly 'feed off each other'. The purpose of this first chapter of the volume, then, is to conceptually re-ask important sociological and geographical questions, such as, what is it like to be urban; what is it like to experience rurality? What is the nature of rurality in post-modern society when hyper-mobilities collide with new ecological vulnerabilities and social inequalities? And, importantly, do these conditions engender a new transition to re-territorialized and, as Latour (2018) suggests, re-territorialized processes as a reaction to global and globalized ecological and economic crisis? Somewhat ironically, rural places again become places to put down roots, almost as an antidote to globalization and ecological crisis.

Further chapters in this book will attempt to explore some of these major cardinal points in this new rural–urban compass and consider key aspects of the academic research agenda as we progress (or indeed re-gress) into the post-carbonized transition, during a period when the coherence and perhaps dominance of the neo-liberal hegemony is now, at the very least, fragmenting (see Tilzey, 2019). Clearly we argue here in this chapter that it is possible to posit that the process of urban or metropolitan domestication has and continues to be a global and somewhat universal process affecting not just urban populations but those in many rural areas as well. Access to diverse consumption patterns, high levels of mobility, the opportunities choice brings, tend now to be accounted as a global universal. In rural areas, however, the dangers are that the very demands that such (urban) domestications place on natural resources significantly affect rural areas.

This is most commonly witnessed by the recent round of rural 'land grabbing' – or the new enclosures. Since 2007, an estimated 220 million hectares has been acquired by foreign investors in the global South (see Chapter 5). Intensive forms of increasingly vulnerable urban domestication are being offset by more intensive and profound forms of financialized enclosure in many rural regions, especially those areas – such as in Africa and Latin America – where pre-existing rules and governance regimes are relatively weak to resist these financialized pressures (Chapter 4). Whilst much has been made of the new rounds of 'land grabbing' as new expressions of hyper-financialization and the expression of 'accumulation by dispossession' (Harvey, 2003) by extracting and exporting primary natural resources, it is also the case that this is indeed a by-product of the intensive process of urban domestication being experienced in countries like China, the majority of South Asian countries and (food and water insecure but rapidly urbanizing) Middle Eastern oil states. Expanding and densely populated cities rely upon vast and increasing ecological and indeed rural 'footprints'. It is argued that London's is the equivalent size of Spain. But this is of course a generality and a metaphor. In reality, cities lie at the epicentres of immense and complex supply chains for natural and processed resources, like water, rocks, minerals, foods and plants and animals.

Thus intensive forms of urban domestication are going hand in hand with selective and intensive forms of new rounds of rural enclosure, now on a globalized scale. Just as the early urban manufacturing cities demanded former rural labour and resource commodification and enclosures in the 18th and 19th centuries, in the 21st this has massively intensified with networks of mega-cities demanding globally extractive enclosures across the globe. See for instance the development of China's 'belt road initiative'. We have to recognize therefore that the growth of mega-urbanization is coming at an increasingly high material and ecological cost. And it is one that may not be sustainable.

If we conceive of mega-urban domestication and rural enclosures as 'two sides of the same coin' at least in hyper-capitalist and carbonist hegemonic systems, this also begins to raise questions of who is enslaving whom, and who is empowering whom? Or to put it another way: what types of power and empow-ering relations are these interdependencies creating? Not all rural areas are caught up in webs of extractive enclosure, with many (in Western Europe, for instance), it would seem, able to create more autonomous systems of empow-erment that enable endogenous social and economic development to take hold. Similarly, in the midst of the big 'high rise' city we find counter-hegemonic forces developing, not least around access to sustainable foods, housing and energy schemes. Indeed the spectre of post-carbonism shows some signs of also encouraging post-capitalist and certainly post-neo-liberal modes of social organization and profit sharing that are 'counter-hegemonic' in that they create the social conditions for social empowerment over consumerist 'enslavement'. Hence we begin to witness counter-movements in both the urban and rural realms, and indeed, as with the food solidarity movements in Brazil and Southern Europe, new emancipatory urban–rural relations that are disrupting our earlier domestication–enclosure dialectic.

We can conceive of this as not so much 'accumulation by dispossession' as new forms of *empowerment by association*. The latter tendency is becoming a more dynamic force in many urban and rural settings and is creating new innovative conditions for social action and sustainability strategies in many rural regions. Hence empowerment by association can be considered a transformative force, as we shall discuss in Chapter 3, not least around agroecology and new empow-ered urban food consumption (Chapter 6). People can, as the transition from capitalist carbonism accelerates, find the space and social power to create new associations and practices that are based upon different and more emancipated forms of organization. Hence the city is not merely a site of domestication and disempowerment, just like the countryside is not merely a place of enslave-ment or enclosure. Therefore, the complex unfolding of the tendencies for both domestication and enclosure now have to be modified and qualified by considering how new sites and networks of association and empowerment can take hold.

Thus in writing this volume we have realized (at the particular vantage point of 2020) that we are witnessing a time when both traditionally exploitative tendencies of urban domestication and rural enclosure are indeed intensifying and diversifying. But, at the same time, we can recognize the power of alternatives and transformative processes counterposing these tendencies. This, we argue, throws up many contradictions and dilemmas for contemporary rural peoples and areas. We wish, in a non-reductionist and open-ended way, to explore these tendencies, as the contradictions and dilemmas play out; and to propose some of the key epistemological and methodological questions and challenges these raise for those engaged in rural (as well as urban) research.

## 2.1    Interlinked systems of urbanized/consumerist domestication and rural enclosure

Nowhere are the linkages and mutual dependencies and vulnerabilities involved in urban re-domestication and rural enclosure more exposed than in the fast-urbanizing (and so-called developing) regions of South and East Asia. In 2014 the WTO estimated that 422 million adults were living with one of the four most prevalent non-communicable diseases (NCDs). In most countries, including Malaysia, this prevalence is increasing. Addressing the key interconnected risk factors for Type 2 diabetes – unhealthy diets, obesity and physical inactivity – is critical in understanding and attempting to tame this rising trend (see Schema, 2017). In turn this requires radical reshaping of urban lifestyles and environments, and it is indeed a recent wave of re-domestication that is highly negative to urban people's health and wellbeing. Let us consider the case of Malaysia, a rapidly urbanizing and developing country that is emerging from its more rural and traditional past.

Diabetes is a major and rising health concern in urban Malaysia, affecting almost one in five Malaysian adults (Li et al., 2019; Lee, 2020). By 2025, 7 million adults are projected to have developed diabetes. Frequency of and opportunities for unhealthy fast food choices are seen as a major cause of this recent growth. Food choices are influenced by convenience and cost. The pressures of urban life, work demands, traffic congestion, and the rise of urban dual-income households have all led to a decline in home cooking and self-provisioning. Now 64 per cent of Malaysians eat at least one meal per day outside the home. Time pressures also reduce the willingness or energy to seek outlets serving healthier food, with many making choices based on time and costs alone. On top of this structural and potentially addictive trend, the average consumption of sugar in Malaysia is 26 teaspoons per day (2005), more than four times the recommended allowance. A large fraction of this sugar comes in the form of local 'kuih', often consumed with meals and as snacks throughout the day, and imported condensed milk, added to tea and coffee.

The popularity of fast food and the now rapid expansion of outlets has especially affected food choices of Malaysian youth. On the one hand, fast food reflects a desire for convenience, and a reduced appreciation of traditional food choices; on the other, accessible affordable fast food increases habituation to unhealthy diets. This is reinforced by fast food advertising and commercials and television programming aims at children. This feeds addiction (like the morning greetings from a fast food giant that tempt road users along a busy highway in the Klang Valley).

Obesity has tripled worldwide since 1975, reaching epidemic proportions in both developing and developed countries; as of 2018, 13 per cent of adults are obese and 39 per cent overweight. Meanwhile, the prevalence of overweight and obesity among children and adolescents has risen from 4 per cent in 1975 to 18 per cent in 2016. The Global Burden of Disease Study (Ng et al., 2014) reported a prevalence of overweight and obesity in Southeast Asia of 22.1 per cent among men and 28.3 per cent among women, with the highest rates in Malaysia at 48.3 per cent and 48.6 per cent for men and women, respectively. The 2015 Malaysian National Health and Morbidity Survey (NHMS) reports similar numbers, estimating the national prevalence of overweight and obesity in adults at 30.0 per cent and 17.7 per cent, respectively, for a total of 47.7 per cent. In just two decades, the prevalence of overweight adults has almost doubled from 16.6 per cent, while obesity has increased approximately four-fold from 4.4 per cent (Institute of Public Health, 1996).

Malaysia has stated its intent to stop the rise in prevalence of obesity by 2025 (Ministry of Public Health, 2016). The US$1–2 billion (RM4.26–8.53 billion) spent to combat obesity in 2016 – including direct and indirect costs – is equivalent to ~10–19 per cent of national healthcare expenditures. Public health messages around nutrition – such as those issued by the Malaysia Health Promotion Board – are important as one of a range of efforts for health promotion and obesity prevention. Yet, despite all these actions, obesity rates have continued to rise sharply.

Failure to halt the dramatic increase in the prevalence of overweight and obesity in Malaysia and worldwide has contributed to increased health risks for NCDs such as diabetes, cardiovascular diseases and cancers and other health issues, leading to higher morbidity and mortality rates. About 8 per cent of total mortality each year is attributed to obesity. Beyond increased risk of obesity-related chronic diseases and poorer quality of life, the healthcare costs of treating obesity-related disease conditions are rapidly escalating. On average, obese Malaysian males and females lose 6–11 years and 7–12 years of productive life, respectively.

It is important to consider how health messages feed into the urban physiological–environmental system that underlies obesity and the conditions necessary for information to be effective in this context. Public health messages aimed at reducing obesity must transcend an implied *information-deficit* model, which assumes that supplying basic knowledge on nutrition is enough to achieve change. Rather, such messages are best understood as attempts to convince a very broad, diverse audience to make behavioural and lifestyle changes that are both difficult and at odds with their contextual cues and incentives. This differs from traditional marketing, which delivers uncomplicated, attractive messages to targeted audiences, and it should be no surprise that health messages achieve lower response rates. This problem is compounded when health-sector messages compete against those from commercial and corporate food and 'health' industries. The latter promote simpler products while also generating profits, allowing the private sector to far outspend the health sector in this context. At present, guidelines for health promotion focus on communication techniques, such as limiting the number of ideas to avoid confusing readers, reducing jargon and technical language, using active voice and conversational style, and providing concrete examples. Indeed, beyond failing to enable healthier behaviour, poorly crafted messages may contribute to negative self-perceptions and, in the process, generate more pervasive problems. Yet, while important, such techniques do not address the broad range of obstacles in the messaging environment.

As knowledge is necessary, but not sufficient, to change behaviour, messages targeted at individual behaviour need to be accompanied by strategies that create contexts where people are encouraged or naturally predisposed to act on these messages. Therefore, health communicators also need to consider how to influence the key actors who shape these environments. For example, the failure of town and transport planners to consider health issues in, for instance, the design of parks, recreation centres, and other public spaces has been seen as a cause of the rise in the prevalence of obesity, NCDs, and sedentary behaviour. A wide range of stakeholders—both public and private, at federal, state, and municipal levels—must play a role in halting the obesity crisis. Physical, social and cultural environments associated with work, food, family, and community all enable and constrain the individual choices and behaviours that affect obesity. For example, in Malaysia, the widespread practice of serving sweet and savoury snacks at morning and afternoon tea at functions, conferences, and meetings enables over-consumption of food and cements frequent eating as a social norm. Working hours, availability of fast food, and school nutrition (SCHEMA, 2018), among other factors, also play key enabling/constraining roles in Malaysia. Health messages and other policy interventions must target these physical, social and cultural environments, connecting actors and creating new feedback links to reshape systems in ways that promote health.

Within Malaysia there is such heterogeneity in sociocultural environments that both the message and the way it is communicated must be tailored to local contexts, highlighting the importance of place-based thinking. Indeed, rates of obesity in Malaysia vary by geographical locations and ethnicity, and these differences are greater than can be explained by simple urban/rural differentiation. Varied diets and cultures imply that the changes needed to achieve healthy and socially acceptable eating habits and lifestyles may be very different for different ethnic and social groups. Similarly, identifying the appropriate form of messages and messengers for a target group is important and requires local knowledge. Acquiring and using this knowledge depends on early and consistent community engagement and participation in both research and policy processes, before problems and potential solutions are formulated. Accounting for the particularities of place will better allow for the development of targeted and tailored messages, programmes, guidelines, and interventions to meet age, gender, culture, socioeconomic, and geographical needs.

## 2.2   Impacts on rural enclosures: examples in Malaysia

The growth in both urban population and dietary changes is having important implications for Malaysian farming and rural food systems. The government, faced with growing costs of imports of basic foods (meat, milk and sugar), is promoting a domestic policy of self-sufficiency. This entails large-scale restricting of some small family farming areas, and the development of largely scale-intensive livestock units. This in turn entails subsidies for high-tech intensive systems to feed growing urban populations and meet the needs of the growing population (of 50 million by 2050). Across much of Southeast Asia this is a familiar story; and indeed we can see here a direct linkage between the reconstituted and unhealthy dietary changes principally occurring in the cities, and the policies of new rural enclosures both at home and abroad that attempt to supply these dietary changes. The intensive livestock industry is also highly dependent upon the procurement of global feedstocks, not least soya and corn based. The reconstitution of the Malaysian diet then becomes a major driver for 'locking in' intensive systems of enclosure both in Malaysia and abroad.

This is currently, despite significant recent policy pronouncements advocating more sustainable diets and production practices (see EAT-Lancet Report,

Planetary Health: Jan 2019), the major development trend in the Malaysian and Southeast Asian agri-food complex, and it is tied directly to an urban and mega-urban model of growth and modernization that, as we see here, creates and re-creates a range of negative feedbacks for urban and rural populations alike. In addition, this re-domestication of urban people holds different social and physical consequences for different ethnic and demographic groups and is also highly gendered. Risks and vulnerabilities are both intense but also highly differentiated across the cities and the countrysides. Bodies and lives are literally re-shaped by these processes, and obesities and diabetes are increased based upon the generation of addiction to particular unhealthy food choices and related car-based lifestyles.

When scholars and policy advocates talk about transforming such systems, then, it is important to stress the high levels of cultural and social 'lock-in' such exploitative and domesticated systems tend to reproduce. This means that we should not discourage talk and ways of transforming these systems. But it also suggests, as we will posit in more detail in the succeeding chapters, that we have to understand the very (post-modern) ways in which domestication and habituation works and has been re-created in urbanized and rural populations, if we are to realistically bring about real transformations and new empowerments.

Here, as Scott (2017:21) historically reminds us, such re-domestications are not un-linked to the role of the state and governance systems (see Chapter 2). Following Aristotle he conjectures that states have always relied on various forms of enslavement and bondage: 'The captives, individually and collectively, become an integral part of the state's means of production and reproduction, a part, if you will, along with livestock and grain fields'. City walls, for Scott, were a symbol not so much of keeping the barbarians and invading peasants out, as an infrastructure for enslaving and keeping a fiscal and hegemonic control of those increasing masses who resided within.

## 2.3    Reflecting on the urban to understand the rural

In the contemporary (especially con-urban) world the boundaries between freedom and captivity are far more complex than recognized in antique periods, but the questions of enslavement and empowerment through now complex and advanced digital and physical forms of control are no less relevant.

Take for example the relatively new use of digital facial recognition technologies. Whilst in the West these are being increasing controlled by security agencies and a small group of digital and social media firms (like Facebook), in the East, especially in mega-urbanizing China, they are becoming literally embodied into civil society actions by the totalitarian communist state (see Lanchester, 2019; and Strittmatter, 2019). The progress in facial recognition technologies and big data is resulting in their use not just for surveillance of popular unrest (as in the now long-running protests in Hong Kong, and indeed one of the main reasons that face masks and umbrellas have become such a crucial defence for the protestors); it is also central to the pilot trials of what are termed 'social credit systems'. This is far extending the West's use of financial credit ratings into what is seen by the state as socially desirable behaviour. Points are awarded for good behaviour, not least communist party organization, and calligraphy lessons, but lost for pouring water outside the house, dog fouling, driving through red lights, etc. In some versions your social credit scores are affected by the types of social networks with which you may be associated, as well as who you travel or congregate with, and where. As Lanchester (2019) argues:

> The China-wide version of social credit is scheduled to go live in 2020. The ultimate goal is to make people internalize their sense of the state: to make people self-censor, self-monitor, self-supervise. Strittmatter quotes *Discipline and Punish* [Foucault] 'He who is subjected to a field of visibility, and who knows it, assumes responsibility for the constraints of power, he makes them play spontaneously upon himself; he inscribes in himself the power relation in which he simultaneously plays both roles; he becomes the principle of his own subjection'. The Chinese version of social credit is the closest thing we've ever seen to Foucault's system in action at a national level.

Social credit is currently most extremely applied in Xinjiang province to monitor and regulate Muslim minorities (Uighurs). Here people are forced to have police-owned GPS systems in their cars, you can only buy petrol after having your face scanned, and mobile phones have a state app on them to monitor their activities and prevent access to 'damaging information'. Religious activity is monitored too, and the state is able to know if you have or participate in foreign networks. DNA and fingerprints are offered in 'free health clinics'. This is a new mega-city, an algorithmic version of state-led re-domestication; and in the West it is being led not only by the state but also by de-regulated digital media companies like Facebook, which already owns patents for customers' algorithmic representations of their faces, and members of their networks' faces. Today, in 2020, this is increasingly what it's like to be urban.

Certainly the rise of urban-based non-communicable diseases, diet-related human health risks, and more intensive expressions of air and water pollution are relatively new forms of urban enslavement that are in turn built upon a density-driven and convenience-driven urban consumption re-domestica-tion of both household and work life. It is argued that pollution of water systems creates conditions also for the rise in urban neighbourhoods of anti-microbial resistance and infertility. High-density and 'high-rise' living come with renewed risks too (consider the example of Grenfell Tower in the richest borough in London), especially as income and social inequalities rise in these dense urban and increasingly privatized spaces (see Chapter 5). Indeed, as Bai et al (2012:465) have scientifically synthesized from a planetary health and human ecology standpoint:

> The health risks associated with the urban environment are diverse. Many cities face at least five types of health threats: (i) [i]nfectious diseases that thrive when people are crowded together in sub-standard living conditions; (ii) [a]cute and chronic diseases such as respiratory disease and pulmonary cancer that are associated with industrial pollution; (iii) [c]hronic, non-communicable diseases that are on the rise with unhealthy lifestyles (physical inactivity, unhealthy diets, tobacco smoking and harmful use of alcohol; (iv) injuries resulting from motor vehicle collisions, violence and crime, and (v) climate change related health risks, for example heat stress and changed patterns of infectious disease, which are considered as one of the biggest health risks in the 21st century and are likely to exacerbate existing risks.

Air pollution has re-emerged as a global urban killer. In the US, it is estimated that it kills up to 200,000 people per year, more than traffic accidents, and combinations of outdoor and indoor air pollution caused one in every nine deaths globally in 2016, far more than those caused by malaria, malnutrition or alcohol (Gardener 2019). Beijing's intense smog in January 2013 (dubbed the 'Airpocalypse') sparked wider political awareness of our urbanized depend-ence upon burning coal, gasoline, diesel, wood and litter. London is not only one of the most unequal cities in Europe; it also has the worst nitrogen dioxide pollution level in Europe. The Mayor in 2016 declared the city a 'public health emergency' and announced a new 'ultra-low' emission zone for Central London. Climate change as expressed in more 'wild fires' in the US and the San Francisco Bay area, meant that this iconic city region had, in 2018, the worst air quality in the world, easily on a par with what the inhabitants of Delhi experi-ence day on day. *This is a form of ecological and biological urban enslavement and embodiment.*

Exposure to fossil exhaust particulates can result in the particulates' pene-trating deep into the lungs, and into the alveoli, the tiny air-filled sacs where oxygen is exchanged for carbon dioxide. The particulates then travel into the bloodstream and throughout the body, lodging themselves on the brain, con-stricting arteries, creating heart attacks and strokes. This can affect the unborn as well as vulnerable persons such as children and the elderly. In 2019, despite

significant denial lobbying and rubbishing of the science by fossil fuel industries and their political supporters, the American Lung Association reported
that 141 million Americans live with unhealthy levels of ozone and particle
pollution, an increase of 7 million since 2018. This is attributed to the exac-
erbating effects of climate change. Ambient air pollution is now responsible
for 8.8 million premature deaths per year, more than double previous global
estimates, and 1.5 million more than caused by smoking.

We can see here, then, that in the context of both climate change, and a long
and contested denial by fossil fuel business interests, urban living is, for many,
an enslavement process involving high levels of metabolic and biological
vulnerability, created and re-produced by an increasingly dense and polluting
ambience that restricts dwellers' environmental rights to natural and (what
should be) 'common pool resources' (see Chapter 5). This is seemingly exacerbated by not only the growing privatization of available green spaces in cities,
but also the still largely unregulated nature of air and water pollution.

Our points here are not just to dwell upon the relatively new pathologies
and domestications of urban life, but to demonstrate the relationships and
discontinuities these trends have with and for their surrounding countrysides,
and in turn concerning rural development (see UN Habitat, 2019). The trends
tend to de-naturalize urban living and the urban condition, which means that
many people, especially inner-city residents, have no or little access to direct
forms of nature: they are indeed naturally and ecologically enslaved. This is,
of course, very different from the rural condition, however much some rural
places are also populated with larger numbers of urban cosmopolitans. For the
richer urban cosmopolitans, such denaturalized urbanities drive various forms
of 'counter-urbanization', expansive suburbanization and what Americans call
'white flight', either temporarily (as exotic forms of tourism), or more permanently in the buying of second or new first rural homes. These are trends well
established in the richer countries and are also being replicated in Asia and
parts of Latin America. Thus the reactions by many urbanites who can afford
it, are to escape the enslavements of urban life, and to re-create a rurality that
holds all of the advantages of the city culture.

Growing and increasingly recognized pathologies of urban life are leading
to a variety of rebound and interactive effects in rural development; and so
we need to tease out the new dynamic linkages between the urban and rural
worlds in times of growing ecological and economic crisis, and a period
when the sanctity of the urban 'growth machine' needs to be seriously called
into question. One implied question becomes, therefore, if new models of
(post-carbonized) growth and modernity are to be designed, how will this affect

our understanding of what rural areas are for? And what forms of rurality can be experienced? So far few have considered the implications of a post-carbon world on the countrysides. Yet we can see here that what happens in the rural domain is intricately bound up with growing global cosmopolitanism, and all of its ecologically driven 'spill-over' effects. These become major drivers for rural change and development, far more nuanced now than in previous centuries of nationalistic colonialism and enslavement. This in many ways sets a context to ask new agrarian questions about how rural development copes with global cosmopolitanism.

## 3.　　Transversal rural development themes: empowerment and association

These global and variable post-modern trends, we believe, create a fertile research ground and agenda in which to explore the new geographies of empowerment and association in rural areas. Up until recently it was generally assumed that generalized capitalist relations have penetrated most of the globe – North and South. With the rise of neo-liberalism in recent decades, many have assumed that rural agricultural producers are subject to the same fundamental forces of capitalist markets, leading to the decline in pre- or post-capitalist modes of production. Byres (2012) calls this a sort of 'world system determinism', with conclusions drawn without close spatial analysis of the internal dynamics of agriculture and its interactions with a range of related production, and without taking account of the particularities of property relations that govern local production systems (see Carlson, 2017:718). Recent evidence suggests that in the Global South at least many regions do not

> appear to be following the general processes of dispossession and differentiation that occurred with the transition to capitalism in the Global North. It would appear that there is still an unresolved agrarian question in the Global South today, and that it remains central to understanding the problem of underdevelopment. The exact nature of this question, however, can only be understood through a more detailed analysis of the rural property relations that govern agriculture in the vast array of societies that make up the Global South. (Carlson, 2017:718)

In the global North too, the persistence of family farms, even if they are reduced in number, and the disproportionate number of small businesses is a strong feature of advanced rural regions. In the EU, the State has attempted to protect the family farm whilst also encouraging the rise of agri-business and corporate retailing. Many rural areas are fostering new social relations of production as well as pre-existing systems, leading again to a more complex picture than that depicted in 'world systems' or global food regimes thinking. We can hypothesize that with both the continuing crisis of neo-liberalism and its attendant global assumptions about subsuming traditional forms of production and property rights, *and* the process of post-carbonism, there will be conditions for further fundamental differentiation of rural production systems. First, there is the traditional but rising trend towards farm-based pluri-activity, which suggests a diversification as well as a re-empowerment of family-based businesses in the rural domain; and second, we also now witness the growth of the agri-energy–tourism nexus (see Marsden and Rucinska, 2019), whereby, as demand inevitably increases for energy and amenity from rural resources, 'farms' become sites for a variety of natural resource, energy and amenity production. In the global South too, in China and Brazil, eco-tourism and amenity provision become significant drivers of rural development, especially around the hinterlands of the expanding cities, and as the domesticated urban middle classes 'rediscover' the need for natural habitus as well as urban habitus. Again the re-constitution of the urban–rural relation, now under conditions of neo-liberal crisis and post-carbonized transition, becomes a critical factor in restructuring the rural realm and, indeed, creating opportunities for differentiated empowerment of rural people, not least the young and the female.

Rural areas are thus facing new processes of reconstitution (see Murdoch and Marsden, 1995), which are shaping their social spaces and locales. This is not contradictory to the continued processes of mega-urbanization, the shifts towards post-carbonism, or the rise of (domesticated, and urban) environmentalism, which in itself creates more demands for rural goods and services, from sustainable foods, natural amenity spaces, agri-tourism, and links and experiences with the rural 'exotic'.

These processes are re-shaping rural areas and indeed making them more aligned and influenced by their particular regional settings. Whilst national and globalized networks and assemblages have a key role in many rural regions (see Woods, 2018) in shaping rural empowerments and enclosures, so too do the local and regional contexts in which these rural regions sit. The relational geographies of rural spaces are made up of combinations of shorter and longer connections, depending upon the nature of the reconstituted socio-natural endowments those rural areas hold. It is this essential process of contingent uneven and combined development that creates the social conditions for their continued survival and/or vulnerability. Natural and physical ecological endowments come to take a renewed significance in the post-carbon transition, not only because they may become attractors for urban amenity and environmental interests, but also because those very physical ecologies become the bedrock upon which more sustainable production and consumption practices can be developed. No clearer case here demonstrates this than, as we discuss in Chapter 6, the rise of agro-ecologies, which in themselves have to be situated and develop and be defined from their own ecological geographies. Similarly, the location of wind turbines, hydro-energy schemes, bio-gas and composting initiatives, solar energy sites, can only be created where there are inherent natural endowments. Thus in the post-carbon transition, relational space meets natural space, such that they are recombined to create sustainable rural development. One cannot exist without the other.

We can see here, then, that the rise of these tendencies and combined complexities of post-modern rural–urban realities tends to confront somewhat outdated or out-moded theoretical and conceptual frameworks upon which we have hitherto relied. 'World system determinism' and its attendant connections with agrarian 'regime theory' seem unable to capture the temporalities, differentiations or spatialities now arising. In a similar vein, after two decades of post-structuralist application in the social sciences, and the particular approaches associated with social constructionism and post-humanism, we now see the need, once again, to combine our nuanced understandings of relational space with the realization that nature, as bio-physical and ecological nature, and natural endowments really matter in the post-carbonized transitions (Clark, 2011). Thirdly, the distinctive nature of rural transformations has so far not been incorporated sufficiently into transitions management theories of change. In subsequent chapters in this volume, therefore, we do not wish to completely debunk these theoretical avenues. Rather we wish to use them as creative springboards to develop new and, we think, more relevant contemporary theoretical positions – positions, indeed, that are needed in order for us to understand the complexities of contemporary rural and urban living and livelihoods.

Thus it seems apposite at the current juncture, and in writing about the unfolding research agenda for global rural development, to point to a need to develop new and potentially more grounded theoretical frameworks that can assist scholars and researchers in their endeavours to understand the potentialities and challenges of rural living on a turbulent and increasingly con-urbanized planet. In this sense the new and revised 'agrarian question' is much broader than its original conception, which was associated with the long-running question of, why does 'backward'-facing agriculture represent a fundamental barrier to industrialization and economic development and progress in societies? Also, why does it seem an obstacle to fully fledged capitalist penetration of agriculture and rural relations? Whilst we may argue that these questions are still of relevance (indeed both in the South and the North), the central question today needs reformulating around the global necessity to assess how rural and agricultural societies can contribute to a (largely urban domesticated) world that is fast running out of material resources for its continued existence, and faces growing climate change vulnerabilities that exacerbate these unsustainabilities. Our answer, as we wish to expand, is that the rural, and rurality, will be fundamental in meeting these challenges of post-carbonized modernization and transformation; perhaps in part because it never completely allowed the appropriation of its natural and social assets in earlier phases of capitalist development. Thus the new agrarian question is far from just a concern about understanding its inherent 'backwardness', as it involves tracing its potentialities for sustainable transformations and innovations.

## 4.    Conclusions: refracting the rural–urban dichotomy for the 21st century

In Sorokin and Zimmerman's classic, *Principles of rural–urban sociology and Systematic Source Book* (1929–32), the authors synthesized and reflected on over forty years of investigative rural and urban studies by concluding:

> Our general conclusion must be that all the principal differences between rural and urban societies – differences in means of communication, in mobility, occupation, total population, and density – are tending to diminish. Rural and urban societies … are approaching a type of rurban society …. Under the influence of steam-power civilization, the two societies became radically different. The use of electricity, however, and such recent inventions as the radio and the automobile have begun to produce a rapprochement that in all probability will develop. [volume 7, p642 and quoted by Granberg (2018)]

These conclusions promoted ongoing fierce debates about the existence or otherwise of a rural–urban continuum, and/or the conceptual redundancy of the 'rural–urban dichotomy' under the conditions of 20th-century progressive modernism (see Granberg, 2018; Andersson et al. 2016). We have argued here, a century on, that rural and urban societies are far more interconnected and diverse; and yet to be rural, or to be urban as we have seen above, can hold very different experiences and life chances. Urban living creates new pathologies for many, with new forms of domestication and environmental enslavement, far more profound than the 'densities' and 'heterogeneities' commented upon by Louis Wirth (1938) in his Chicago of the 1930s. Rural development today, as we struggle towards a post-industrial and post-carbonized world, represents both a site of potential continuing enclosure (e.g. of exclusive houses, landed estates, exploitative and intensive practices) and of *a new socio-cultural and ecological enlightenment* – a place for the potential re-creation and empowerment of social autonomy and participatory community by association (Milone et al. 2015).

The next chapters – on governance, power and transformations, financialization, land and property, agroecology, family farming, and markets – will explore these deep rural dilemmas, tensions and contradictions, these new 'agrarian questions', in more substantive detail. It is important to conclude, then, that global rural development today represents both a scholarly and re-politicized sociological potential, essentially a new framing that could and can obviate many of the destructive and unsustainable cosmopolitan forces that continuing capitalist, often authoritarian, and industrialized con-urbanism still manufactures and exudes.

# 2. Changing questions of governance: reflexive and disruptive governance in the Anthropocene

## 1. Introduction: new governance dimensions in times of crisis and transition

What is a new conceptualization of governance? Where are rural and agri-food politics? How do they now impinge on agri-food and rural development? What is the nature of new forms of institutionalization and de-institutionalization? These are long-running questions in rural development debates, but they now take on a new context and significance given the (somewhat unfortunate) confluence of neo-liberalized economic and political crisis on the one hand, and the rise of the recognition of the Anthropocene, and all of its ecological and carbonized urgencies, on the other. This chapter will set out some of the key parameters of a new and contemporary agenda regarding questions of rural development and agri-food governance that emerge from recent debates in the scholarly literature.

We shall do this within what we regard as a useful and contemporary framing of disruptive governance, exploring how governance systems are changing or about to change as a consequence of these combined macro changes. Some of these shifts are associated with the rural realm directly, but in many cases they are part of broader political, economic and ecological shifts, which bear severe and profound consequences for rural development as well as other spheres of the economy and polity. Disruptive governance can be either positive or negative; first, we will look at how disruptions are occurring, taking first Europe and then more specifically the UK as our reference points. Then we will posit the struggles of creating disruptions in order for making and reinforcing sustainable transitions in the rural realm. This sets an important and fruitful agenda for rural development scholars, not least because it is argued that without such disruptive innovations in governance systems and processes, sustainable transitions will not necessarily be achievable. However, before we explore these matters, let us ask, what do we currently mean by rural and agri-food governance? In Box 2.1, we list a set of composite definitions.

| General |
|---|
| 'The institutions, practices, power relations, technologies and actions which are involved in managing resources, managing change and the resources needed to regulate change'. |
| 'The architecture of 'the state' and its political, democratic or otherwise, processes and actions which reproduce concent and legitimacy'. |
| Government and Governance: institutions, networks, assemblages. |
| The processes of Policy initiation (e.g. interest group activity), processing (e.g. enacting policies) and implementation (impact on the ground). |
| **Food Governance:** |
| The operation of governance processes (both food related and non-related) which condition and regulate food systems. |
| **Sustainable food governance:** The operation of food governance processes with the INTENTION of creating and managing renewable ecological resources for this generation and future generations, including the ecologically efficient production, processing and consumption of food goods. |

**Box 2.1**      General definitions of Governance

*Source:* Terry Marsden (2018).

A dominant perspective regarding rural and more specifically agri-food governance has been to adopt a historical world systems 'regime approach', whereby capitalism has shaped governance regimes in ways that most effectively provide a basis, or an accumulation terrain for appropriation (see Freidman and McMichael, 1989). In a very abstract and structuralist sense these evolving regimes (Imperial, Fordist, post-Fordist) provided a coherent regulatory system in which global food systems could be sustained. More recently the rise of highly concentrated corporate and financialized capital (see Chapter 4) has led to what has been termed a 'corporate and environmental regime' dominated by globalized food firms and a neo-liberalized state regulatory system, which has stimulated corporate retailers, food processors and input manufactures. As we shall see below, this has not necessarily reduced the role of the state, but it has meant that the state has become more conducive to, and some would say dominated by, both industrialized and financialized forms of global capital (see Chapter 4).

There is now clear recognition that the levels of conceptual and empirical coherence experienced under the evolving regimes has significantly weakened due to at least two forces of disruption. First, the severe and combined financial, fiscal, food and fuel crisis that erupted in 2007–8 created significant disruptions to these regimes, not least because, as Moore (2015) contends, industrialized capitalism reached severe and unprecedented limits both in its own accumulation strategies and in terms of its ecological impacts. Second, the rising acknowledgement of the emergence of the Anthropocene, and climate change specifically, created a new politics that began to fight against industrialized carbonism.

As we shall see in the rest of this chapter, these two governance trends are clearly affecting rural and agrarian questions, suggesting the rise of significant disruptions in established regulatory systems. For instance, Latour (2018) has recently argued:

> The hypothesis is that we can understand nothing about the politics of the last 50 years if we do not put the question of climate change and its denial front and centre. Without the idea that we have entered into a New Climate Regime, we cannot understand the explosion of inequalities, the scope of deregulation, the critique of globalization, or most importantly, the panicky desire to return to the old protections of the nation-state – a desire that is identified, quite inaccurately, with the rise of populism. (Latour, 2018:02)

We can argue and postulate here what these disruptions mean for our understanding of rural and agri-food governance, and to what extent they usher in threats and opportunities for more democratized forms of environmental governance. Purdy (2015), in *After Nature*, argued powerfully that the onset of the Anthropocene needs to lead to deeper forms of political democracy. He recalls Amartya Sen's proclamation that no democracy has ever suffered a famine: 'Famines are not natural products of absolute scarcity, but political products of distribution.' For Purdy:

> A democratic Anthropocene would mean a few things. First that the world of scarcity and plenty, comfort and desperation is not just where we live; it is also what we make. Second is a premise of equality: if Anthropocene ecologies are a political question, then no one should be left out of the decisions that shape them... It should be everyone's authorship politically... Democratic sovereignty through discursive practices in exemplary sustainability science. (pp49–50)

Latour's, Sen's and Purdy's arguments see a strong link between the social and political reactions the onset of the Anthropocene now brings and the potentialities it creates for necessary and indeed more re-territorialized forms of governance. How relevant, we may ask, are these arguments for rural and agri-food governance and development in the contemporary period? This chapter asks, what trends and counter-trends are emerging?

## 2.    Disruptive governance

Since the financial and combined food and fuel crisis that disrupted world markets in 2007–8, many scholars have begun to link this economic and indeed accumulation crisis as a basis for more unstable and disruptive forms of governance. Jason Moore (2015) sees these conjunctions as a historically pivotal moment in capitalist world ecology whereby severe and growing limits are placed upon capitalist accumulation and expansionism; and when, as the world in fact grows smaller and more heavily urban populated, severe limits are reached in the carbonized exploitation of natural resources – including foods, minerals, water, soils and indeed socio-natural resources such as human labour. In these conditions, he argues, the capitalist (and carbonized) world is running out of 'cheap natures'.

This ongoing crisis has profound political and sociological implications over and above the economic effects and reactions that are often those of denial, 'business as usual', and further intensive financialization based upon the very nature of the growing natural scarcities (see Chapter 4, which addresses financialization and vulnerabilities in more depth) (see also Lanchester, 2018). Many national governments, and perhaps most famously the EU, facing the need to 'prop-up' their over-financialized banking and investment sectors, adopted something of a re-enforcement of the crisis by introducing severe public sector financial cuts in their welfare and local government funding regimes. This led to what is now commonly called a prolonged period of 'austerity', whereby government expenditures were cut quite radically for the purposes of reducing financialized government debts created by their bank bail-outs. Neo-liberalized governments, in the EU, Germany, the UK, Brazil and Argentina, thus compounded the financialized vulnerability of those in the lower socio-economic classes by reducing state welfare programmes. This, inter alia, created the rise of food and energy insecurity amongst a greater proportion of the population, a situation that is worsening as we write today in 2020.

It is important to recognize that these sets of conjunctions have had severe and long-term sociological and political consequences, which, in short, have created two related conditions associated with the rise of 'disruptive governance'. First, there was and is a crisis of the political left, in how to provide viable and legitimate alternatives for their political constituencies. In the US, UK and Brazil we have seen the failure of the political left to mount a viable and electable strategy to counter the dominant neo-liberalized austerity politics. Second, this has meant that the steady rise of post-carbonized politics, or what Latour called the 'globalized climate regime' (2018), has faced severe obstacles in making or mounting real sustainable transitions. In addition, and crucially, politicians on the right, faced with economic failure of their neo-liberalized model, focussed on a renewed and nationalistic promotion of the politics of blame and scapegoating as a form of nationalist populism. This only re-enforced and re-legitimized social, spatial inequalities and ethnic and gendered 'scapegoating' and marginalization. Just at a time when there was a profound need for a new or renewed public and governance contract to be formed between governance systems and the public in order to resolve both the combined neo-liberal and ecological crisis, the over-riding response, at least by national and supranational bodies like the EU, was to preside over a period of allowing a new populist authoritarianism to take hold, especially in countries like Brazil, the US and the UK. As a result, left and green–left political coalitions have been fragmented and attacked, whilst populist right politics has renewed its forceful denial of climate change by re-enforcing carbonized corporate interests like oil and agri-business firms.

Rather perplexingly for many of those on the (green) left, it has been interesting to ask why the rise of right-wing (and carbonized) politics has found so much support in rural areas and heartlands. This is the case in the US, Brazil and the UK, as shown in the electoral results and not least by the UK referendum on Brexit. Although not comprehensive, this demonstrates something pertaining to a new rural–urban political divide, for instance in the US and to some extent in the UK. The divide has been analyzed by Paul Starr (2019) and J. Rodden (2019). As the latter writes, 'The geography of partisan support matters a great deal … in countries (like the US and UK) using single member districts that are winner-take-all. Underrepresentation of the urban left in national legislatures and governments has been a basic feature of all industrialized countries that use "winner-take-all elections"' (p38).

Whilst the actual system of 'first past the post' electoral governance may go some way to explain this urban–rural divide, Starr believes that its origins and recent re-emergence is also connected to political and sociological 'lags' associated with the long-running historical and economic geography. He argues:

> The political geography of cities followed their economic geography. Parties of the left – originally socialist and labour parties in many countries, later the democrats during the New Deal – organized workers in the urban core, while conservative parties dominated areas further from the city centres. Remarkably, while the economies of cities have changed, their political geography has persisted. When manufacturing departed, the old neighbourhoods filled up with the poor and minorities, and sometimes students and artists – and they supported the parties of the left. The result is a paradoxical relationship of the left to industry and industrial workers. Democrat votes today, are geographically correlated with manufacturing employment a century ago, while republican votes are correlated with contemporary manufacturing. Today, the democrats are the party of urban, post industrial America, and the republicans receive more votes in ex-urban and rural places where manufacturing activity still takes place. (p39)

In the British Brexit referendum of 2016 again it was those non-gentrified, non-ethnic and white ex-mining and manufacturing areas and rural areas that returned most anti-EU Brexit votes, and it has been in these areas where right-wing populist sentiment has been greatest. This was re-enforced in the general election of December 2019. Why are these interconnected relations between neo-liberal economic crisis and their sociological and political effects of significance to our understanding of contemporary rural development? The consequences have particular implications for a range of governance and regulatory disruptions that are now occurring. Let us list some of these here, before looking at the processes of governance disruption in more depth.

First, and indeed foremost, disruption has taken place in those policy areas – trade, food policy, agricultural and environmental and immigration policy – that have been mostly prone to political attack and de-regulation by the populist right. In Trump's US and Bolsonaro's Brazil, climate and environmental policies and migration issues have been key priorities for reform and, one can argue, disruption. Both wish to deny climate change existence, or more indirectly wish to irresponsibly rely on other countries to adopt mitigation and transition strategies whilst they continue to over-exploit carbon-based resources and exacerbate carbon emissions. This privileges carbon-based corporate agri-businesses and oil-related businesses, and opens up rural spaces (like Mato Grosso in Brazil) for more industrial and intensive farming systems whilst marginalizing small family farming, agro-ecological practices and the land rights of indigenous rural communities. The rise of right-wing populism is leading therefore to governance disruptions that not exclusively but particularly affect rural sustainable development, whether it is new restrictions on migrant farm labour in California, or more trade protectionism, or the further deforestation of the Amazon by favouring logging and agri-business firms over environmental protection measures and interest groups.

The Brexit process in the UK is a populist right-wing attack on the very Europeanized areas of policy that the earlier rounds of de-regulatory reform-ism under Thatcher failed to unsettle. These are EU-integrated trade, environ-mental, and food and farming policies. All of these hold profound impacts for future uneven governance arrangements for rural businesses in the growing, selling and supplying of rural goods and services (see Lang et al. 2017). Under these disruptive governance conditions, existing and long-standing governance institutions and their practices become far more destabilized. Environmental agencies come under attack and there are reductions in funding and powers (e.g. the EPA and the FDA in the US[1]). Regulating agencies for food standards and agricultural extension have publicly funded budgets restricted and subject to growing control by private sector bodies (e.g. the Food Standards Agency, UK; the EPA, US; and EMBRAPA in Brazil[2]). Private interest bodies become more influential in driving policy inside what is supposed to be the publicly democratically organized government.

As we shall see in the conclusion to this chapter, disruptive governance, whilst being a strategy to de-regulate established structures and processes that were originally put in place to protect the public interest, can also provide a basis for more positive sustainability actions and movements, as reactions and counter-movements to these very disruptive trends. We shall explore some of these potentialities in the conclusions to the chapter. Now let us examine in more detail the processes of recent destabilization of governance that has been occurring in the rural and agri-food policy field, especially in the European context. Of course Europe has been the home of widespread innovation in environmental, food and trade policies over the past thirty years. These series of environmental action programmes, family farm and rural development policies, and more recently stronger carbon emissions and climate mitigation policies, have been leading the world. In mainland Europe these sentiments and policies are still strong and robust, for instance in the areas of renewable energy and the growing significance of the circular economy. But it is impor-tant to examine how these forms of governance and indeed more reflexive forms of governance are increasingly contested in some regions and countries of Europe. There is thus a contested co-evolution of sustainable pathways emerging, between governance and associated policies that are addressing the need to speed up and substantiate the necessary post-carbonized transitions, which recognizes the need to address the effects of the Anthropocene, at the same time as disruptive forces are in evidence, as outlined above.

At the heart of this contested governance terrain lies a philosophical divide between individualism and a reliance on markets on the one hand, versus new forms of collectivism and associational development. The latter is indeed essential for collectively tackling the post-carbon transition, but it is the very abhorrence of emerging forms of collectivism and associationalism that fuels both climate change denial and, in turn, disruptive forms of governance. Disruption, then, is continually fuelled by the need to attack and neuter emerging forms of collective and associational practice, and indeed more democratized forms of political ecology (see Purdy, 2015). This is why we might here counterpose the surge for individualized disruptive governance on the one hand and the rise of a more collective and place-based development of a new climate change and transition regime.

Figure 2.1 below thus counterposes the interconnections between the limits of carbonist capital accumulation, its political and sociological ramifications (post 2007–8) and the rise of nationalist and populist 'disuptive governance' in the succeeding period. At the same time we witness two-co-evolutionary processes: the continued 'race' for even more difficult carbon and mineral resources, on the one hand, and the struggles to develop a post-carbon transition, not least in the agri-food energy nexus on the other (see MaCarthy, 2015; Marsden and Rucinska, 2019). These processes create the basis for different levels of disruptive governance.

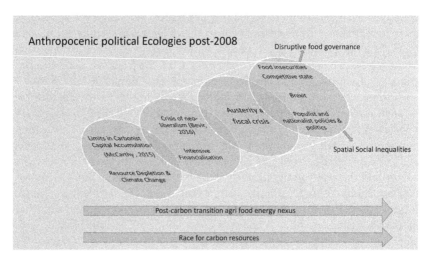

**Figure 2.1**    Anthropogenic political ecologies post-2008

*Source:* Terry Marsden (2018).

# 3.    Empirical examples of the disruptive process

## 3.1    Rebuilding sustainable food systems in Europe

The European food system currently stands at an important crossroads. It is, on the one hand, still significantly harnessed and embedded in what can only be regarded as outdated and increasingly dysfunctional governance and regulatory systems that had their origins during a significant period of economic growth and plenty experienced in the later parts of 20th century. On the other hand, and as we shall see, an entirely new and alternative paradigm is taking shape (see Marsden and Morley, 2014), built upon a more diverse set of actors and initiatives, and governance arrangements that are commonly called 'Alternative food systems'. But this 'crossroads' is fraught with contestation regarding food politics, policies and effective regulatory systems.

In many ways, adopting a regulationist approach, particularly resonant since the onset of the food, fuel, financial and fiscal crisis starting in 2007–8, we can characterize the current and foreseeable future of food policy in Europe as one that is losing its means of coherent social regulation. This means that current and dominant forms of the food governance and economy are progressively losing their means of social and political legitimation. They are beginning to lose their powers to reproduce themselves and to justify themselves. Whilst the burgeoning literature on alternative food systems often too readily celebrates its heterogeneous and explosive development as a new paradigm, such a movement can only have real transformative potential if, at the same time, we can see significant evidence of the collapse and weakening of prevailing conventional and hegemonic food governance systems. It is important, therefore, in analyzing the potential transformative potential of 'alternative food systems' that at the same time we consider the evidence of the inherent and contested demise and decline of prevailing hegemonic food governance systems. Transformations in food systems thus entail studying the crisis of prevailing systems simultaneously with exploring the anatomies of new, more sustainable systems.

In beginning to approach this 'dual task', this section starts by mapping out the current nested natures of the three major forms of food governance currently operating in Europe during this more volatile geo-political and economic period since 2007–8. This is a period of growing food insecurities and vulnerabilities, as much of the empirical evidence in the EU-funded project TRANSMANGO (2015–19) has depicted. As such, it is a period in which the interlinkages or potential synergies between food security, sustainability, sovereignty and their effective governance can no longer be taken for granted;

indeed the evidence shows that these components are now more fragmented and working against one another in many ways (see Moragues Faus et al., 2020). For instance, over a quarter of UK citizens are presently experiencing some form of food poverty, and the EU as a whole has been losing one out of three farms over the past decade.

The past synergies between the regulation of production and mass consumption of relatively 'cheap' foods has come to an end, with the reversal of 'Engel's Law', whereby now the proportion of household income expended on food and fuel is increasing, not decreasing. We thus have a food crisis today that is affecting both ends of the food chain, whilst the highly concentrated corporate sector continues to abstract the highest proportion of economic value from both its increasingly 'dedicated' suppliers (farmers and processors) and its increasingly impoverished and under-nourished consumers. Therefore, since 2007–8, Europe has been facing something of an unprecedented rise in food insecurity with its interconnected ecological, social and political dimensions. This is, we shall argue, *primarily a crisis of food governance*, as existing and longstanding governance regimes are no longer capable of delivering effective and long-term food security and sustainability.

## 3.2   The anatomy of food insecurity: three interconnected regulatory models and their disruption

It can be argued, as indeed Marsden did with colleagues in a longitudinal study of European food regulation ending in 2009 (see Marsden et al., 2010), that for much of the period between the 1980s and 2007–8 Europe enjoyed the benefits of a post-cold war and strong policy synergy between a private-interest governance regime on the one hand, and a corporatist EU state-based regulatory regime on the other. The former allowed, through the adoption of neo-liberal principles, the corporate retailers, caterers and food manufacturers to control and police the food system through developing their own private systems of quality control, hygiene management, and the development of logistical systems that allowed the cheap transport of goods across large distances. This empowered the corporate food sector to be the archetypal private deliverer of relatively stable food prices and quality on behalf of the state. This 'flattened' the significance of natural seasonality and food geographies, and created massive expansions in just-in-time delivery systems.

The latter, the development and maintenance of a Europeanized agricultural policy, supposedly developed to protect producers and consumers, continued to provide public financial support for farmers in order that they could pass on lower-priced goods to the corporate sector, and created a baseline regulatory system to support food consumers (through the development of the European Food Safety Agency, for instance). In addition, and often ignored in these accounts, there was the role of national social welfare programmes for low-income groups, which for a long time enabled food poverty for the lower-income groups to be kept at bay. Together with the vast expansion of relatively cheap imports (not least in fresh fruit and vegetables and fish) from around the world, driven by the corporate retail global sourcing strategies, these regulatory frameworks between the state, farmers and the corporate sector created stability in food security.

The onset of the 'FFFF' crisis in 2007–8 significantly disrupted these domi-nant and historically stable food regulatory systems, but it did not stop their operation, or their attempts, as we shall see, to re-define the growing problem of food insecurities. Faced with increasing fuel and food costs, more inter-national instability in geo-politics and food supply (such as the Arab spring and the Russian food embargo), the renewed fiscal crisis of both European and national member states, and the emergence of 'austerity' agendas in social welfare programmes, the historical synergies between the established regulatory systems started to fall apart. We can see this as part-and-parcel of the beginnings of the end of 'cheap food' (see Moore, 2015), and indeed as a segment of wider governance crises in capitalist world ecologies.

The rise of a third, what we might call, civil regulatory assemblage, that around alternative food systems, food welfare initiatives, sustainable food cooperatives and buying groups etc., has emerged very much to fill the gaps left by the partial collapse of the dominant regulatory systems. This has been fuelled, as much of our empirical evidence has shown, by a much more variegated set of actors involving civil society, small independent businesses, and some farmers and landowners, and is based upon more cooperative and collabo-rative models of governance (see for instance cases like the UK Sustainable Food Cities network, AMAPs in France,[3] CSAs in Flanders,[4] Coops schemes in Wales, peri-urban consumer–producer alliances in Spain, as examples). Some consistent features of these alternative regulatory assemblages are that they are place-based, and sometimes translocal in character; they are based on developing 'shorter supply chains' between producers and consumers; they are non-corporate in organization; and they define themselves by being outside of the two dominant food regulatory regimes outlined above. Moreover, they explicitly address and wish to solve local and regional forms of food insecurity and sovereignty, as well as often having strong ecologically sustainable goals and visions.

We can see, then, that in the current period of food insecurity the rise of new and alternative assemblages are being given significantly more energy and fertility, as indeed the older regulatory regimes progressively lose their legitimacy. Nevertheless, the degree to which these assemblages become potentially transformative will partly depend upon the continued adjustments and actions of the dominant regulatory structures. This in turn will partly depend upon how malleable and flexible these dominant structures are, and the degree to which alternative assemblages can become more embedded and institutionalized without losing their inherent integrity and autonomy.

It is important to recognize that as we depict the rise and proliferation of alternative food assemblages in Europe this is occurring in a changing policy context with regard to the two major established governance systems outlined above. For instance, the private interest model, during the period of crisis, has attempted to continue to drive down costs in its supply chains in order to continue to make cheap food available in its stores (especially through discounting strategies). This has further pressured the producer and small processor sectors, who have had to absorb much of this pressure (for instance in the now more deregulated dairy sectors). In addition, many corporate food retailers and manufacturers have attempted to embrace the sustainability and food security agenda by creating green sustainability initiatives with their 'dedicated suppliers'. PepsiCo, Nestlé and Tesco, as examples, all now have 'partnership' schemes with their suppliers, which monitor reductions such as in carbon emissions and water usage. As the food crisis has deepened, therefore, we see the private interest governance model – one that is also becoming more highly financialized – attempting to regain public and consumer legitimacy through corporate greening strategies. Greening is presently only one challenge for the private interest model, however. The rising health agenda associated with obesity, diabetes and undernourishment is meaning that the corporates are having to continue to lobby governments to maintain their traditional relations with government and their level of control over food safety and quality regulation. They are finding it necessary to continue to articulate their role as the real and trustworthy custodians of the consumer.

The corporatist state regulatory system is also, in combination with these changes, struggling to maintain its legitimacy. One fairly immediate reaction to the emergence of the food crisis was to regain a justification for productionism, or, as it was framed, 'sustainable intensification'. Armed and aligned with several influential scientific bodies, the renewed emphasis and policy direction for 'solving' the food security problems was again focussed on neo-productivist approaches. This has been aligned to various R&D EU and national funding schemes and agro-industrial strategies. In the UK, for instance, a new agri-industrial strategy was announced in 2013, linked to new government/ private sector partnership funding programmes. The emphasis is on sustainable intensification, and increases in 'productivity' through the application of a new round of digital and precision farming practices.

It is important, then, in considering the 'transformative potential' of alternative assemblages, to recognize how the dominant governance systems have attempted to reposition themselves given the end of 'cheap food'. In one sense all three of the governance models espouse sustainability and food security; and this places pressures upon the alternative movements, particularly in maintaining their integrity, and in resisting co-option and appropriation of the activities *inside*, as opposed to *outside*, these dominant regulatory systems. These *boundary problems* between the three interlocking but significantly contested governance systems are a major issue with regard to assessing the transformative potential of the alternative assemblages. For, as we will see below, the sub-alterns need indeed to engage with and be part of the deliberations in established governance systems if they are to become more empowered and embedded.

## 3.3    Towards new food regulatory landscape: opportunities for transformational potential and empowerment

In order for the new food assemblages to become more empowered and potentially transformative, then, our evidence suggests several areas of action and opportunity that need to be addressed.

First, there needs to be far more recognition and opportunity for these assemblages to be brought into and indeed made part of the decision-making structures of the existing multi-level state-based regulatory and policy frames. This means, as we see in the case of the Welsh Government, the recognition and prioritization of food poverty alleviation as an area of government action. The Welsh government has funded the Community Food Co-operative Programme and has created a food poverty alliance. At the EU level discussions are now taking place about the next reform of the CAP (Common Agricultural Policy) into a much wider Common Food Policy or Framework. At city municipality levels, many authorities embrace food policy councils and are now (as London is) setting sustainable food targets for local authorities. Hence a key empowering and potentially transforming process involves the proactive participation of assemblages into a more reflexive, strategic and deliberative food governance.

A second challenge is to enrol farmers and their unions into the food sustainability and security paradigm. This is a major challenge and obstacle, as the majority of conventional farmers are still highly dependent upon the two dominant regulatory regimes outlined above. They are dependent on retail and catering corporates for their price and quality setting; and far too many are still also dependent upon EU state subsidies. It is thus not surprising, then, that they feel alienated from many of the sustainable and food security movements given their 'lock-in' and dependent status on these historically reliable regulatory systems. Brexit in the UK and the debates about potential radical reform of the EU CAP after 2020 may present a political opportunity to unify the farming lobbies with the alternative food movement, and to significantly modernize agricultural policy along a wider set of food and nutritional security principles associated with quality food provision, bio-diversity enhancement, and health and wellbeing.

Thirdly, a major government role is to create and encourage new forms of both physical and social infrastructure, or what we term the 'missing middle', which currently provides the weakest links in creating the transformative potential of alternative food systems. This means creating a greater number of physical hubs for the more distributed rather than concentrated nature of their food networks and shorter supply chains. Alternative food assemblages are distinguished partly by their distributed (rather than concentrated) geographies of both production, processing and consumption. They do not abide by the same logics as the retailer-led logistical and concentrated chains. Thus far, many have suffered through their difficulties in getting goods to market, or meeting urban consumers' demands. In addition, government bodies also tend to deliver programmes and procurement contracts to large and concentrated delivery agents, rather than to groups of smaller and distributed actors. This is particularly a problem for the much-needed growth in fruit and vegetable production and supply, which requires not only local and distributed levels of pump-priming funding, but also a more diverse set of retail and consuming outlets.

## 4.    Empirical examples of the disruptive governance *process*

### 4.1    The UK and Brexit

These challenges for the UK agri-food sector are currently far from being resolved or even adequately debated. It is as though few can believe the damage or uncertainty or frustration (one chooses which it is, according to political predilection) that might follow. Rational policy options and developments (whether dealing with future trading, food or rural development policy) are being neglected in the febrile atmosphere of what we term *disruptive governance*.[5]

Disruptive governance is often advocated as if it were an end in itself. That, however, is almost always a misrepresentation, except in relation to a handful of anarchists. Most frequently, disruptive governance is intentionally pursued, with the aim of shifting the governance system to a radically different type of future; and in the context of Brexit, the hoped-for future is a radically neo-liberal one, with entrepreneurs unencumbered for example by EU regulatory restrictions, so that they can enjoy a regime allowing for the free movement of resources, goods, capital and services, but not labour. Another, not entirely distinct, variant of disruptive governance is a decidedly nationalistic, rather than globalist, perspective that insists on rules and regulations, just as long as they serve particular national, or at any rate nationalist, agendas. These aspirations are, of course, not confined to the UK or to Brexit. It can be seen in varied forms in North America, with the election of Donald Trump, re-writing of NAFTA trade arrangements, and the abolition of US environmental protections, and in Latin America with fiscal austerity and the corporatization of government, not least agri-business, for instance in Argentina and Brazil. Those disruptions are leading to higher levels of food insecurity for consumers, and greater vulnerability for farming families.[6]

Given the historical centrality for the EU of the agri-food sector, which accounts for around 40 per cent of all EU-wide expenditure and legislation, Brexit is hugely important to farmers and urban consumers and the entire UK food sector. In Wales, this is particularly so. Should a food company stockpile? Yes or no? Should one invest, or delay, or re-locate? While farmers might continue their daily and annual practices, hoping (and/or praying) for the best, off the land the questions are more urgent and immediate. Labour flows, not just capital, have become uncertain. The Seasonal Agricultural Workers Scheme (SAWS) was ended by the UK government in 2014, maybe only to return for just two years from March 2019, and then only for 2,500 workers whereas the past SAWS had recruited tens of thousands. No wonder some horticulture firms are relocating their production to West Africa. This new disruptive governance exposes the extent to which the UK agri-food system has been ordered by the EC/EU-wide regime during the last half century. Europe provided a combination of agreed measures to stabilize agricultural markets, and to establish practices that are all now being disrupted. This has effects, of course on markets, as well as on institutions and their regulatory practices. As we argued elsewhere, to disrupt just-in-time (JIT) food supply chains is folly. Yet, at present, the systems stumble on, threatened by growing uncertainties. The new order is disorder; and it seriously affects future markets, investment and economic outcomes.

Critics have already commented that there is little clarity from the government about the way forward for the UK food system. The Guidance Notes on food only began to be published in late summer 2018 (HM Government, 2018). The government has no Food Plan or Strategy, just a dawning recognition of the prospect of accelerating disruption with many unintended consequences and an inability to control anything. Rising concern from one corner is countered by, 'It will be alright eventually' or 'They'll sort it' from another corner. These fissures rather than attempts to find a common good and ground have become the *leitmotif* of both governance and policy.

For example, when the Food Research Collaboration published its *Feeding Britain* report in July 2018, drawing on the Government's own figures on UK reliance on food supplies from other EU Member States, its concerns were dismissed by Defra; then, just 48 hours later, another Secretary of State admitted there was contingency planning underway, and a few weeks later came the astonishing leak that the Transport Secretary of State was planning to hire a flotilla of ships to bring in food supplies! (See Parker and Blitz, 2018.) This, in the sixth-richest economy on the planet. No wonder food industries are alarmed. Disruptive governance is underway, actively attempting to shatter the prevailing regulatory structures and processes, in the belief that eventually this will create wider opportunities for creative actions. But if that were to occur, it would only be for the few, not the many.

Disruptive governance is thus a deliberate political strategy, the eventual goal of which is not always acknowledged by its advocates. The governance arrangements that have been in place in recent years are increasingly portrayed by enthusiasts as disrupting those arrangements as if they were outdated and illegitimate (Marsden et al. 2019). Old-fashioned political narratives focussing on the primacy of nation states, the benefits of liberalized markets, and the burdens of regulatory 'red tape' are emerging in the rhetoric of 'taking back control', but without being explicit about what is to be controlled, how or by whom. In this context, agri-food is being collaterally embroiled in a new politics – a politics that sits between rationalist and clearly worked-through evidence-based perspectives on the one hand and populist ideological promotions on the other.[7] The former proposes more integrated and systems thinking about food security, while the latter promotes more fragmentation and disruption, which would seriously compromise food security in the UK.[8]

For Wales, a small country with limited powers, the Brexit crisis disrupts the established ways in which it can operate within the *multi-level* governance frameworks that apply in the UK and the EU (Sjoblom et al., 2012). In disruptive governance, the political and territorial tectonic plates perturb their locations and what can be done at different governance levels, from the local to the global. Fast forward over a decade from the financial, food and fuel crises of 2007–8, and, while enduring financial austerity, disruptive governance is further destabilizing weakened regimes.

The UK's legislative approach to leaving the EU legislation ostensibly just rolls over EU rules into UK laws, but there is no clarity on how the laws will be interpreted or implemented. In July 2017 Lang et al. explained that there are dozens of links with food-related institutions and regulatory frameworks that will be disrupted if and when the UK leaves the Single Market and Customs Union. Ministers might profess commitments to high standards, but the UK's compliance will no longer be monitored by the European Environment Agency, and devolved administration will receive no European Regional Funds for help with finance. The UK will no longer have access to EU-wide research networks providing relevant data, nor support from the European Food Safety Authority, and also little or no bargaining power in trade negotiations or at international forums.

## 5.    The disruptive governance paradox: de-regulation or re-regulation?

Amongst these multiple disruptions and discontinuities, we also detect a *new disruptive governance paradox*: hope amidst the turmoil. On the one hand, the UK is creating uncertainty as a new norm, and nobody knows for how long it will last. Uncertainties are unavoidable when ministers protest they are committed to retaining 'high' food standards, while beginning to try to pre-negotiate trade deals with countries, such as the USA, that have lower food standards. On the other hand, severance from the EU could offer new opportunities to all, or parts, of the UK to forge a radically better direction for our agri-food systems. Simultaneously, farmer and environmental interests argue for new subsidy and support-payment systems, and food consumer groups and some trade unions are pressing for higher welfare and food quality standards. In the agri-food system, therefore, *disruptive governance may indeed unleash significant public counterforces that eventually undermine its plausibility*. This is a paradox of disruptive governance; *it could lead to the very opposite effects to those originally intended: more public and institutional regulation rather than less, as food producers and consumers recognize the harm that such disruption will cause.*

For years, evidence has emerged from civil society, academia and progressive agri-food sectors that radical change is needed in how the British are fed; there has also been evidence in official reports (e.g. Food Matters, 2008; The Global Future of Food & Farming, 2011). The scale of the changes needed is considerable. If the recent IPCC warning were taken seriously, the government and the food industry would recognize that there are just 12 years to contain average temperature rises to within 1.5 degrees centigrade (IPCC, 2018). Given that Wales is a major animal and dairy producer, and that livestock farming is a major contributor to greenhouse gas emissions, Wales ought to be helped to change. Considerable change is required across all of the UK, encompassing everything from the scandal of food banks to the food system's adverse impacts on the environment and public health.

Essentially a Great Food Transformation is needed, on a par with what was accomplished in the post-Second World War period of reconstruction. Now, the redesign should focus on, for example, lowering carbon dioxide and other greenhouse gas emissions, while diminishing dietary inequalities and health outcomes; substantially increasing consumption of fruit and vegetables, while producing more at home; shortening food supply chains where possible; shifting more of the £204 billion UK consumers spend annually on food and drink to primary producers under a 'fair returns' policy, rather than subsidizing farmers; encouraging young people into decently remunerated employment on the land. But no such vision has yet emerged from any of the three main Westminster political parties.

If Brexit was really about UK citizens 'taking back control', policy would be directed towards enhanced food security, in the sense of a system that more reliably provides a food supply that is sufficient, sustainable, safe, nutritious and equitable, but that is not the preferred direction of the most enthusiastic pro-Brexit disrupters. The signals from Defra's Agriculture Bill are weak and disturbing. It barely mentions health or devolution or indeed food. An Environment Bill is promised but unlikely to surface until well into 2020 (Environmental Protections and the EU Bill, 2018). Creating 'hollow' statutory bills and acts seems to be a political tactic of disruptive governance, and it needs to be challenged in the wider public and consumer interest, for it will encourage increased political and ministerial latitude in a post-Brexit and transitional landscape.

In relation to food, the rhetoric of Brexit is laid bare. Food, like ecosystems services, crosses borders, so 'taking back national control' is a recipe for detachment. If the UK chooses to set its own rules, it can do so, but that would disrupt the international trading on which our system relies. The UK could import any foodstuffs that satisfied our rules, but the UK is only able to export foodstuffs that satisfy the importers' rules. The UK has to be a rule taker, not a rule maker; the only questions is, which rules and whose rules? Those of the EU, the USA or the WTO; there are no other realistic options. The UK's food problems cannot be solved by parochial action. Even the EU needs to negotiate with other jurisdictions. Birds that winter on the farmland or shores of Wales often come from Scandinavia. Those summering in Wales may have flown from Southern Africa or farther. Biological isolation is entirely unrealistic; avian flu, for example, readily crosses borders and even oceans. The cultural messages that entice people to eat junk foods and unhealthy diets are bought by giant corporations, not by the EU. Without the EU, Wales' capacity to transform its obesogenic environment will be weakened, and the same is true for all parts of the UK.

## Conclusions: what does all this mean for rural areas? Vulnerability versus sustainability in rural transformations

We have shown above how established governance regimes, many of them developed after the Second World War, are now being transformed, either by relatively slow and piecemeal changes (as in the EU), or by more radical disruptive changes (as being experienced in the UK in the Brexit process). The lessons we are learning are that rural and agri-food governance systems are both indirectly and directly affected by far more than specifically rural policies alone. They are being affected by macro-governance shifts associated with the decline of state welfarism and the rise of neo-liberalism since the 1980s, or the more recent rise in neo-right 'disruptive' governance systems since the financial crisis and its political aftermath in 2007–8.

At the same time some opportunities are being taken to develop more reflexive and experimental forms of governance that foster more sustainable processes and practices for rural development. Since the turn of the century, we have seen the rise of new institutional arrangements and governance systems, developing at the local and regional scale (such as protected geographical origins for local and regional foods in the EU), or local and regional food procurement systems based upon linking local sustainable food practices to school feeding programmes (see Rossi et al. 2019; Morgan and Sonnino, 2011).

In addition, the city is now becoming a major actor in developing sustainable food strategies (Blay-Palmer et al. 2014). These countervailing trends beg two important questions at this critical juncture. First, do these more variable and place-based reflexive and experimental forms of rural and food governance represent a viable and potentially scalar beginning to rural and agri-food transformations? Second, if they do, will we see a continual decline in former established state regimes, such as what Friedmann (2005) has called the corporatist–environmental regime in the food sector? We currently do not have the answers to these questions, and a major area for further research concerns tracing the contestations and pathways of these co-evolving governance arrangements (see Marsden and Rucinska, 2019). We need improved conceptual and empirical tools by which we can study these competing governance frameworks.

A further observation, also highly critical to the outcomes that may emerge from these contestations, lies with a focus upon the rise and pathways of both rural and agri-food politics. Earlier regimes created their own systems of political legitimacy that created a coherence and at least some form of stability and working arrangements amongst the key actors. This could most explicitly be seen in the rise of post-war agri-rural policies around the world, but especially in Europe. This coherence was built around a compact or contract that balanced and promoted the production of relatively cheap but abundant amounts of standardized and quality regulated food for consumers with explicit protection measures to maintain family farm incomes and livelihoods. This was often termed the period of agricultural productivism, a regime that needed the explicit role of the state to intervene to stimulate agri-food systems and rural development. Such a compact was severely tested but interestingly not totally broken by the Thatcher–Reagan period of early neo-liberalism. Thatcher may have tried to challenge mainland European vestiges of state support for agriculture, but she largely failed to shift European policy in this area, or indeed in related areas of trade, environment and food standards policy.

With the rise of neo-liberalized disruptive governance and politics since 2007–8 we witness a refreshed and more profound attempt to disrupt earlier political assumptions about the role of the state in agriculture, rural development and food policy. It exists exactly in the opportunities Brexit brings to reform these policies, fuelling wider anti-European politics – almost to attempt to complete the de-regulatory job that Thatcher started. Bolsonaro's Brazil is a clearly different context but nevertheless one that is seriously attacking state interventions in food, farming and rural development in the cutting of funding for school feeding programmes and family farming cooperatives, and is challenging the future of the state support research and agricultural extension service (EMBRAPA and EMATER[9]). Food politics in particular has risen in importance as a result of these disruptive tendencies, and the realization by many urban consumers as well as rural producers that, faced with the unshackling of former well-established systems of governance, it is necessary to act politically in a policy arena that for a long period could be taken for granted.

Here, then, we see a shift in scholars' thinking, to the realization that we can no longer assume a de-politicization or a post-political stance in our research practice and theorizing. Food and rural development are becoming highly politicized, as established and long-running assumptions about the role of the state in these fields become more contested and based upon political ideologies of the right, left and green. This demonstrates opportunities as well as threats, and it also links much of this politics to wider environmental and sustainability questions in what Latour (2017) has termed the age of the new 'global climate regime'.

Whether the age is as coherent as the term 'regime' inevitably suggests is indeed an open question. But the parallels Latour makes between the largely right-wing climate deniers and the increasing assemblages of climate activists (like the Global Climate Emergency and Extinction Rebellion), and the politically contested fractures existing within the agriculture, food and rural development politics, are currently very relevant to our rural development scholarship. This needs not only to take on board the more politicized nature of governance and policy in the field, but also to recognize that 'the field' itself is being increasingly entwined into the wider sustainability and political dynamics associated with dealing with the Anthropocenic and global challenge. Studying rural and agri-food development, then, needs improved tools with which we can critically examine both politicized governance and integrated transversalities between the rural and the global environmental crisis. This is another reason why our research and epistemologies need to be both transdisciplinary and interdisciplinary. They also need to be 'more than rural' and more than food, for they have to incorporate the tensions and dialectics in the highly contested and contradictory politics of the 'global climate regime' itself.

Part of the picture of contemporary agri-food and rural governance has been the gradual weakening and demise of agricultural and farming political interests since the productivist period (see Self and Storing, 1962). Farmer power in government has waned, even in the most politically conservative governments, being squeezed by a combination of metropolitan environmental interests on the one hand, and corporate agri-business and food retailing interests on the other. It is only now that we are, however, seeing new alliances being built between farmers (such as the small farmers' Landworkers' Alliance in the UK, and more broadly different parts of translocal movements like Via Campesina) and urban consumers, and different shades of food sovereignty and solidarity movements (see Chapter 7 on family farming). These new alliances are largely outside of the main productivist farmers unions, which still mainly cling to their historical productivist ties with central governments. A key area of research is needed in the area of farmer politics, in a period of growing food insecurity and rising urban political movements for food justice.

## Notes

1.  Environmental Protection Agency; Food and Drug Administration.
2.  The Brazilian Agricultural Research Corporation.
3.  Associations for the Support of Peasant Agriculture.
4.  Community-Supported Agriculture.
5.  It is important to point out that this concept is by no means restricted and indeed applicable well beyond the UK Brexit conditions. Most notably, and built upon a rise of populist nationalism, we can see wider geo-political variants of disruptive governance in the ensuing NAFTA reorganisation of trade in North America; G20 resolutions on significantly reforming the WTO and its rule-making powers; US–China trade re-organisation and disputes; and EU–Russian trade embargoes and especially Ukrainian relations. In this sense there are wider and multi-layered levels of disruption to which a Brexit UK (and Wales) will be further exposed, post March 2019, whatever the actual shape of the Brexit 'deal'.
6.  For an analysis of this wider perspective, see Marsden et al., 2018.
7.  There is clearly a strong and scientifically sound set of arguments that has been developed by many agri-food experts (not least embodied in the FRC series of Brexit Briefing papers) for adopting a normative systems perspective for food, based upon a wealth of knowledge, and indeed linked to wider sustainability, and UN Sustainable Development Goals. The point is that disruptive governance needs to at least side-step, marginalise, fragment this science, very much as fossil energy supporters challenge and attack recent IPCC climate change evidence. This is, as history has shown most recently with Exxon and earlier strategies in the tobacco industry, a political strategy that attempts to question the status of overwhelming scientific evidence. That is another critical element of disruptive governance – to diminish public science.
8.  See, for instance, RSA, 2018, as one of many reasoned accounts of food system integrated thinking.
9.  See https://www.embrapa.br/; http://www.emater.pr.gov.br/

# 3. New power configurations and transformations

Power relations between the city and the rural and within the rural world itself have always been a key theme in rural studies, from the studies of antique towns to contemporary situations. From Marx to Duby or Braudel, historians and economists have long showed how power relations are inscribed in both economic relations (cities' provisioning, commodification of food, etc.) and political ones (authority, taxation, etc.). The relations between the city and the rural have been more recently reframed along the modernization era (from the 1960s to the late 1980s) and in the periods of so-called 'reflexive modernity' (Giddens, 1990), and/or, even more recently, of the *Anthropocene*. The current period is characterized by the development of new and contrasted ways of living, producing and consuming, and thus of articulating the urban and the rural as well as connecting the different actors within the rural areas. The aims of this chapter are to explore how social scientists have addressed the issue of power relations and reconfigurations within and around the rural in the modernization period and in the last decades, to discuss some recent approaches and their applications to French, British and Brazilian cases, and finally to define the priorities in terms of a research agenda.

## 1. Contrasted perspectives on power transformations

### 1.1 A rural world dominated by the urban?

The agricultural modernization period (from the 1950s to the late 1980s, at least) amounted to a devaluation of the peasant model, which had to give way to a rational and modern agriculture while rural communities lost their specificities and got 'urbanized'. In France, agricultural modernization processes resulted in a dramatic decline in the active agricultural population, from about 40 per cent in the immediate post-war period to 20 per cent in about 1960 and then 6 per cent in 1988 and 3.5 per cent in 2015. In the UK the trend was even more pronounced, with agricultural workers and farmers declining through-out the modernization period (to below 2 per cent), especially in the more productive lowland regions of England. In addition, the gross value of agricul-ture as well as its employment potential was strongly characterized by national and regional planning bodies as a 'declining sector'. Likewise, demographic changes in Brazil have been dramatic since the 1960s, when the process of agri-cultural modernization began (with the creation of the National Agricultural Credit System in 1965, that of the public extension company in 1970 and of EMBRAPA, the Brazilian Agricultural Science Corporation, in 1972). In 1950 the rural population represented 63.8 per cent of the total (51.9 million), in 1970 it decreased to 44 per cent, in 1991 to 24.5 per cent and in 2010 it reached only 15.7 per cent of the total of 212 million inhabitants of the country.

In the 1960s and 1970s, these profound changes gave way to sharp debates within rural sociology, especially in France. Henri Lefebvre and Henri Mendras would distance themselves from the then-dominating devaluation of the peasant model, showing the 'sustainable' specificities of rural communities, highlighting the role of social regulations that are played out in interpersonal relations without the mediation of institutions. H. Mendras argued there was a specific peasant 'social system', which integrated partial systems: family, economic, power, and inter-knowledge (Jollivet and Mendras 1971). He con-sidered that this social system was characterized by traits common to all the peasantry of Western Europe, from the medieval era until it was challenged by the industrial system. Edgar Morin, based on his work in Brittany at the same time, also concluded that the forces of homogenization at work did not lead to the disintegration of legacies of the past and local diversities (Morin, 1967). Certainly, rural societies were modernizing, but also retaining some historical structures.

This perspective was criticized by other scholars who saw it as idealistic and naive, for it supported the idea of a closed community dominated by 'internal' interconnectedness, global harmony and cohesion (Eizner 1974). Adopting a more critical approach anchored in a Marxist perspective, they suggested linking the processes at play in the rural world to external structural transfor-mations rather than 'only' approaching them in terms of internal logics, as in the notion of the peasant social system of H. Mendras. Their main question was no longer about the maintenance of peasant communities and social systems, but about the future of agriculture and the rural world in a capitalist country and in a context of globalization (Jollivet 2009).

Since 1975, the sociology of the rural world has been much less centered on the scale of the village of the previous generation. Certainly, the rural community is no longer 'the village' as it was studied at the time of Morin, Lefebvre and Mendras: contemporary phenomena are based on other scales and induce other questions related to urbanization, work and leisure migration, increased mobility, and the resulting changes in the intensity and diversity of links between town and country. Admittedly, the rural can no longer be identified with an area of social cohesion and inter-knowledge; it becomes a space of desire under the notion of 'country' (*campagne*) (Hervieu and Viard 1998), and of diverse leisure and residence uses for the urbanites (Alphandéry and Billaud 2009). The country's reinvestment dynamics even lead some authors to assess a certain 'ruralization' of the urban, parallel to the 'depeasantization' of the rural (Alphandéry and Sencébé 2009). For other authors, rural society – in the sense of a social group linked to a space by a culture, values, norms defining the ways of living and producing – no longer exists, and only 'rurality' remains, which is seen as embodied by 'qualities' rather than by people (Mormont 2009). However, the sharing of values and norms in a locally anchored society, which characterized peasant society for Mendras and others, retains its relevance for a revisited notion of rural community, which should encompass the diversity of social profiles present in rural areas and that of their practices. Today, processes of construction of 'new' shared values and norms might well impact ways of living and producing in rural areas, in line with the rise of environmental concerns.

In the UK, the processes of counter-urbanization began to dominate rural sociological and geographical debates from the 1970s (Pahl, 1965; Newby et al. 1978; Clout, 1972), as indeed suburbanization of the countryside selectively expanded under a strong post-war planning and agricultural policy based upon the twin aims of containing urban areas, and leaving farming outside of planning control and designated to the further intensification of production (see Marsden et al. 1993; Murdoch and Marsden, 1995). In this context there were significant transformations in power relations in rural Britain. Former landowning and farming classes were still dominant in some areas (see Murdoch et al. 2003; Newby et al. 1978) but were ceding power and control to the new ex-urban arrivals in the villages (what Pahl (1965) characterized as 'Urbs in Rure'). These powers to control local planning and create 'nimbyism' both widened and deepened throughout the 1970s, through to the 2000s (see Murdoch and Marsden, 1995, for a detailed sociological analysis of rural Buckinghamshire, where new 'class spaces' were being carved out and protected through selective planning control, and a parallel transformation in the rural economy occurred, away from agricultural income and employment to rural amenity, and high levels of diversified economic activity in income and employment terms).

Such transformations were typified by the concept of the 'consumption coun-tryside' – a countryside whose increasingly predominant ex-urban population wished to preserve the aesthetic and landscape qualities of a quaint rural 'idyll' at the same time as prospering from highly mobile non-agricultural labour markets and career trajectories. This was, as Ambrose (1975) called it, 'a quiet revolution'; one based upon the construction of highly positional rural housing markets, which often meant, ironically, that traditional local rural families could no longer afford to live in the villages their forefathers had indeed re-created.

In these transformed and 'preserved' countrysides, the very power to socially re-construct their character was strongly in the hands of the new ex-urban middle classes and not the yeoman farmers or landowners. The former were politically influential both at the local level, increasingly and vociferously popu-lating the local councils and planning committees with anti-growth and devel-opment politics, and at national political level, with the rise of Thatcherism, which stimulated both selective 'white-flight' counter-urbanization in the countryside, and the privatization of housing (see Phillips and Smith, 2018). This meant that much of the rural council housing stock (and farms; see Chapter 5 for more detailed discussion of this), the bedrock of traditional agricultural workers' housing, was sold off at a relatively cheap rate to existing tenants. This cut off the supply of low-income housing for rural workers and further exacerbated local housing shortages for those not able to afford the expensive costs of new rural housing developments. Thus, by choking local supply of public housing and allowing only restricted private development of new builds, the social transformation of rural England was strongly re-enforced throughout the 1980s and 1990s. The problems for 'homes for locals' became a common cause in rural development debates.

The farming population was in this period becoming numerically smaller, even if it was usually sitting upon substantial capital and landed assets. Faced with further mechanization and intensification, farmers were able to convert, lucratively, many of their traditional barns for grain and livestock into 'barn conversions', which attempted to keep the rustic aestheticism despite the significantly changing occupancy. Many village farms thus disappeared during this period, being amalgamated into larger farm consortiums; nevertheless, the built environment of the village still retained artificially the rustic appearance, as buildings had been re-furbished to resemble images of them in the 19th and early 20th centuries.

Therefore, between the 1960s and the end of the 20th century, much of the social transformation of the British countryside was largely complete with the growth of ex-urban middle-class power relations replacing traditional productivist interests. Farmers and landowners were also, in parallel, being affected directly by changes in the power relations associated with the food systems to which they were connected (see below). Productive spaces were thus about to be more controlled at a distance by external actors in the food system. A process called farm-based subsumption was also taking pace, already acknowledged in the 1980s (see Whatmore et al., 1986a and b). These two socially transforming processes in the British countryside in the latter parts of the 20th century – middle-class counter-urbanization and agricultural sub-sumption relations – tended to dominate rural sociological debates from the 1980s until the turn of the century (see Lowe and Bodiguel 1989); and served to contrast with the debates in mainland Europe. This was indeed the intellectual as well as the policy framing of 'post-productivism'. It wasn't until the 2000s that food production and wider questions of rural sustainability became major concerns in the UK (see Marsden 2003; Marsden et al. 2010).

In both French and UK cases, there are diverse and complex phenomena of reappropriation of the rural and 'counter-urbanization', whereby new inhabitants are attracted by the amenities (Woods 2006); this brings dramatic change in the rural population, and leads to the emergence of new rural inter-est groups, new disputes and conflicts, but also new alliances. In this context, the environmental question can appear either as the avatar of a secular urban domination over the countryside or at least as a strategy of investment in space by different social layers, or as the basis/foundation of a post-materialist reac-tion to the 'dominant' capitalist system (Billaud, 2012).

### 1.2   A rural productive space controlled by corporate external actors?

Another significant perspective on power relationships in the rural world is that offered by approaches focused on the rural space seen as a productive one. In such perspectives, like the one developed by food regime theorists, the focus is on power relations between unequal economic actors (such as corporate companies or big players in general against small farmers) rather than between social groups (such as a farming population versus urban newcomers), as was discussed above. Many studies have shown how farm strategies are determined by corporate food chain actors, even though some productive and marketing choices may illustrate other options. Food Regime theorists have analyzed the transformation of regulation of agricultural and commodity markets on the large scale and their key principles (standardization, durability, etc.), and theorists have highlighted the negative trends in global food relations and their effects on poor farmers (Friedmann and McMichael 1989). They have also analyzed the ways in which the global food system adapted to the growing criticisms it had to confront, as exemplified by the emergence of a 'corporate environmental food regime' (Campbell 2005).

This Food Regime theory, originating from 'world systems' approaches, takes a long historical as well as wide spatial focus, arguing that power relations are the result of different combinations of corporate and state interventions over different time periods. Transformations, like that from an Imperial regime before the wars to a post-war Fordist regime, have their roots in changing processes of rural enclosure, organization of production and consumption systems, and the onset of different rounds of globalization and financialization (see Chapter 4). The latest manifestation of the 'corporate environmental food regime' provides a significant critique of current processes of global agri-business and the new interconnections in trade (for instance between China and Brazil). The 'Soya-izeation' of Brazil, for instance, has indeed been a transforming agri-food force since the 1990s and represents new sets of global demands for basic food commodities as a result of population growth, economic development and associated demographic transitions with more meat eating and intensive livestock production.

## 1.3   Empowering rural actors: new territorial visions of rural development

Faced with these 'critical' traditions, some adopt more comprehensive (in the Weberian sense) post-structural approaches that are also more 'liberal' in the Anglo-Saxon sense. Indeed, by looking at the meaning given by farmers to their choices and actions, these approaches defend the idea that these farmers are active in negotiating the change imposed both by globalization and by the need to 'green' agricultural models. They suggested, for example, the emergence of an endogenous development model, which views rural development as resulting from local resources and driven by local collective action (van der Ploeg 1993), and, more recently, of a neo-endogenous development (Ray 2000) or of an 'integrated' rural development paradigm following the productivist paradigm (van der Ploeg et al. 2000; Marsden 2004). These perspectives acknowledge diverse redefinitions of rural identities around the valorization of specific territorial resources and social relations of proximity, in rupture with the principles and policies of the modernization project. In these perspectives, agricultural activities are still key to the visions of the future that are built, but other activities such as nature and landscape conservation, tourism, care, and education are also involved (van der Ploeg and Marsden 2008).

In Europe, LEADER programmes are emblematic of these perspectives that started to be conceptualized in the 1990s. The LEADER programme was launched in 1991 within the second pillar of the Common Agricultural Policy; it aimed at supporting bottom-up processes and involving civil society in contractualized projects, and reinforcing local and participatory democracy (Dolowitz and Marsh 2000). It relied on a strong premise that was the existence of territorial communities able to identify their own priorities and resources (Buller, 2000). Before this European programme, some countries had already implemented national programmes aimed at supporting local development strategies, such as rural development plans that were encouraged from the 1970s on in France and the UK, for example. The hypothesis of an endogenous development conceived on a territorial rather than a sectoral basis, was already key to these pioneer programmes. Within LEADER, an important principle was to allow the participation of local actors in the conception of their own development strategy and its implementation, through the key governance tool created by this programme, which is the local action group, supposed to gather local actors (local authorities, private actors, farmers, civil society organizations, etc.). This expresses the strong will to decentralize public action. Therefore, the LEADER programme has been seen as a new stage in the development of European rural areas (Osti, 2000), whereby local communities became sources of legitimacy (Bruckmeier, 2000).

Of course, the programme was not equally applied in all EU countries. Despite the fact that the local development framework defined at the European Union level is applicable according to the same procedures, each country assumes its aims according to its own priorities (Chevalier and Dedeire 2014). Over time, the network of active local action groups had densified, and in 2014, 1,800 LEADER regions (2,800 in 2020) would cover nearly 40 per cent of European rural areas and more than 60 per cent of the rural population (ibid.), with strong differences between countries with a high number of local groups as is the case in France (300 groups) and even more in Central Europe where in some countries nearly all the rural areas are covered, in contrast with the UK or Scandinavian countries where the spatial grid of LEADER areas is much less dense. It seems that prosperous agricultural regions that are also strongly inserted in agro-industrial chains, are less covered by LEADER programmes than less 'integrated' agricultural regions, but the presence of local actors able to launch such projects seems even more determinant. In other words, the dynamic of LEADER programmes is less correlated to local socio-economic dynamics and needs than to the political will to foster endogenous develop-ment approaches. Institutional perimeters seem to influence more the defini-tion of LEADER regions than the physical, historical or cultural unity that is advocated by the EC.

In France this has to be understood in the context of national planning policies that have favoured the definition of new perimeters for public action from the 1960s on with the Regional Natural Parks (PNR) – for a limited number of areas – and in the mid-1990s with the 'pays', aimed at including the diversity of rural areas. Indeed, French legislation requires LEADER regions to coincide with the perimeters of PNR and pays (RDR, 2007). In the French case, interestingly, these relatively new 'project territories' (as they are generally named in France) do not superpose with the 'old' institutional perimeters (regions, department) and thus are less submitted to electoral logics than in other European countries (like in Hungary). This may also be a weakness in the current trend of simplification of public action, as they are not the most supported scales of public action.

Even though, in the European philosophy of local development, the LEADER programme is supposed to favour actors' participation (included in the definition of their territory's perimeter and needs), in many cases it has become a mere territorialized policy, i.e., a form of territorial regulation by the national states, that sometimes leads to a standardization of local development, far from the idea of a local definition of public problems. In some countries, like Portugal, it has become a 'single window' policy. Moreover, the composition of LEADER programmes' steering committees is strongly framed by new public management principles, which leads to standardization and to the formation of a project class (Kovách and Kučerová, 2006), once again far from the initial will to 'reflect' social realities.

To a certain extent, influenced by European territorial development programmes, especially LEADER, in Latin America and Brazil public policies for rural development also began to be permeated by the territorial approach from the 2000s onwards. Brazil is an emblematic case due to the creation of national programmes such as Sustainable Development of Rural Territories (2004) and Territories of Citizenship (2008), both under Lula's term in power. Despite the many limitations and problems, the general assessment of scholars is that those initiatives might be understood as challenging experiences in a political context in which government centralism on the one hand and rural clientelism on the other were questioned in some territories on the construction of participative planning actions and decision making based on democratic procedures (Grisa and Schneider, 2014).

## 2. Rural specificities when addressing power and inequality issues

### 2.1 Specific issues of social justice and inequalities

Social inequalities and poverty have distinctive features in the rural world, which are much less known and studied than in urban contexts. Social inequalities are often less visible, as is rural poverty, due to the fact that it is often spatially scattered or even sometimes hidden (as in the case of precarious housing in some rural areas). The concurrence of multiple problems is an important factor in processes of rural marginalization, feeding into a vicious circle of decline. Loss of employment and services encourages further out-migration, which puts services and business even more at risk (Bock 2016). Power relations are also often interlinked in a systemic and even organic way as land, family, gender, economic, work relationships strongly interfere. In such contexts, it is often more difficult to detect and locate inequalities and social justice issues.

### Box 3.1   The fragilities of social action: an Ardèche case study

Southern Ardèche (in the south-east of France) is a rural region with a strong cultural identity, linked to its history and to its more recent reputation as an alternative region with a high proportion of neo-rurals. A variety of initiatives have developed over the decades, often launched by these (then) newcomers in interaction with local farmers and inhabitants. This region has undergone a strong loss of agricultural land and farming population; however, local agriculture has resisted and maintained some diversity, and about 15 per cent of the farms are organically run in 2018. Even though the articulation of diverse initiatives (emanating from civil society, farmers' networks and agricultural institutions) has supported a process of ecological transition, this hides a much more complex situation and raises issues of social (in)justice. Most initiatives indeed reached rather wealthy and/ or committed consumers – whether local ones or tourists in the summer season – and excluded poorer social groups while they would not address the main farmers' difficulties (especially small farmers' ones). In the recent period, several civil society organizations have started to tackle the issue of consumers' access to local quality food and of farmers' access to land, agricultural knowledge and support.

Among a larger diversity of initiatives, an example is a local box scheme, which is part of a national network of social enterprises that market vegetables produced by formerly unemployed people, who work on 2-year contracts during which they are accompanied in their future professional projects[1] (4,000 employees and 25,000 boxes at the national scale, on 120 different units, 24 employees for the local unit). Operating within a national project, this scheme also develops 'solidarity boxes' that are delivered to poor families, in interaction with local social services and with an educational programme about diets and food practices. In 2018, this initiative reached only about twenty-five families (besides the dozens of boxes that are sold at regular prices to local households who can afford them), and its possible extension to more households as well as its impact on families' food practices and on their links to their territory has still to be assessed. Another initiative was launched in 2015 by a local farmers' organization based on the observation that about 30 per cent of local fruits and vegetable production was not marketed because the products were too small, too ripe, or because the harvest period is limited due to work organization constraints. A 'gleaning project' was developed with the support of local social institutions and local farmers, where low-income households would go into the fields with the farmer, harvest the remaining fruits and vegetables, and also take part in cooking or processing workshops.[2] A third initiative aimed at setting up appropriate ways to support farmers or future farmers who are not well assisted by the conventional agricultural services because of their rules and frames, based on innovative tutoring networks linking experienced farmers and new or future ones.

However, the last two pioneer initiatives were financed through public funds that have been redirected to other priorities in a context of political change at the larger regional scale (in 2015), which shows the fragility of such initiatives, due to their dependence on public support. For the same reasons, a local network aimed at creating farm incubators in order to facilitate young farmers' access to land and training, has not yet succeeded in creating such innovative structures, in contrast to the nearby Drôme Valley, where such a project has benefited from a strong support from the local authorities (Bui et al., 2016).

Of course, the Ardèche case study (above) and the initiatives reported above only reach a limited part of local consumers and farmers, but they should be considered as social experimentations aimed at tackling social justice issues and likely to be a basis for future dissemination as well as exchanges in the region and between rural areas.

While there is strong evidence today of the need to combine civil society and public action in order to address social justice issues, a major issue for future research is to investigate the necessary complementarity of (i) lobbying work that aims at discussing and disseminating paradigms and visions that take into account social justice; (ii) social experiments forged with and by (and not only for) disadvantaged groups (poor farmers, farm workers, women farmers, poor families, or others); and (iii) tailored public policies that can support these initiatives by adapting or reinforcing appropriate legal and administrative frameworks.

*Source:* Based on Lamine et al. 2019.

## 2.2    The role of women and youth in rural development

Many works acknowledge the increasing role of women in rural transformations: whether this is or not distinctive of rural contexts, women lead a good part of rural initiatives and represent a large part of local staff in alternative and rural development organizations. However, the fact that initiatives, projects and networks are set up by women, youth, alternative farmers or any 'marginalized' social group does not mean that they are socially inclusive, and their actual social inclusiveness has indeed to be assessed and discussed.

For example, in an ongoing project focused on rural youth in the rural Ardèche (AJIR project), social inclusion is defined in terms of participation (a key principle is, for example, to include 'the voice of the young people' in the governance of the project), and not in terms of actual inclusion of marginalized or fragile groups and individuals among the large category of 'young people' that is aimed at by the project – an aim that would also require specific approaches to identify and mobilize these groups and individuals. In other words, this project addresses participation rather than social justice issues. As a consequence, the project tends to focus on the part of the youth population that is rather skilled and socially inserted as opposed to more marginalized young people. However, and linking to the discussion above about the role of LEADER programmes, the participation focus has led to innovative and radical changes such as a specific edition of a LEADER call for which the evaluation of the submitted projects was carried out by young people (instead of the 'usual suspects' of LEADER commissions, bringing together local public institutions and civil society organizations), which was a way to give the local youth a power of decision that is usually denied to them.

## 2.3    Rural social innovation

Social innovation is receiving particular attention in discussions on rural development and sustainable transformation processes (Neumeier 2012). Like sustainable transition, it has become a buzzword in policy and social movements discourses. One of the often-cited definitions of the notion refers to the satisfaction of unsatisfied or alienated human needs and 'to those changes in agendas, agency and institutions that lead to a better inclusion of excluded groups and individuals in various spheres of society at various spatial scales' (Moulaert et al. 2005: 1973). It is seen as a motor of change rooted in social collaboration and social learning, which appears as a response to unmet social needs as a desirable outcome. In a context of the longer trajectory of rural development in public policies in diverse countries, social innovation has often been introduced as the new panacea for realizing development and growth while, at the same time, warranting social inclusion and counteracting social inequality, as is the case in the EU context (Bock 2016).

Advocates of social innovation cherish the opportunity for civic initiatives to empower and to promote the renaissance of the cooperative movement. Critics view social innovation as justifying or stemming from state withdrawal and condemn the shift from public towards private responsibility. The extent to which social innovation may help to effectively fight rural marginalization, is still a matter of debate. Rural social innovation is distinctive in its dependence on civic self-reliance and self-organization due to austerity measures and state withdrawal, and in its cross-sectoral and translocal collaborations. Social innovation calls for a *nexogenous* (and not only endogenous) approach to rural development that departs from the importance of reconnecting and binding together forces across spaces (Bock 2016).

Some recent works have explored the specific mechanisms of rural social innovation. This led to identifying crucial aspects such as urgent societal challenges and ways to increase rural attractiveness, and to discussing appropriate forms of social innovation including new forms of social service delivery, empowering mobilization of vulnerable groups such as rural immigrants in social service design and delivery (Lindberg 2018).

Other authors, while not ignoring these specificities of rural social innovation, have rather insisted on the importance of rural–urban links and the significance of external contacts with other environments (Noack and Federwisch 2019). In this perspective, social innovation in rural regions can be inspired by cross-border constellations of actors and can build on bodies of knowledge and practices widespread in urban areas. This re-joins the argument of a combination of local resources and external impulses as a fundamental basis for rural dynamics (Ray 2000).

## 2.4    Projectification and territorial inequity as blind spots

However, these dynamics take place in a larger 'projectification' context (Sjöblom and Godenhjelm 2009), a notion that describes the transformation of governance systems and the increasing reliance on temporary project organizations: projects have become symbols of efficiency, innovation and adaptability (Boltanski and Chiapello 1999); they are expected to be flexible instruments, making it possible to cope with unforeseen situations, but they are also expected to provide means of co-ordination and policy coherence (ibid.). The 'projectification' context raises other problems such as temporal scale mismatch (Cash et al. 2006) as well as democratic accountability.

Based on the experiences with LEADER programmes, some authors point out that only the most resourceful rural areas may be able to develop social innovations, which suggests that social innovation may reconfirm existing inequality and promote further spatial disparity (Bock 2016). Comparative studies also suggest that rural development dynamics are unequally supported by such public programmes (Chevalier and Dedeire 2014) that are implemented at the national and regional scales in very different ways (with 'redistributive' versus 'elitist' strategies), as are other types of rural development programmes.

In sum, the 'projectification' context generates risks of territorial injustice or inequity, whereby territories where there are skilled stakeholders and where the civil society networks are active (i.e. attractive territories) are more likely to adapt to this context and develop diverse types of projects. Of course, the role of the state is precisely to guarantee some territorial equity in order to counterbalance these trends (Cañete et al., 2018).

At a larger scale, territorial inequity also refers to the ecological unfairness of economic exchange, as has been showed about agricultural exports, for example, through the exports by poor regions to richer ones, of diverse kinds of products, at prices that cannot include the local externalities generated by these exports nor the resource depletion (Martínez-Alier, 2002). Although these phenomena start to be addressed especially in the field of political ecology, it still appears as a key research gap.

## 3.    A pragmatist perspective on power relations in ecological transitions

The issues linked to power relations and governance have been amply discussed in the literature about food and rural systems transitions and within different theoretical strands. An overview is presented in Table 3.1.

Table 3.1    Overview of conceptual frameworks to analyze change mechanisms in food systems

|  | Food regime theories | Sustainable transitions | Alternative food networks studies | ANT & pragmatist sociology |
|---|---|---|---|---|
| Theorists | Friedmann, McMichael | Smith, Geels, Schot, etc. | Marsden, van der Ploeg, etc. | Latour, Callon, Boltanski, Céfaï, Chateauraynaud, etc. |
| Interpretation of transition mechanisms | Transformation of regulation over time and of power relations | Destabili- zation of the current regime under landscape and niches pressures, stabilization of a new socio- technical system | Combination of grassroots initiatives and emergence of alternative paradigms | Redefinition of alliances under the effect of enrolment processes and controversies |
| Scale | Large scale (global food system) | Large scale (socio-technical system) | Small scale | Meso-scale of actor networks and relations |

*Source:* Adapted from Lamine et al. 2015.

Power issues are much more central to food regime theorists and critical alternative food networks scholars who have analyzed in depth the processes of domination and exclusion but also resistance and alliances that characterize food systems. They are less central to transition and actor–network theories (ANTs). Although the role of power struggles and conflicts in transitions is widely acknowledged in the transitions literature (Geels and Schot 2007), this literature has been criticized for falling short in its understanding of power, especially in food systems (Rossi et al., 2019; El Bilali, 2019). Often power is addressed through niches and regimes interactions, although it is actually rather dispersed across actors at different levels than concentrated at regime level. However, an increasing number of recent articles deal with 'transition politics' (Avelino and Wittmayer 2016), and power has become central to the research agenda of the transition studies network, which has suggested three main perspectives on power: a socio-technical one focused on power struggles between niches and regimes as mentioned above; a governance one concentrating on institutional transformation; and a politico-sociological one (Köhler et al. 2019).

## 3.1   The combined effects of diverse niches on power relations

Some recent work has attempted to combine transition studies and ANT frameworks in order to address food systems transition (Barbier and Elzen 2012; Diaz et al., 2013) and better assess the transformations of power relations.

---

### Box 3.2   The Drôme valley case study

The Drôme valley is a mountainous rural area in Southeast France, located between the Alp foothills and the Rhône valley, with quite a strong local culture, as well as a strong attachment to the territory. Due to the diversity of farming systems involved (field crops, seeds, fruits, garlic, goat, sheep, aromatic and medicinal plants, vegetables and wine are locally farmed), there is little intensive use of chemical inputs in local farming. Organic farming accounted for 30 per cent of cultivated areas in 2017.

A diversity of initiatives has flourished in the agricultural networks and in the civil society, among which is Court-circuit, a for-profit association founded in 2009 by local parents to raise elected officials' and other parents' awareness in order to develop local and fresh food procurement for school canteens in place of agro-industrial catering. The parents rapidly realized that trying to raise awareness of incumbent actors was not sufficient and that school canteens wishing to purchase local products faced logistical barriers. They then decided to diversify their actions and to contribute more actively to overcoming these barriers, so they created a procurement platform, following a feasibility study that showed such a tool was missing from the structure of local food chains. This second organization, named Agricourt, was created in 2011 with a board comprising consumers and farmers who worked together on drawing up principles and rules; these were formally laid down in a Charter in 2012, which included ethical criteria such as lower trade margins on local and small-scale farming products to offer local farmers higher prices and at the same time encourage customers to buy these products. Public financial support allowed for the rapid development and professionalization of the activity: in 2015, Agricourt employed four people to provide 60 per cent of local school meals.

Over time, farming issues were integrated into the project, as this issue is critical in the Drôme valley, as elsewhere, in link with another initiative aimed at supporting the setting-up of young farmers and small-scale agriculture, a farm incubator where future farmers could test their project's feasibility for one or two years and build up a social network, launched in 2008 by another organization, Compagnons de la Terre. This was identified as a 'missing link' within the conventional farm set-up system, handled by mainstream agricultural actors. In 2012 the initiative moved to a larger place where project developers are provided not only with land and farming equipment, but also with storage, processing and marketing facilities such as an on-farm marketing point. In link with the local authorities and to favour land access, this organization also set up a Land Intervention Fund.

*Source:* Based on Bui et al. 2016 and Rossi et al. 2019.

These initiatives (and others; see Bui, 2015) not only bring technical and social innovation, they also have a transformative power. Indeed, their capacity to articulate different components of the territorial agri-food system (farmers, consumers, retailing, training, public institutions, etc.) laid the foundation for a new socio-technical pathway and for the co-construction of a more systemic vision that gained legitimacy and led to a mutual redefinition of narratives, strategies and activities and a larger transition of the local agri-food system.

What is the potential impact of these changes at broader levels? This region is highly publicized and often cited as an example in both academic and political arenas at the national and international scales (IPES-Food 2018). The collective empowerment process that took place in the Drôme valley is just one case of transition towards decentralized, locally embedded, sustainable agri-food systems (Stotten et al., 2017). Other case studies related to participatory plant breeding of diversification in agri-food chains have allowed for exploring the mechanisms underlying the reconfiguration of power relations in agri-food systems and for highlighting the need for a more variegated and dynamic configuration of power relations, as transformations depend on the variety of interactions that may develop among the actors involved (Rossi et al. 2019). These diverse recent studies have also highlighted some conditions that are necessary for such sustainable transitions, which are not present in all rural areas: the presence of skilled actors both in civil society and in local public institutions, and the capacity to mobilize public funding. This once again raises issues of territorial equity that require further research.

## 3.2    Towards polycentric and distributed perspectives on governance

Rural development and agri-food system governance are often tackled in the social sciences through the 'governance triangle', composed of the state, market and civil society (see Chapter 2), a concept that helps in distinguishing key institutional mechanisms that may give 'structure' to collective human behaviour within society (Rhodes 2007; Wiskerke 2009). While *the state* mainly corresponds to public regulation in order to structure collective action, the *civil society* governance mechanisms refer, for example, to the active citizen's participation and democratic control. *The market*, on the other hand, relates to market regulation mechanisms such as prices and rules for market liberalization or privatization as means to govern market partners' actions. However, recent works suggest that governance should be addressed through a dynamic perspective, and that the 'state' as a category that defines public action should be adapted to the specific context of relationships between national, regional and local public authorities and policies (Rey-Valette et al. 2014).

The question of how to govern multi-scale problems, as are those linked to sustainability issues, has given rise to diverse approaches and ample debates. While monocentric governance approaches claim that an ideal scale might be found to tackle such problems, alternative approaches have been developed, that favour multi-level governance or adaptive governance (Termeer et al., 2010). Multi-level governance approaches assume that the dispersion of governance across multiple levels is more efficient and more appropriate than monocentric governance and focus on cross-level interactions. Adaptive governance or 'co-management' approaches (Olsson et al., 2004) focus on the necessity to match scales (for example, ecological scales and social ones, knowledge and decision-making ones). Successful co-management, involving governments and local communities, often arises from the adaptive, self-organizing processes of learning by doing rather than from an optimal power sharing across levels. These authors also show the role of leadership (that spans levels) to develop and communicate a vision that can frame and give direction to the processes. A key argument of these diverse approaches is to match governance systems with problems relating to socio-ecological systems and to favour institutional diversity (Ostrom 2012; and see Chapter 5). In such polycentric conceptions, boundary or bridging organizations (Guston 2001) should play a key role in facilitating cross-scales interactions.

### 3.3    A need for contextualization: different rural (and territorial) realities and epistemologies

Territorial approaches are tackled differently in different national and cultural contexts. Recently, diverse approaches have been suggested to tackle sustainability transitions at the territorial scale, especially in link with agro-ecological and food sovereignty concepts. Vaarst and colleagues have suggested a conceptualization of 'agroecological food systems' based on the extension of the main agro-ecological principles (minimizing inputs, resources recycling, resilience, multi-functionality, complexity and scale integration, contextualization, equity, and nourishment) from the scale of agricultural systems to that of agri-food systems (Vaarst et al. 2017). This approach calls for a strong integration of social and ecological dimensions at the scale of 'city-region food systems', within a concentric perspective that may not apply to rural territories (Lamine et al., 2019). Wezel and colleagues (2016) have suggested the concept of agro-ecological territories, defined as places where a transition process towards sustainable agriculture and food systems is engaged. This approach, based on a combination of agricultural science, landscape ecology, and social science, defines food systems as 'socio-technical networks linking people, natural elements, and artefacts that interact with food issues' (Wezel et al. 2016). However, although these authors rightly underline the problem of scale mismatches between ecological and social processes, they do not propose to explore the functional links between these ecological and social processes that could support the reconnection of agriculture, food, environment and health, and remain in an 'impact-based' perspective (Lamine et al., 2019).

Of course, the territorial scale does not take the same meaning in different national and cultural contexts. In France, there are five to six jurisdictional levels as opposed to three in many countries (state, region or province, and municipality), as is the case in Brazil, for example. The complexity of the public governance system probably leads to higher 'transaction costs' but is also a sign of a democratic thickness that translates into the existence of various arenas of debates and allows for redundancies and subsidiarity. Of course, the articulation of these levels remains a key issue, as is that of intersectoral articulation – what some authors call vertical and horizontal interplays (Cash et al. 2006; Termeer et al., 2010).

In Brazil, territorial perspectives have been increasingly advocated by and used in experiments within social movements, as well as in the recent period in public policies (with programmes such as Territories of Citizenship – *Territórios da cidadania* – or Ecoforte, set up during the Lula era). They are also increasingly present in academic circles and in larger arenas. In the Latin

American context, though, territory is seen not as much as a policy action category than as a social struggle one (Escobar 2003). The proliferation of struggles that makes territory a strategic instrument for a diversity of 'deterritorialized people' leads to reaffirming the close link between the concept of territory and the space/power pair (Haesbaert 2018).

Territory is an analytical category but also a normative one, linked to policy/ political instruments that may lead to imposing the hegemony of certain visions. The reinvention of territories may be hegemonic and top down rather than bottom up. Moreover, while discussions over territorial approaches often follow an opposition between symbolic or cultural dimensions and power ones, these dimensions are indeed related, in the sense that the enactment of an identity would, for example, empower social groups, as was the case with the ecologization paradigm in the above case study of Drôme Valley.

## Conclusion

As the 'blind-spot' issue of power relations remains central despite the diversity of local and territorial initiatives and transition experiences that have been analyzed in the recent literature, reflection about rural futures should be inspired by two concepts that recently gained importance in the research agenda on agri-food systems. These are: 'food democracy', which refers to the ways (and extent to which) consumers, producers, and citizens can take part in decisions regarding agri-food systems; and 'food justice', which qualifies the ways (and extent to which) diverse social groups and categories are included or excluded from agri-food systems transition benefits (Gottlieb, 2009).

Should we then not also talk of rural democracy and rural justice? These are important not least in terms of the wider range of rural-based resources beyond food (e.g. nature, soils, water, minerals and property rights; see Chapter 5). Rural justice has mostly been framed in terms of 'agrarian justice' in relation to land access issues and/or in continuity with the concept already elaborated in the late 18th century by Thomas Paine, and amply discussed in diverse contexts of agrarian struggles and reforms in Latin American contexts, for example. But we can suggest that a larger conceptualization of rural justice should be considered. The rich experience of Brazilian academia, public policies and civil society action in terms of rural education and development, based on emancipatory approaches such as the theology of liberation, and on lasting experiences such as that of 'Educação do campo' public university departments, should represent a key contribution to this necessary conceptualization.

In this chapter we have attempted to bring together the necessary, but often overlooked, linkages between understanding the processes of transformation and the role of power relations. These are indeed very much the same part of the 'horse and carriage' – each driving each other. Yet new conceptualizations and empirical explorations are needed to understand these linkages in the 21st century. This is because there is, as many of the other chapters of this book recount, currently both a considerable amount of social flux – that is, which way should the carriage go, and what sort or combinations of 'horses' – state, civil society, markets – should be pulling it? At the same time there is also much contestation and dialectics in the process of transformations, such that it is less clear or coherent today than it was in the 1980s, about what types of dominant 'regimes' or hegemons there really are. This is also where we need to revamp multi-scalar territorial approaches to rural development, because we are seeing that former, what seemed to be coherent, globalized regimes are giving way to re-territorialized processes of empowerment and transformation, as the (rural) world becomes a smaller but more vulnerable place, which demands both care and hope.

## Notes

1. See http://www.leterreau.org/, http://www.reseaucocagne.asso.fr/english-version/
2. See http://civamardeche.org/Glanage-social

# 4. Financialization and nested vulnerabilities: the rise of fictitious capital in placing agrarian change

## 1.    Introduction: the rise of fictitious capital

The 2007–8 financial crash became a signature moment for the global capitalist system, and not least we are still feeling and indeed reeling from its affects a decade later. In this chapter we want to explore financialization and the variety of what we term nested vulnerabilities this engenders for rural populations and, in particular, the agri-food system. There has, partly because of the crash and its consequences, been a resurgence of scholarly interest in financialization by rural and agri-food scholars; and we want to explore this here in this chapter, suggesting that it is a rich area to further explore, both in itself, but also as a driving mechanism for affecting wider social and economic trends in rural development. Also, as we shall see social resistances to it – what might be termed re-agrarianized processes are also a rich area for further research. The first part of the chapter then explores some of the long-running conceptual issues involved in the process of financialization; and we then explore recent trends and effects especially in the case of Brazil and Latin America where it is unfolding as a major feature of structuring agrarian relations.

Financialization in capitalist systems has a long history. Recent French and European theorists (such as Tooze (2018a, 2018b) and Durand (2017)) have re-invigorated the significance of financialization in late capitalism. Adam Tooze's recent treatise: *Crashed: How a Decade of Financial Crises Changed The World* (Tooze 2018a:28) examines in detail the technical workings of financial markets and asset-backed commercial papers. Tooze writes:

> Political choice, ideology and agency are everywhere across the narrative with highly consequential results, not merely as disturbing factors but as vital reactions to huge volatility and contingency generated by the malfunctioning of the giant 'systems' and 'machines' and apparatuses of financial engineering.

It is a major force of uncertainty and disruption for governments and peoples around the world, especially as recent bouts of neo-liberalism have indeed stimulated its circulation and intensity of function. Durand re-introduces and indeed re-models the relevance of 'Fictitious Capital' (2017). A term first coined by the Bishop of Liverpool, Secretary of War in George III's North Administration in the UK, the concept was developed as a central lubricant of capitalist processes by successive scholars like Ricardo, Marx and Hayek, and more recently by Harvey (1982) in his treatise: *The Limits of Capital*. Tooze gives a more up-to-date account of its central presence in fuelling the global capitalist economy both before and during the latest financial crash of 2007-8. He defines:

> Whereas in normal times rising prices weaken demand in the real economy, the opposite is generally true of financial securities: the more prices increase, the more these securities are in demand. The same applies the other way round: during a crisis, the fall in prices engenders fire sales, which translate in the acceleration of the price collapse. This peculiarity of financial products derives from the fact that their purchase – dissociated from any use-value – corresponds to a purely speculative rationale; the objective is to obtain surplus-value by re-selling them at a higher price at some later point …. The self-sustaining price rise fueled by agent's expectations is further exaggerated by credit. Indebtedness increases prices, and since the securities can serve as the counterpart to fresh loans, their increasing value allow agents to take on more debt. On the way down … 'as asset bubbles start to burst' economic agents trying to meet the deadlines on their debt repayments are forced to sell at discounted prices. Unleashing 'a self-sustaining movement towards depression which only the state can interrupt'. (Tooze 2018a:29)

This is a very clear summary of fictitious capital, and lends itself to ask: how have these financialized dynamics affected the rural domain over the past decade? Since the deregulation of capital flows in the 1980s there has been a huge expansion of financial markets over and above more productive manufacturing capitals. By 2007, the total (notional) value of derivatives was some ten times that of global gross domestic product (GDP). By 2013, after the state-supported rescue of much of the financial sector, the value of purely financial transactions outclassed those of trade and investment combined by a factor of 100 to 1. According to IMF calculations, between the autumn of 2008 and the beginning of 2009 – the height of the most recent financial crisis – the total support extended to the financial sector by states and central banks of the advanced capitalist countries was equivalent to 50.4 per cent of world GDP (Tooze 2018b:69-71; Anderson 2019). This represents probably the most explicit state-based support for neo-liberalism that has ever existed in global capitalism. And it brings into sharp relief how the amalgams of power relations between private finance and 'deregulated' state policies have conspired to protect neo-liberalist ideologies and practices.

We want to shine a light on how these global processes have indeed affected and in some cases absorbed much of the rural and agri-food economy, raising some important conceptual and empirical pointers as to the undfolding agenda for scholarly research.

## 1.2    The ongoing squeeze on agriculture: a *longue durée* of creating vulnerability in the farm sector and rural sector

Notwithstanding the growth and significance of financialization, a significant trend associated with globalization is that a limited number of globally operating agro-industrial firms have gradually gained more control over the performance of agriculture across many sites and places. This concentration of power occurs up- and downstream of the farm and is irrespective of farm type, size, location or farming system. The production and distribution of added and surplus value in agricultural commodity chains has thus progressively been shifting away from primary production units to up- and downstream corporate entities. This process is also framed by many as 'accumulation by dispossession' (Harvey 2003).

The process has brought about a 'squeeze on agriculture', which refers to the ongoing narrowing of margins in primary production: increases in the cost of production outstrip increases in the price of farm commodities (Marsden 2003; van der Ploeg 2008, 2010a). At the national level, low agricultural commodity prices on global markets are transmitted to the domestic market through trade liberalization policies that are regulated by World Trade Organization agreements. The effect has been a decline in agricultural incomes worldwide. This 'squeeze' is also a major driving force for an ongoing scale-enlargement in the Global North, but also in selected countries of the south, notably the BRICS (Brazil, Russia, India, China and South Africa) countries and middle-income countries (MICs) (Edelman et al. 2013; Cousins et al. 2018). The 'race to the bottom', as Marsden (2003) describes the impact of the squeeze, has similarly and certainly intensified global competition between producers, regions and countries, spurring and deepening processes of social differentiation.

As we shall see in this chapter, the squeeze on primary production has most recently also been associated with the growing financialization of upstream and downstream food corporations and the globalized commodity markets upon which they depend. We argue here, with reference to both advanced economies in the north, and emergent economies in the south (particularly Latin America, Brazil) that there are two important parallel processes at play regarding the new rounds of financialization of agrarian change: the continuing 'squeeze' upon land-based production and its productive capital, on the one hand, and the spectacular growth in 'fictitious' capital markets in agri-business on the other. Faced with the inevitable and long-running obstacles in controlling and completely appropriating land-based production systems due to their natural and ecological constraints, financial and industrial capital has attempted to create conditions upon which it can create surplus value in developing complex financial instruments linked to futures agricultural commodity prices and market volatilities. It seems, moreover, that the very conditions of crisis which ensued during 2007–8, only exacerbated these processes of fictitious capital formation and investment. This is particularly relevant for agrarian spaces in the south (like Latin America and parts of Africa), whereby highly mobile forms of capital investment could be directed in new land grabs and agri-business investments. Such processes come, as we see below, however, with considerable vulnerability costs and impact in these very agrarian spaces.

## 2.    Agro-industrialization, financialization and vulnerabilities

Agriculture is thus in a constant, if contested, process of being increasingly both industrialized and financialized, which has brought about a disconnect between farming, nature and locality. Growth factors provided by 'nature' are increasingly being replaced by artificial factors generated by means of industrial and financialized processes. This has made farming more dependent on external inputs, new technology, expert knowledge and industrial, credit and financial capital. All of these are commoditized factors of production and they not only raise the costs of production but re-arrange and re-configure the control of markets, thus contributing to the squeeze on farm margins. Control over land, labour and capital by corporate structures is fundamentally different from that in family or peasant farming (van der Ploeg 2010b; Hirsch 2012) with the result that their dependency on external resources is different. Yet much of family farming (as we depict in Chapter 7) is indeed directly and indirectly affected by the mobility of financialization.

In recent years following 2007–8, the food system has witnessed the intensive application of complex financial products whose 'fictitious' value is linked to fixed and ordinary assets, like farm land, bushels of corn or wheat, or the myriad of products placed upon corporate retailers' shelves. This re-commodifying and 'rebundling' process in the face of growing food shortages and price rises has been centrally facilitated by neo-liberalizing states (as in the UK, Marsden et al. 2018), which contemporaneously withdrew public systems of welfare support (austerity) whilst stimulating private-risk finan-cialization. These co-processes of neo-liberalizing governance and corporate financialization have combined and held far-reaching effects not only upon the food production sector, but also on consumers and the complex varieties of rural firms and actors operating between producers and consumers. In short, this points us in the direction of needing to trace the contextualized and nested linkages between: (i) neo-liberalizing food governance, (ii) the socio-political impacts of financialization, and, (iii) the relatively recent deepening of nested vulnerabilities both for producers and consumers. Isakson (2014:571) attempts to link the (re-)production of vulnerabilities (among farmers) with finan-cialization arguing that 'Vulnerability is contextual and dynamic'. It is pro-duced through evolving social relations and articulated within a specific socio-ecological setting.

As we shall witness below, this very process of construction of nested vulner-abilities is not unique to producers; it also heavily affects the food security of consumers.

## 2.1    Interpreting the tendencies

Processes of deagrarianization and depeasantization are predominantly the-orized as inevitable outcomes of past and contemporary processes of agrar-ian transformations. Global, capitalist expansion has restructured effects on farming, the way farming is practised, the composition of the family and the provision of (family) labour; the intergenerational transfer of farm assets; urban–rural interactions; the natural environment and landscape; and the supply and provisioning of food. Scholars predict the demise of what is referred to in the policy and scholarly literature as 'small-scale' or 'smallholder farming', 'family farming' or 'peasant farming'.[1] We will indeed deal with these questions in more depth in Chapter 7 where we focus on the role of family farming. Globalization and neo-liberalism are said to work against or at least complicate sustainable pathways that revolve around family farming (see Hebinck 2018 for a state-of-the-art review these issues).

The expansion of a capitalist 'world-ecology' on a global scale continuously (re)shapes highly differentiated forms of agricultural production and repro-duction processes and investment and consumption patterns, affecting the forces at work at the level of the farm, family and rural and land-based liveli-hoods to the extent that the reproduction of family farming is jeopardized. As a result, some argue that family farming and any non- or pre-capitalist forms of production are on a linear path to extinction and destined to be subsumed by capital (Bernstein 2004). Some even call for rural development pathways that no longer place small-scale agriculture at the centre; seeing them as largely redundant and a dwindling sector in comparison with the power and influence of financialized corporate agri-business (Sender and Johnston 2004; Bernstein 2016). In Europe, where there is still considerable farm subsidy, farm livelihoods are in crisis. From 2003 to 2013 more than one in four farms disappeared from the European landscape; 48 per cent of farm holders were aged over 55 and 25 per cent were over 65; urban-based speculation has sky-rocketed, particularly close to towns and cities. This further consolidates farm land occupancy and potential conversion to residential and construction uses. From 2006 to 2012, some 107,000 ha/year were converted to strictly non-agricultural use.

Deagrarianization is broadly referred to as a process producing social, material and bio-physical conditions that are not conducive to the reproduction of agrarian and land-based livelihoods. Strictly agriculture-based modes of liveli-hood, it is argued, will become rare in the near future. Agriculture increasingly provides insufficient income and employment opportunities, pushing rural people to work off-farm, to migrate to the cities in search of work, and/or to engage in marginal 'subsistence' agriculture which is doomed to render endur-ing rural poverty from which people only wish to escape. Deagrarianization manifests in an occupational shift, ultimately resulting in a further reduction of the share of small-scale or family farming in total agricultural production. Depeasantization, on the other hand, manifests in development situations where farming is predominantly becoming organized by corporate entities (e.g. plantations) and/or by medium-scale, commercial, entrepreneurial forms of farming. Depeasantization entails the disappearance of the peasantry whose livelihoods are tied to the land, or their being dispossessed and replaced by outgrowers and contract farming schemes, or corporate large-scale farming operations. Depeasantization also means that the resource base of (any form of) farming is increasingly disconnected from the locality, from activities on- and off-farm and the immediate natural environment. 'Capital' (i.e. agri-business companies) increasingly structures agrarian relations, determin-ing how farming is and should be done, what resource-use efficiency is, how added value is distributed and how rural incomes are constituted.

Considering global tendencies in the agriculture and rural development process, we cannot, realistically, deny that deagrarianization is a real trend; nor can we refute that processes of rural livelihood diversification occur, or that the continuity of (family and peasant) farming is challenged. There are many processes at play that push rural people off the land to a marginal life in cities. There is thus no doubt that capitalist expansion and restructuring of markets and resources governance systems poses new threats and continuously forces us to rephrase existing sets of agrarian and rural development questions, and that it simultaneously generates multi-faceted agrarian and rural-based crises that challenge the continuity of farming and the strengthening of rural livelihoods.

The predominant trend in Africa and elsewhere in the Global South and North may well be that agriculture as the basis of rural livelihoods is increasingly being squeezed and challenged because of land issues and conflicts as well as more financialized and chaotic markets, which in turn fuel a combination of farm closure, fallowing of land, depopulation and migration to the city in the hopes of earning additional income to feed back to homes in the rural area. This trend is well documented in the literature about the Global South (Marsden 2003; Roep and van der Ploeg 2003). However, a complete disconnection from the rural base does not occur. Rural people continue to (re) engage in a range of rural and land-based activities and forms of agriculture.

## 2.2    Financialized land grabs

Large-scale land acquisitions have received substantial attention in recent years. This phenomenon is also framed as 'grabbing' and occurs at a global scale (Borras and Franco 2013; Fairhead et al. 2012). Land grabbing is clearly associated with the corporatization of agriculture and the ongoing process of financialized agro-industrialization. As land is increasingly commoditized it changes in meaning, rights and usage. New land markets have developed (see Chapter 5), and the re-registration of land titles to individuals or groups has facilitated land deals. In the Global South, where land rights are often uncodified, large-scale land acquisitions have forced many people to vacate land, often without consideration for either their cultural rights to land or proper compensation. Communal land rights and their related resources are frequently ignored or abused. In the northern and western parts of Europe, land acquisitions have made land more expensive and machine-servicing more costly.

Corporate interest in farmland is fuelled by financialized speculation and the expectation that land prices will rise in relative terms to other investments, especially in periods of recession. The rising importance of 'flex crops' and a variety of precious metals (not least lithium in Chile and Bolivia) are also significant in explaining the global interest in land by corporate capital groups and local elites. Flex crops have multiple uses (food, feed, fuel, fibre, industrial material, etc.) that can be flexibly interchanged in response to market prices and other incentives, such as carbon credits (Borras et al. 2016:2). They can also be profitably produced on large, mega farms that can swiftly respond to the increased global demand for flex crops, such as maize and sugar.

Although our interest is more directly the issue of land, it is important to highlight that there is already an important literature on the issue of 'green grabs', which refers to the process of appropriation, control and restriction of access to natural resources such as water, fauna and flora (Fairhead et al. 2012: Sauer and Borras 2016). In some countries, and especially in specific rural territories, green grabbing is, in fact, the main process of what Harvey (2003) called 'accumulation by dispossession'. It is worth noting that in some countries and particular situations, the interest in land is secondary, because what really matters is the appropriation of the resources that are under the ground or on the surface.

This re-commodifying and 'rebundling' process in the face of growing food shortages and price rises has been centrally facilitated by neo-liberalizing states (as in the UK). This contemporaneously withdrew public systems of support (austerity) whilst stimulating private-risk financialization. Following and developing a food *system* perspective, therefore, signals that these co-processes of neo-liberalizing governance and corporate financialization have combined far-reaching effects not only upon the food production sector, but also on consumers and the complex varieties of firms and actors operating between producers and consumers. In short, this points us in the direction – as much of the succeeding analysis demonstrates – of needing to trace the contextualized and nested linkages between: (i) neo-liberalizing food governance, (ii) the socio-political impacts of financialization, and, (iii) the relatively recent deepening of nested vulnerabilities both for producers and consumers.

What we can postulate here is that there is the need to conceptually and empirically explore the revised and systemic interconnections between these three spheres. Isakson (2014:571) in a special issue of the *Journal of Agrarian Change* devoted to financialization, attempts to link the (re)production of vulnerabilities (among farmers) with financialization:

> Vulnerability is contextual and dynamic. It is produced through evolving social relations and articulated within a specific socio-ecological setting. The commodification of agriculture and agrarian relations, the deterioration of ecological conditions and growing inequality resulting from agricultural modernisation and the rollback of state protections under neo-liberal restructuring ... combined, these processes have helped produce a global peasantry, that, in many ways is highly vulnerable to the contemporary risks emanating from climate change and increasingly volatile market conditions.

He concludes (p557): 'Financial means cannot substitute for the socio and ecological foundations of security.'

The recent conjunctions between neo-liberalist food governance, new rounds of financialization, and indeed its relationships with setting off a wider and deepening set of social vulnerabilities is creating, overall, as we shall analytically examine below, a food landscape which is far more volatile, not just in market terms. For as Visser et al. in the same special issue (2015) suggest, key areas needed for further research on financialization involve tracing thoroughly the very social vulnerabilities and volatilities which it inherently creates; and identifying the diversity of 'actors in context' who promote the drivers, strategies and discourses of the processes as they unfold. They argue (2015:547):

> To what extent are these drivers, strategies and legitimating discourses simply about the management of risk, and to what extent are they about generating profit at the expense of others? Such research is crucial in order to gain a deeper understanding of the rise of finance in agriculture, and the possibilities and limitations of regulation.

As we shall witness below, this very process of construction of nested vulnerabilities is not unique to producers; it also heavily affects the food security of consumers.

## 3.    New volatilities and nested vulnerabilities in the food system for both producers and consumers

The recent uneven growth of financialization emerging from 2007-8 has led to the rejuvenation and reproduction of a series of interconnected food system vulnerabilities that cover both food unsustainabilities *and* food insecurities. Both the production and consumption arenas in the food system have become more systemically connected and more vulnerable over recent years. Since 2007-8, it can be argued that *both* the sustainability and security dimensions of food have diminished compared to earlier governance phases, when both the security and sustainability of the food system was at higher levels. Now both realms are seen to be in crisis. The combinative nature of this crisis has been documented for some time both in Europe (see, for example, Marsden et al. 2010) and in North America, where the corporate private-interest model has recently been discussed as an expression of a wider crisis associated with a persistent neo-liberal form of food regulation (see Wolf and Bonanno 2014). As Bonanno (2014:27) argues:

> The limits of neo-liberalism are theoretically clear and empirically evident. Arguably, the crisis of the regime can be seen more as a demonstrated fact rather than a hypothesis. Additionally, existing contradictions make it problematic to argue about the existence of an organised system. Neo-liberalism appears more like a project in crisis, rather than a regime. Yet, and despite claims of economic unsustainability and lack of substantive democracy, neo-liberalism remains the dominant ideology and, in many instances, the preferred political choice of the second decade of the twenty first century.

The food system is a central subset of these new contingencies, and it is one that, as we shall delineate in this chapter, openly displays their contradictions and vulnerabilities, thereby reducing the overall legitimacy of the neo-liberal food regulatory system as a whole (see Ostry et al. 2016).

We can identify and discuss the onset of interconnected food vulnerabilities through a focus on the food system in the EU and UK, where, since the start of the combined financial, fuel, food and fiscal (FFFF) crisis, we have witnessed both the rejuvenation of the private-interest, corporate-led governance model, and an intensification of its social impacts and vulnerabilities; such that a renewed discourse around 'food security' has emerged (see Feeding Britain Report 2014; UK National Report, Transmango Project 2015). This is leading to a new set of conjunctures which are far more unstable in comparison with the late 20th century, which delivered what seemed to be abundant and socially legitimate food provision at a relatively cheap price for the majority of the population. Under the current conditions, by contrast, we can expect more volatile and nested vulnerabilities in food nutritional and provision systems operating at the same time and in parallel spaces. For instance, as we shall depict, we are witnessing the continued intensification of production and supply of food and the consequent removal of formerly viable farm businesses, at the same time as a growth in alternative food networks (AFNs) is occurring as a reaction to these trends. What is clear, and UK governance seems particularly prone to this, is that there is a lack of coherence and proactivity on the part of the state to act (and especially to positively intervene) in and on behalf of the wider public interest; over and above its private-interest obligations to corporate (and increasingly financialized) private food interests.

These dynamics are tending to devalorize and disempower significant groups of consumers and producers, such that value is continually abstracted from both by the more concentrated and financialized corporate manufacturing, catering and retailer sectors. This is more evident today than it was a decade ago, when the dominant private-interest food governance model could rely upon fairly stable and abundant procurement of food materials from around the world at a relatively cheap (albeit externalized) cost. At the same time, general levels of economic growth and universal state welfare spending also tended to uphold the effective demand and consumption of food goods for the majority of the low-income population. Prior to the ongoing FFFF crisis emerging from 2007-8, whilst there was a general recognition that the food system was increasingly ecologically unsustainable, its ability to secure food for the majority of the population was largely taken for granted.

As Moore (2016) and Marsden and Morley (2014) have recently pointed out, today the emerging conjuncture of resource depletion, on the one hand, and the continued withdrawal of national state welfare nets on the other, together with the upholding of a continuing neo-liberalizing and financialized corporate food system, have led to the production of a new set of nested and recombinant food security vulnerabilities.

The current conditions have also further stimulated the corporate controlled 'financialization' of key aspects of the food system, as growing scarcities have led, in turn, to new rounds of speculative financial investments in land and key natural resources (see Ouma 2016). New forms of market instruments and investments are developed for financial and investment gain, thus often promoting short-term and ephemeral gains and volatilities in agri-food markets (see Birch and Lawrence 2009; Clapp and Fuchs 2009; Fairburn 2014; Isakson 2014). One reaction to the crisis has thus been to continue to shift financial resources to resource-based 'safe-havens' and 'land grabs', further reducing social and public-good investments that target vulnerabilities and inequalities.

These transformations, we argue here, will require innovative forms of food governance to replace the current withdrawal of national-state food policy in the face of the dominant corporate and financialized food governance model. The related postulates underpinning this argument which we begin explore in this chapter include the following:

(i)    Since 2007-8 and the emergence of the FFFF crisis there has been a political metamorphosis between national state polities and corporate financialization. A common effect of this has been a further concentration of control over natural resources, infrastructure and food-based capital.

(ii)   This process is deepening and reproducing food vulnerabilities and inequalities, while at the same time promoting separate and autonomous 'trans local assemblages' in the wider NGO and civic sectors. This is an outcome of ongoing efforts to ameliorate some of these vulnerabilities and to create new social and physical infrastructures that enhance (in the medium to long term) food system resilience.

(iii)  The dual and contested transformation process at play is creating new territorialized 'niches' at the same time as the neo-liberal financialized model becomes a source of basic vulnerability itself in that it tends to deepen both food unsustainability and food insecurity.

(iv)  Both financialization and its nested vulnerabilities in food systems need empirically grounding in more fine-grained analyses that tease out the economic and social relationships and dependences these concepts imply. For instance, in order to re-build more resilience and adaptive capacity in food systems it is necessary to fully address the embedded ways in which vulnerabilities and financialization *are working together*. This provides a more integrated conceptual basis for understanding vulnerability (see Adger 2006) as 'the state of susceptibility to harm from exposure to stresses associated with environmental and social change and from the absence of the capacity to adapt' (Adger 2006:26).

(v)  Critical in mediating the changing balances between the onset of nested vulnerabilities and the (potential) creation of adaptive capacities and resiliencies is the question of the types and modes of food governance. These even in their most neo-liberal forms, play a critical role in conditioning these balances. As even the conservative International Monetary Fund has recently come to recognize:

> In sum, the benefits of some policies that are an important part of the neo-liberal agenda appear to have been somewhat overplayed. In the case of financial openness, some capital flows, such as foreign direct investment, do appear to confer the benefits to growth claimed for them. But for others, particularly short-term capital flows, the benefits to growth are difficult to reap, whereas the risks, in terms of greater volatility and increased risk of crisis, loom large. (Ostry et al. 2016:40)

(vi)  It follows from these postulates, as we will address in the conclusion, that the elimination or reduction of nested vulnerabilities in food systems, and their attendant capacities to build more resilience, will require systemic and governance attention, and indeed a shift and innovation in how the financialized 'markets' are managed within (as well as beyond) their specific institutional contexts.

(vii)  The case of Brazil and Latin America can be taken as paradigmatic of the confluence between these three processes that gravitate around financialization. The neo-liberal governments that have taken over the governments of Chile, Argentina, Paraguay, Colombia and also Brazil are largely supported by the rural elite sector identified with the so-called agri-business (Sauer et al. 2018). Because of the strong economic insertion of these countries into global commodities markets, such as soy and other agricultural products, these political groups advocate the liberalization of international trade and, above all, the deregulation of access to land and other natural resources such as water and seeds. In Latin America, private interests and neo-liberal governments are creating proper conditions for the development of the neo-extractivist model of economics, which is based on political coalition based on exploitation of natural resources and exports of raw materials (Veltmeyer and Petras 2014; Wolford et al. 2013; Ye et al. 2019).

(viii)  While there are many reasons for disenchantment and resignation, given the oppressive power and omnipresence of the signatories of this model in all spheres of the political and institutional status quo in these countries, there is also room to believe that this power might be more apparent than real. Or at least, it is less unbreakable than it looks at first glance. Evidence of fragility emerges from the environmental risks posed by (neo) extractivism, particularly in the face of the increasingly significant restrictions and resistance of consumers and importers of food and feed products from regions and areas that have suffered deforestation or environmental impacts (Ye et al. 2019). The recent episode of the burning in the Amazon region of Brazil and the reactions of the EU governments, clearly expressed by French President Emmanuel Macron and German Chancellor Angela Merkel, are consistent indications that there is ongoing global surveillance, which may represent some brake. It can be argued, as the mainstream business as usual does, that these statements are only resistances to the EU-MERCOSUR trade agreement. On the other hand, it can also be said that these initiatives might sum up to the new green activism of young people around the world, very well represented by the actions of Swedish Greta Thunberg and her strike for the climate.

## 4.    Financialization in the Latin American context: a case of expanding financialization in the midst of the financial crisis

With inherent structural limits to the growth of production and consumption of physical commodities – whether for environmental or supply and demand reasons – there is a greater incentive to use financialized derivatives in agri-food systems. Without any physical limits, commodity derivatives are 20 to 30 times more than the value of the physical production of commodities.

Commodity assets under derivatives grew by 450 per cent, from US$10 billion dollars at the end of the 20th century to US$450 billion dollars in April 2011. Financial investors now account for 85 per cent of the commodities futures markets. Such investors do not trade on the basis of fundamental supply and demand relationships in single markets. There is a strong correlation between commodity futures markets with prices in other speculative financial markets rather than supply and demand of physical commodities.

Financialization in agri-business has produced a gap between the sphere of production, whether agricultural and livestock production or agro-industrial production, and the control of that production (Clapp and Fuchs 2009). There are two aspects that contributed to the increase of this distance. The first has to do with the greater number and types of actors now involved in global agri-food chains (trading companies, pension funds, investment agents and other institutional investors, shareholders, securitization and other companies). The second aspect is that food is also abstracted from its physical form into highly complex financial products such as derivatives of agricultural commodities (Clapp and Fuchs 2009). Such products are considered investments which provide an opportunity to diversify financial portfolios without the need the physical purchase of products.

Not only banks but also the large trading commodities are strongly involved in the agricultural derivatives market, as is the case of ADM, Bunge, Cargill, and Louis Dreyfus. Pension funds also make up a major player internationally. They hold between five and fifteen billion dollars in assets linked to rural areas (Clapp and Fuchs 2009). Calyx Agro Fund, for instance, seeks explicitly to identify, acquire, develop, market and sell land to large institutional investment funds, such as AIG that has a focus on Latin America. Elsewhere, Emvest and Silver Street Capital funds established investment funds aimed at agricultural assets in Africa.

However, the influence of these actors and the results of their investments is not something transparent depending on the distance that financialization provided. Decisions and their weight on the allocation of investment in agricultural and livestock production do not appear in the aggregate statistics; they are very privatized systems of financial management.

The financialization from large corporations also occurs in the downstream tiers of the agri-food chain with a high concentration of capital in food retailing. The market share of supermarkets in food retailing in Latin America increased from 10 per cent to 20 per cent in 1990 to 60 per cent in 2001 (Isakson 2014). The five largest supermarket chains accounted for almost two-thirds of food sales on the continent. In addition to the weight of the capital markets of these retailers, they offer financial services such as credit cards, insurance, transfers and payment services (Isakson 2014).

Moreover, the large retail chains seek internationalization and financialization as a growth strategy and response to a market with an increasing concentration of capital. The increasing interconnectedness between financial and non-financial markets and among regional markets extended the reaction to market shocks such as the recent financial crisis and economic stagnation. Market liberalization has also coincided with the expansion of emerging markets that are important vectors in the development of commodity markets.

In Latin America and elsewhere, as pointed out by Ye et al. (2019), financialization is also related to the deepening of the neo extractivism economic pattern, which represent a new way of production and reproduction that captures important sectors of emerging economies and subordinates them to global accumulation. The key point is the extractivism could not be possible and would not work so well without the alliance of financialization, which becomes a strategy to hide the ownership and the flows both to avoid control and regulation as well as taxation.

These circumstances have increased opportunities for financial market participants to enter these markets and the large trading companies to expand their physical assets. Thus, there is an aggregation effect on the financial returns of commodities overlapping with the returns of other financial assets, leading to a strong correlation between commodity prices and the financial ratios. Price volatility reduces the incentive for the accumulation of physical capital. Despite being in line with historical patterns, volatility has increased in recent years.

As a result, financialization caused more vulnerability of commodity markets in relation to fluctuations in the financial market. The size of the trade in commodity futures markets has tripled since 2004. This size reached its peak in 2012 with the sale of three billion contracts. It is noteworthy that the sale takes place in a very concentrated form. There are now only a few global market infrastructures for commodity futures markets. One is European, four are Chinese and two are American. The market share from Chinese companies is 50 per cent. The further consolidation of these companies is under way and there may be even greater concentration. This tends to worsen the problem of forming trusts in the global commodity futures market. Most investment funds in commodities and land started their investments within the last decade in their home markets and preferred mature markets. However, in the past nine years, there has been an increasing shift to emerging markets. The geographic focus of these emerging markets has been the South American and the African continents. Traded funds have provided the opportunity for investor participation in large beef cattle production scale operations, milk, vineyards and permanent crops. In the last decade, these funds have expanded to Eastern Europe. In general, private corporations raise funds from families, wealthy individuals and financial institutions in order to acquire and manage land.

With institutional investors, the management and the ownership of land and agricultural assets are separated along the same lines as in the large corporations. The reason is that the management and the scale of operations can be performed more effectively in a wider platform of assets managed by third parties. Brazil, according to the surveyed funds, has a legal system that facilitates foreign investment in land and a relatively light regulatory environment. Managing companies as third parties resort to a number of different practices and strategies, mobilizing different instruments and repertoires.

Both conditions have attracted foreign investment in land and it is estimated that a third of the funds operating globally have investments in Brazil. In a kind of south-to-south globalization, fund managers have leveraged the Brazilian know-how in South Africa where costs of land acquisition are much lower. However, the control of capital is rather unstable, multiple and far from being transparent (Fairburn 2014). There are two examples given by Fairburn (2014) which clearly illustrate these complex arrangements. One is the joint venture between the US-based pension fund TIAA-CREF and the Brazilian agri-business giant COSAN in 2008 that created a rural estate company called Radar Propriedades S/A. Another example is Adecoagro S.A., a publicly traded company from Luxembourg whose holding company headquarters are in Delaware. It owns 270,000 hectares across South America. It is probably more accurate to describe this type of capital control as transnational and global rather than generically foreign.

When considering different aspects of financialization as a whole, and especially in the case of agri-business, certain risks are unveiled. On the one hand, there is the argument that it has a positive effect on the amount of money capital and liquidity, in a Marxian sense, available for investment. On the other hand, there is a risk of increased inequality in the distribution of resources in the agri-business value chain detrimental to productive capital and in favour of finance and short-term profit gains.

The enormous concentration of power in large retail corporations and their growing financialization raises the issue of power relations within the production chain (Isakson 2014). The financialized actors take ownership of a larger surplus value generated and this has clear implications for key issues like quality (tends to be lower due to the pressures for cost reduction), sustainability (greater pressure on resources without the knowledge of environmental parameters) and working conditions with the emphasis on low wages to keep the lower production costs.

## 5.    Financialization in Brazilian agri-business and the bio-economy

When compared to North American agri-business, the emergence of the Brazilian agri-business is more recent.[2] The development of Brazilian agri-business can be divided into three major stages. The first stage refers to a strong agricultural modernization which started in 1965 and went on until 1985. The second stage covers the period between 1985 and 1995. The latter is regarded as a period of crisis and restructuring that unleashed the beginning of an 'economy of the agri-business'. This stage is marked by a greater presence of private capital in the credit operations and agricultural financing as well as a higher concentration of agricultural output in a few crops by a few very large farmers.

The third stage has its onset from the 21st century and is still ongoing. The major feature of this stage is a rapid internationalization process of the commodity production for global markets. This is especially true in the case of soybeans. As a result, Brazilian agri-business exports increased fourfold between 2000 and 2014. They rose from US$20.6 billion in 2000 to US$96.7 billion in 2014.

In its turn, the financialization of the agricultural sector in Brazil is in the second stage of the agri-business development. It has one of its origins in the evolution of securities circulated on the domestic market to generate capital liquidity through advances in financial resources or inputs that led to the Rural Product Note (*Cédula do Produto Rural* – CPR in Portuguese), a type of forward contract, enacted by a 1994 Federal Government Act. The CPR has an exchange rate basis which can be tradable and is subject to judicial execution. This changed former dominant logics of 'planting first and selling later', into a more 'financialized buying and selling futures whilst planting'. Initially, the CPR was intended to ensure the physical delivery of commodities demanded by grain processors and traders. But later it has become a vehicle for investment and making short-term profits often before the actual physical commodities are traded. This is a new version of fictitious accumulation with attendant levels of high risk and high investment gains by those selective firms and agencies who are capable of knowing and operating in these veiled markets.

Among large farmers with capital surpluses to invest, there is increased financing provided by large trading companies. In their turn, such companies are quite active in financial products, as can be seen from their commodity derivatives operations. In addition, the largest farmers gained a foothold in the financial markets through hedge operations for their commodities (cattle, coffee, corn, and soybeans) as well as an increasing number of derivative contracts. Such behaviour may be surprising considering that the futures markets in Brazil are still relatively young. Additionally, Brazil's futures market differs from the profile of its competitors in the US Midwest, where the monitoring of the futures market has been active for generations.

There has also been a wave of Initial Public Offerings (IPOs) by large Brazilian agri-business corporations over the last ten years. Over 70 per cent of the Brazilian food and milk processors, ethanol and agricultural companies at the major Brazilian stock market (BOVESPA) opened their capital after 2005. A greater presence in the stock market is consistent with a growing power of shareholders making companies more prone to follow the market short-termism.

The Brazilian institutional investors (investment funds, pension funds and 'hedge funds') and non-financial corporations (particularly in the case of trading companies, agrochemical industry, and cooperatives) have been playing a major role. During the recession in the US between 2007 and 2009, these trading companies no longer supported the producers, but that did not mean that they appealed to federal or private banks. Input suppliers continued to finance their customers and part of the production was financed with farmers' own resources. According to data from Agrosecurity Consulting, input suppliers' share in the rural credit ranged from 13.1 per cent to 35.9 per cent in the largest soya producers counties in the Brazilian South and Midwest. This apparently comfortable situation deserves to be carefully determined, but all reflect an evolution of the access of farmers to financial markets.

According to the Brazilian Futures Market Bourse (BM&F), the number of futures contracts and commodity-related options increased from 670,000 in 2000 to 2.65 million in 2011, a rise of nearly 400 per cent. Within the contracts traded on the BM&F, about 80 per cent of the contracts had physical delivery and about 20 per cent were financial contracts in 2000. This figure is reversed in 2011 with 71 per cent of financial contracts and 29 per cent of contracts with physical delivery.

The agri-business sector in Brazil has had the highest share among all publicly traded companies with 21.2 per cent, followed by IT companies with 19.2 per cent. The percentage is consistent with the wave of IPOs (Initial Public Offerings) that took place between 2005 and 2008 in Brazilian agri-business companies.

In addition, there was an increase of the foreign capital share in the Brazilian stock exchanges between 2003 and 2013. The share of foreign companies nearly doubled in this period going from 24.1 per cent in 2003 to 42.1 per cent in 2013. It is important to realize that the stronger growth from 2011 coincides with a shift from institutional investors to financial assets linked to natural resources, especially in the case of commodities, as seen by the performance of the investment funds that specialize in agri-business. Moreover, there has been an astonishing evolution of bonds in Brazilian agri-business. This evolution was a consequence in the de-regulatory and privatizing legal environment concerning the credit to agriculture. Farmers and agricultural enterprises were allowed to obtain credit directly from the financial system with less dependence on public credit. The state permitted the creation of five different types of bonds: Credit Rights Certificate in Agri-business (*Certificado de Direitos Creditórios do Agronegócio*), Letter of Credit in Agri-business (*Letra de Crédito do Agronegócio*), Certificate of Receivables in Agri-business (*Certificado de Recebíveis do Agronegócio*), Certificate of Agricultural Deposit (*Certificado de Depósito Agropecuário*), and Agricultural Warrant. The creation of these financial instruments was crucial to the expansion of private credit and a greater dependence on agricultural production and farming families on the financial markets.

Partly as a result of these privatizations and deregulations, the financial amounts involved grew by fifty-eight times from 2.4 billion reals (1.11 billion dollars) in June 2006 to 140 billion reals (41.3 billion dollars) in June 2016 in real value. The sharp rise was much stronger after 2011. Between 2012 and 2015, the financial volume grew seven times, from 19.7 billion reals (10.9 billion dollars) in 2012 to 145.4 billion reals (44 billion dollars) in 2015. The larger share of the agri-business bonds is a relevant indicator of financialization of Brazilian agri-business. There was a substantial increase in the average value of the bond from 79,898 reals (37,383 dollars) in 2006 to 249,036 reals (72,820 dollars) in June 2016.

At the same time, there has been a declining role of the state in public agri-cultural finance with a falling share of public investments in agriculture and agrarian policies. Between 1990 and 2015, public investments in agriculture and agrarian institutions, on average, accounted for 2.12 per cent of the total federal government expenditure in Brazil. However, this percentage dropped to 0.88 in 2015. The highest percentage was in 1995 with a share of 5.29 of total expenses. The Agriculture Budget (*Função Agricultura*) includes the federal public expenditure with rural credit and trade policies, sanitary and phytosan-itary measures, public agricultural research and others. The Agrarian Budget (*Organização Agrária*) includes the federal public expenditure with agrarian reform and other expenses related to farmers' settlements. A smaller budget indicates less public investments with larger room for private banks and inves-tors in the Brazilian agri-business.

Another aspect of financialization is the conversion of land into a financial asset. This is also associated with financialization in the sense that financial actors and financial logics operate. As with Fairburn (2014), the financializa-tion of land may result in land booms and busts due to the presence of financial investors with their enormous pools of capital. 'Land grabbing' has had an impact on land prices over the last decade, with the entry and growth of institu-tional investors in the Brazilian agri-business. Foreign Direct Investment flow into agriculture jumped from 2.4 billion dollars in 2002 to 13.1 billion dollars (Sauer and Leite 2012). The average price per hectare for first crop land in the state of São Paulo increased nearly five times between 2003 and 2015, from 6,000 to 25,000 reals. As shown by Sauer and Leite (2012), São Paulo is also the state with the highest percentage of foreign-owned rural land at 35.8 per cent. One example is the Radar Rural Real Estate Inc. (*Propriedades Agrícolas S.A.*) that was created in 2008 and is active in the rural real estate business. Radar Rural Real Estate Inc. has a portfolio of 392 big farms amounting to an area of 151.5 hectares.

Between 2008 and 2011, a major feature concerning the financialization of the large agri-business corporations in Brazil was seen in the 'hedge' operations with exchange derivatives as a source of financial gains. The derivatives mirror a typical zero-sum game. So, if the cash price of the currency exchange value (dollars and Brazilian real) is above or below the derivative contract price, one party or the other incurs a loss and the other an equal gain as in a zero-sum game. Under the assumption of a world featured by perfect markets, tradi-tional finance theory had cast derivatives in marginal terms. In competitive commodity and financial markets, prices should stabilize with no need to increase hedging and no profit from speculation. This would be consistent with a zero-sum game and derivatives should remain marginal, but this was not what happened in the high exposure from Brazilian agri-business corporations with exchange derivatives. With the exponential growth of derivatives, they also became a source of profit rather than solely operations of hedging.

In the years 2008 and 2009, soon after the onset of the global financial crisis, some of the largest Brazilian agri-business corporations suffered huge losses due to financial speculation with exchange derivatives. Initially conceived of as a hedging tool to protect from exchange rate volatility, foreign exchange derivatives have rapidly become an important source of financial gains for companies.

Within the same time span, the largest multinational in the protein business, the Brazilian JBS-Friboi, was able to make a profit of 722 million dollars with foreign exchange operations in 2009. In a similar way to a financial institution, JBS set up an operations board with ten highly trained financial executives to make daily adjustments on derivatives operations. The JBS operations board had a financial flow of more than US$1 billion per month and were responsible for at least 20 per cent of the cattle futures contracts at the Brazilian Futures Stock Market (BM&F).

Curiously, a larger flow of financial assets into the Brazilian agri-business did not lead to a stronger agri-business in terms of added value. An indicator to measure the share of added value in agri-business is the ratio of agri-business GDP and agricultural GDP. This ratio has declined from more than four to nearly three between 1995 and 2015. Besides the value of agricultural and livestock production, the agri-business GDP includes the value of inputs, industrial transformation, warehousing, and distribution. This ratio has declined with the commodity price boom and a larger share of non-value added agricultural exports.

Changes in the ownership structure of Brazilian agri-businesses is due to the entering of powerful financial actors such as financial investors and a growing dependence on the production and transformation activities on financial operations. This shift signifies agrarian changes in the country. In 1998, the amount of arable land owned by foreign companies in Brazil was 726,000 hectares. This amount increased to 4.3 million hectares in 2010. It was a huge growth of 600 per cent.

There are some key facts that point to a looming financialization of Brazilian agri-business and its wider bio-economy. In summary, there are three elements that make the case for the strengthening of a financialized regime of accumulation in Brazilian agri-business:

- The growing importance of capital markets for large agri-business Brazilian companies with all its implications for a control structure based on the shareholder value maximizing ideology, although blockholding is still very strong.
- The considerable increase in funding for agricultural production through financial or financialized companies (as in the case of large trading companies and input suppliers) and the growing presence of financial instruments in these financing operations such as CPR, CDA, and hedging.
- The entry and growth of institutional investors in commodity futures markets, commodity derivatives and the use of hedge operations according to the logics of a rentier behaviour. In recent years, one has to stress the land grabbing phenomenon with the acquisition of land by large investment funds.

It is worth noting that this moment of deepening the financialization of agriculture focused on the production and export of commodities, especially soy, sugar and meat, also implied a new institutional governance and reorganization of power. This eventually removed the space of political representation of family farming in Brazil through the elimination of the Ministry of Agrarian Development (MDA), which was extinguished in 2016, having been created in 1999 as a result of pressures from the family farming movements (see Chapter 7). In Brazil, this implies the emergence of new forms of governance that leave out actors who were important in the 1990s and 2000s to construct the main policies for rural development and food security. At the present time there is resignation and some paralysis of these actors in the face of the political prominence and permeability of agri-business elite representatives in state power, who take advantage of the economy's dependence on exports and never tire of shout that this should be the path of insertion of Brazil and South America into globalization (Niederle and Ioris 2019). Is shows that the alliance between financialization and agrarian elites is conferring unprecedented power both to impose a model of economic insertion based on deepening primary production and deconstructing another that relied on promoting the inclusion of family farmers in a rural development strategy.

## 6.    Financialization and sustainable productive capacities in Brazil

It can be considered that the theoretical and conceptual elements raised, as well as the stylized facts based on recent data about the increasing importance of financial actors and their assets, can contribute to the understanding of the risks of this phenomenon in the Brazilian agri-business. Since its industrial formation with a capital accumulation process driven by the state, Brazil failed, unlike the East Asian latecomers, to form entrepreneurial and innovative elites that would place technological development at the heart of their strategies. As revealed in several studies of ECLAC and Brazilian economists devoted to the study of innovation in the country, there is still a long process for the Brazilian industrial upgrading allowing exports with higher technological content, even in the agri-business.

There is a risk that the *rentier* tradition of the Brazilian economic elites finds a powerful ally: financial capital as the bearer of interest rates and all other speculative activities associated with financialization. The euphoric attitude towards the achievements of Brazilian agri-business with the increasing agricultural productivity, exports and investment in technology, often overshadows a crucial reality. Almost all countries that achieved industrial upgrading, even in industries linked to natural resources, managed to do that with greater development in intermediate goods (goods that are used as input to final products). Rather, Brazilian agri-business value chains are heavily concentrated in large economic groups and transnational corporations. The entry of foreign institutional investors and international financial capital in acquiring domestic companies will possibly deepen this trend. This means that it becomes more difficult to transform the Brazilian agri-business economy into one which creates endogenous forms of economic value and productive capacities, rather than as an agrarian economy still based upon the export of primary extractive agricultural products. In short, financialization in Brazil benefits its own capital accumulation which then can be directed elsewhere.

Tellingly, the proportion of non-monetary financial assets in relation to productive capital in Brazil increased from 4 per cent in 1991 to 40 per cent in 2010. The unregulated action of non-bank financial investments can produce increased inequality in the distribution of resources in the agri-business value chain actors in favour of the financial markets.

Together with the growth of financial assets associated with agriculture, there is a more prominent role for institutional investors in the ownership of agri-business corporations and a more prominent role for financial activities in such corporations. Moreover, there is the growing importance of financial instruments in providing credit to agriculture.

If Brazil wants its agri-food system to be a driver of economic development, and not just something to compensate the losses of deindustrialization and the low productivity of the factors of production of its economy, it is necessary to build an incentive structure. Such a structure would allow for alignment with agri-business growth and the technological development of domestic companies, increased participation of large and medium enterprises in the value chain, better working conditions, more investment in vocational training systems and environmental responsibility as well as strengthening its family farming sector.

This is not a mistaken dichotomy between advocates of efficient self-regulated markets and advocates of state intervention to tame the markets. It is much more a matter of complementarity between these coordination mechanisms of the economy, the market and the state. In this sense, a powerful idea that proved empirically consistent in the capitalist economies of social democratic orientation can be summarized as 'beneficial constraints'. Competitiveness and innovation can get more from social and political restrictions in the form of regulation and control than from rational interest-maximizing enterprises and individual economic actors.

The field of finance is uneven in different institutional varieties of capitalism, even though it is a general trend in almost all advanced and emerging economies. However, the unevenness of power of financialization signals that different countries can develop their own institutional forms of regulation. This is not a self-fulfilling prophecy or an inexorable fact. It has to do with the actions of the actors and their choices.

The question is which political and economic actors are willing to engage in forms of regulation and social control that align financial incentives with the environmentally friendly and socially responsible production. Recognizing the risks of the problem is the first step. Courses of action and suggestions can be only rhetorical if they are not preceded by a greater understanding of the phenomenon.

# 7.    Conclusions

The chapter has attempted to make a strong but dialectical link between the continuing and persistent 'squeeze' upon land-based production, and the emergence of spatially uneven, but increasingly mobile forms of financialization in agricultural commodity, land and infrastructures. The financial and food crises which ensued from 2007–8 seemed to only exacerbate the process of financialization of rural land and commodities as it created new forms of 'scarcity' upon which investments could be made and then 'hedged'. In countries like the UK and now Brazil, neo-liberalized state governments sufficiently sought to continue to deregulate and privatize their financial sectors such as to aid far more internationalized investment in property and commodity markets. In the Brazilian case, as we suggest, this reflects wider structural difficulties in the economy. This is associated with developing its own agri-business and bio-economic base (including bio-fuels as well as food manufacturing), despite the inherent richness of its massive natural resources. This is, in both the British and Brazilian cases, the rise of a renewed *rentier* economic hegemony, which, as we see in Chapter 5 on land and property rights, extends across both food and wider natural resources and urban and rural land speculation.

What this partly tells us more generally is that these processes tend to increase both the vulnerabilities and volatilities experienced especially by smaller local producers, and it leaves them more exposed to highly controlled markets which are managed by not just agribusiness but the more detached financial sector. This is, as in the case of the EU and especially the UK, being currently exacerbated by the removal of state support mechanisms which have formerly supported farmers against market volatilities. Removal of subsidies and support for market failures is increasing the vulnerabilities of many family farmers, and they are encouraged to attempt to offset these risks by taking more privatized systems of risk insurance (see Marsden et al. 2018). Farmers are encouraged to become more 'business-like' and to enthrall themselves further into financialized credit and insurance schemes, where once the state would have protected them from these risks.

The role and potentiality of governments to intervene, as we somewhat briefly saw in the Lula governments in Brazil of the early 2000s, can act as a major supporting mechanism for fostering small family farming and a wider endogenous research and development base necessary for the post-carbon transition. Yet in many countries, like Brazil and the UK, deepened financialization has been a key process in further concentrating the control of agribusiness whilst continuing to 'ratchet-up' the farm-based 'cost-price' squeeze.

Whilst there has been a considerable amount of recent research concerning the new forms of financialization affecting agribusiness and farming, this chapter has attempted to make the links between these processes and wider processes of vulnerability and state action to which they are linked and indeed embedded. Clearly financialization may aid the fluidity of agribusiness investments but it continues to curtail local and farmer-based control and autonomy over their operations, and it seems to create more uncertainty and risk in farming operations, further 'locking in' those farmers who are providing commodity and export-based food products. This 'lock in' increases with credit needs amongst a larger group of commercialized farmers, and, not dealt with here in great detail, also locks them into packages of agricultural technologies which in themselves demand regular replacement costs (GM seeds, fertilizer and pesticides and new machinery and equipment). Neo-liberalizing states and much of the finance sector see the farm and rural sector thus as just another potential market for the selling of their financial products. These are now accompanied by control over individual farm data, business planning and accounts. Many British supermarkets demand to regularly review their farmer suppliers accounts before agreeing supplier contracts; multinational seed and machinery firms automatically collect farm data on daily farm practices and livestock feeding regimes. The age of big (privatized) data could be appropriated and thus 'enclosed' within financialized agri-business. As a result a key research agenda here is to follow how these battles of autonomy, control, and state interventions link to new forms of financialization, commodification, or indeed re-agrarianizing through stimulated new forms of social resistance. A theme which we will now develop in the next chapter in considering land and property relations.

## Notes

1.   'Small-scale', 'family farming', 'smallholder' and 'peasant' farming are used interchangeably in this summary text. Despite their respective differences in the potential to describe or to analyse, these notions convey that rural production is predominantly organized through employing family labour on family land.
2.   This section was initially developed by Moisés Balestro and Sergio Schneider in a working paper entitled 'Financialization and institutional change in the Brazilian agribusiness' (2017). An updated version of this work is available for consultation as preprint at https://www.academia.edu/42309188/Financialization_and _institutional_change_in_the_Brazilian_agribusiness_Working_Paper_Preprint.

# 5. Re-claiming land: questions of land rights and the management of the bio-sphere

## 1. Introduction: The new agrarian question: towards new political ecologies of resource governance

Questions of land rights, control and use of the land and the bio-sphere are becoming central again given both the need to reduce and remove carbonized systems of production and supply, and at the same time the need for established interests to secure land rights in order to maintain profits from unsustainable resource practices. Rural land and its control thus becomes a fulcrum for the intense competition between depeasantization and re-peasantization as the contestations between traditional and endogenous landed communities face new rounds of pressure of dispossession in the face of continued and in many cases heightened accumulation strategies. This is clearly taking place in what have formerly been seen as global commons (like the Arctic and Greenland ice cap) or the indigenous lands of northern Canada or Brazil, which are under pressure for resource exploitation for forest products, precious minerals and tar sands. They are expressed in Latin America and Africa, as global agri-business and mineral firms attempt to dispossess indigenous communities. Even in Europe the privatization of former public lands is rapidly occurring in some countries, further commodifying former public access and commoner rights.

As we see below, therefore, these are by no means new phenomena, for they raise the spectre of a reformed and renewed agrarian question. *That is how will, or can, local communities and landholders resist and build more sustainable pathways of rural development amidst such exogenous and appropriating forces?* This, though now is a question far more profound in that it is taking place in the pressured context of severe (global) resource depletion on the one hand and the necessary and indeed urgent search for post-carbonized alternatives not least in the energy agri-food and material fields on the other. The new land question is thus at the centre of these debates. It calls into question of course the extent to which existing holders and users of land and bio-spheric resources can maintain their rights over their resources. But in an increasingly urbanized and cosmopolitan world it also questions what rights non-land (urban) holders should have to access the natural resources they indeed require for their survival. We can no longer frame 'the agrarian question' as earlier thinkers did around the protection or projection of narrowly defined owners and occupiers rights. Access to land rights and the commons now have to become a global concern and right for all, however close or distant many are to those resources. The new agrarian land question is thus part of the new global question of how to allocate natural resource rights, and moreover, how to govern those rights. This chapter explores this new agenda by making reference to these global trends in Europe and Latin America. Before we do this, however, it is important to explore both the historical antecedents of the new agrarian question more fully, and second, to position this within a more financialized (see Chapter 4) contemporary context.

In recent papers and books we have been advocating the development of a revised and refreshed political ecology of agri-food and rural development (see Moragues Faus and Marsden 2017; Marsden 2017, 2018). This chapter significantly extends this analysis by incorporating agri-food and rural development into a wider re-conceptualization of political ecology, and indeed global geo-political crisis, caused by the confluence of both a continued limits in (financialized) neo-liberalism and a growing and deepening global climate and resource crisis. This (unfortunate) confluence is leading to both new forms of agrarian resistance and innovation at the new intersections of the agri-food/energy nexus as well as within the transformations within the agri-food system itself.

This chapter, using international reference points and evidence from Europe and Brazil, brings together theories and approaches from both political ecology, environmental studies and peasant studies literatures, and welds these to the relatively new resource governance and transformation studies which suggest nexus and post-carbon approaches. It suggests some key building blocks for new 'post-carbon' agrarian theory which interestingly places some of the early agrarian theory – associated, for instance, with the focus upon the obstacles to capitalist agrarian development, the distinctiveness and resilience of farm-based production of both energy and foods, the disparities of labour time and production time, the centralization of markets, and depeasantization and financialization – in a new post-carbon, and potentially post-corporate post-capitalist light. Critical here, we argue, is a focus upon the re-configuration of power relations, both between agri-food chain actors and, increasingly between these and other forms of concentrated and corporate capital (see also Chapter 3). We argue that for real and long-term agri-food transformations to occur, distributed actors need to re-assemble power relations through the re-appropriation of ecological resources. This can begin to reconstruct new modernities for distributed economies and small land-based business development in the new management of rural natures; a period when cosmopolitan societies will need to procure most of their means of sustenance from the bio-sphere.

The role and interconnected development of hybrid and diverse agroecological systems is critical here to envision and enact new political ecologies of resource governance (see Chapter 6). This 'new agrarianism' needs to integrate agro-ecological production to its very reproduction not least through trans-local market developments, the use and application of digital technologies and the development of place-based skills and investments, new procurement and standards, and rules over common resources (like water, air and waste) that ultimately bring forth new organizational forms and processes of a more cooperative and transformative nature.

## 2.    The new agrarian question: the new political ecology of resource governance

The ongoing (2007–8) financial, fuel food and fiscal crisis means that we have entered a constant and dialectical process of combined economic and ecological crisis which in turn is creating a radical shake up of both political and sociological structural moorings (as discussed in Chapter 2). In a world of climate change and decreasing natural resources, and with the convergence of the continuing neo-liberal crisis, we are facing as a planet severe pressure on the political ecology of resources. This is threatening established democratic and institutional structures, as well as longstanding regulatory processes developed to protect civil societies from economic and ecological vulnerability. These convergences are, as we know, of anthropogenic significance; and the implication of this must be to search for ways in which human actions and practices can begin to overcome these global constraints and threats (see Marsden 2018; Purdy 2015). Earlier theorists have recently talked about the post-political tendencies in recent political ecology; here we wish now to state how we are needing to create a new politicalized political ecology. It is in this context that we now need to urgently address the question of new agrarian transformations: from neo-liberalist late capitalist agrarianism to a potential post-capitalist and post-neo-liberalist set of diverse conditions.

It is the contention and thesis of this chapter then that rural societies, and in particular in their increasingly diversified and distributed agri-food/energy complexes and forms, are now at the potential forefront of this highly contested and dialectical process (see Marsden and Rucinska 2019). This is of such profundity, we may argue, as to parallel what Kautsky called *Die Agrarfrage* (The Agrarian Question) a hundred and twenty years ago, indeed as the 20th century began. His problematic project somewhat infuriated the more conventional Leninist oligarchy of agrarian Marxism of the time, by asking; 'whether and how capital is seizing hold of agriculture, revolutionising it, making old forms of production and property untenable and creating the necessity for new ones'? (1988:12). His main concern, in the midst of uneven but rapid capitalist and carbonized industrialization and urbanization, and the new imperialist globalization of agriculture (Friedmann and McMichael 1989), was the continued role of pre-capitalist and non-capitalist forms of agriculture in capitalist societies (Kautsky 1988:3). The limiting and spatially variable nature of the soil, with land of course being non-reproducible, retarded the processes of concentration and centralization in agri-food, leaving household (peasant) production as continuously structurally distinct. Lenin and later Stalin saw their persistence, not least in their attempts to obliterate the Ukrainian kulaks, obstinately 'awkward' and an obstacle both (in the west) to further capitalist concentration, or (in the east) to the further embedding of a state-led socialist monopolization of the agrarian means of production. These constraints did not of course stop concentrated capital (in the west) or the authoritarian state (in the east) continuing to attempt to penetrate and transform distributed peasant production; and indeed this has been a continuous process of contested transformation throughout the 20th century (see Goodman et al. 1987).

Kautsky's legacy has new credence today. He took the combination and distinctiveness of the material and biological worlds seriously; such as the immovability of land and perturbations and human risks associated with biologically based agrarian domestication and climate vagaries over time and space. He was, along with other agrarian scholars like Chayanov and Kropotkin, prepared to identify the potential sustainability, or at least persistence of household production and the peasantry; whilst at the same time being under no illusions about the increasing intensity and spatial velocity of concentrated agrarian capitalist development. He came to see these multiple determinations and contingencies as the great agrarian paradox of the day, whereby the peasantry interrupted and resisted capitalist penetration not least because of its practices – notably in its ability in the *longue durée* to harness the very disparities between natural and land-based production time with the disparities of labour time. He also saw the peasantry as having 'two souls in the breast', in that they could vary their political allegiances away from the binary

conflicts between capital and labour occurring in the cities, whilst in other contexts also promoting the collective actions of resistance by supporting political
democracy (Levien et al. 2018). Kautsky unleashed over the succeeding century
a continuing debate among Agrarian Marxists about explaining the persistence
and empowerment of what seemed to be the anomalous structural location of
the peasantry (see Marsden 2017).

So why are these interpretations of value today given our current and combinative sets of crisis rural development conditions; and why is it valuable to
critically re-insert them into our interpretations of crisis over a century later?
We want to argue, first for the need for a new neo-Kautskian viewpoint – one
which distinguishes now a radically different set of external conditions than
those which Kautsky experienced; but also, second, to suggest some theoretical
continuities – not least with his abiding *liefmotief* – that is, the *longue durée*
distinctiveness of natural-social material production processes and practices
in the face of advanced (corporate) capitalist penetration. And indeed, more
particularly, the continuous re-activation of ecological and metabolic factors in
creating opportunities for farmers and related food and rural actors to assem-
ble and re-configure power relations amidst processes of capitalist penetration.
First let us consider some of the changing conditions and continuities.

## 3.   Changing conditions: theoretical continuities and additions

First, we can delimit clear distinctions in the changing crisis conditions in
contemporary agri-food capitalism (post 2007-8):

Now, agri-food systems, we can argue, are in ecological and economic crisis
and one can posit that conventional agrarian capitalism shows all the signs
of 'running its course' throughout most of the 20th century. In fact, it has
patently NOT been able to overcome the distinctive organic and metabolic
nature of production after over a century of attempts through not least successive rounds of subsumption, appropriation and substitionism. Indeed it
has resorted to high and more abstract forms of financialization which are in
the long term doomed to failure. Moreover, whilst agrarian capitalism indeed
predominates in many parts of the world (see Greenberg's (2018/19) fascinat-
ing depiction of appropriated intensive production in California's San Joaquin
Valley), and continues to penetrate and privatize rights and access to formerly
common resources in much of Africa and Latin America, overwhelming
evidence now appears to support that this process is: 'rarely found to lead to

simultaneous positive eco-system services and wellbeing outcomes … This is particularly the case when ecosystem services other than food provisioning are taken into consideration' (Rasmussen et al. 2018). Hence, we can argue that both in terms of its endogenous features – super exploitative labour, social and animal welfare, destruction and extinction of bio-diversity, and due to a range of wider external (landscape) factors such as highly volatile markets, financialization, consumer boycotts and drought, the industrialized model of agri-food is confronting a far more serious complex of Kautskian constraining factors today.

Moreover, it can thus also be argued that, indeed, the ecological world has 'closed in' and become more limiting for conventional agrarian capitalism, as formerly 'cheap' resources, labour and raw material (phosphates, minerals etc.) have become harder to procure, and particularly their negative externalities harder to spatially fix and legitimize. In this sense the 21st century capitalist world ecology is, after a series of successive Imperial, Fordist and corporate, neo-liberalized and financialized globalizations (see Jason Moore's arguments (2015)), a much smaller and vulnerable place.

Of course human-induced climate change and the negative effects of intensive agricultural capitalism did exist and were recognized by the end of the 19th century (see Kropotkin 1904; Davis 2018); but this was largely ignored or denied until the final decades of the 20th century. This was based upon the assumptions that: (i) agricultural intensification could continue unabated in world development not least because technological advances would continue to deliver gains in productivity and continue to overcome any natural obstacles (at least for the foreseeable future); and (ii) a wider and deeper neo-liberalized globalization process (especially from the 1980s onwards) was continuing to allow capital and indeed the state to create distanced 'spatial fixes' in food production and consumption which conveniently located the ecological externalities far away from northern consumers who were increasingly environmentally and health conscious about their food intake and provisioning (Morgan et al. 2006). Think for instance of the rapid (post-1980s) growth in Europe of imports of all-year-round exotic fruits and vegetables and fish. These conditions in the latter parts of the 20th century and the first decade of the 21st, continued to provide the means by which Kautsky's concerns specifically – and ecological crisis and climate change more broadly – could continue to be both conveniently denied and side-lined. This favoured the continuing state and corporate support of carbonized capitalism, even though many of its largest global corporations (like Exxon) internally recognized that these problems were indeed occurring but continued to undermine public scientific evidence which suggested otherwise.

However, the political conditions have also in many places structurally shifted with the decline of state socialism, the rise of right-wing populism and new forms of trade wars. Such forms of disruptive governance are now also affecting the demise of agrarian capitalism. Greenberg (2018/19) documents, for instance, not only the ecological crisis in San Joaquin, but also with neo right deportations of Mexican labour, and the related humanitarian crisis leading to structural shifts in agri-food, he argues:

> As things stand, there is a labour shortage the magnitude of which hasn't been seen in the last ninety years. It has prompted growers to rip out labour intensive fruits like table grapes and plant almond trees, which require few workers. Housing costs, especially in the Coastal Valley, have made it even harder to attract and keep workers. In recent years millions of dollars of unpicked crops have been ploughed under or left to rot in the fields. (p93)

Whilst the conditions above did create a long period of 'plenty' regarding food supplies and choices at least in the advanced countries of the north, since 2007-8 we have witnessed the severe rise of food insecurities and associated political turmoil around the world. This is demonstrating again the limits of conventional agrarian capitalism and much of its supportive state structures and regulatory processes, even in the relatively rich and consumerist and environmentally conscious regions of Western Europe (see Marsden et al. 2019). Increasingly then, most recently seen in the negative politics of meat eating and the wider concerns about health as well as climate emissions (see EAT-Lancet Commission Report 2019), it is increasingly recognized that conventional food systems are not delivering and are indeed 'dysfunctional'.

As we shall evidence below, despite these trends, we now also witness both at a global state level (Paris COP21 and UN sustainable development goals), and indeed in terms of recent financial investment and disinvestment trends, the contested rise of post-carbonized transitions in the fields of energy, transport, infrastructure and indeed agri-food. These trends were not in evidence in the onset of Kautsky's agrarian capitalism, nor were they deemed necessary under the assumptions of an inexhaustible assumption about the unfettered spatialized growth of exploitable carbonism.

## 3.1 Second the continuities

Given these significant differences in the structural conditions which now surround us since Kautsky's time, one might argue of the limited value in pursuing any suggestion or postulation that his writings have any relevance today. Yet, in many ways we wish to argue here that the current ongoing transformations in both the agri-food nexus and rural development suggest that his original overall focus upon how agrarian transformational processes occur are still of conceptual value. This is principally because the onset of a post-carbonist and potentially a post-capitalist regime in the 21st century actually refashions and indeed substantially extends some of Kautsky's central tenets. In particular we can now see, for instance, the new potentialities for land and bio-sphere 'holders' – if you like the 'new peasants'; and indeed new consumer-based alliances actively empowering themselves around these rural development nexus processes. As such, as Kautsky recognized, the re-casted ecological metabolism, now (laterally) extending both from new production to mass consumer actions and practices on the one hand, and from (vertically) the bio-sphere and the lithosphere on the other, returns as an active and empowering force partly because of the increasing and necessary reliance in post-carbonist transitions in assembling a wider variety and indeed diversity of human and ecological resources upon which to materially meet, create and recreate energy, food and material needs.

Thus we can posit that once we move off an exploitative carbonized track of development Kautsky's metabolic features indeed come more forcefully into play; and indeed any such related assumptions about the continued 'metabolic rift' have to be conceptually replaced given the inherent post-carbon ecological necessity to integrate and manage the social with the ecological in post-carbon transitions. We will explore these re-integrations in more detail below. In short this is beginning to be recognized in the recent literatures relating to:

- The recognition of the contemporary processes of re-peasantization and depeasantization occurring at the same time (see Hebinck special issue, JRS 2018).
- Re-emergence of the metabolic significance of agri-food in urban as well as rural settings (see Friedmann 2018).
- The emergence of new and indeed more distinctive nexus material practices between food energy, water and air for renewable energy and food production.
- The contemporary more diverse re-conceptualizations of 'capital-to capitals' themselves. That is the understanding of capitalism now, at the very least, as a series of heterogenous and regionally oriented but interconnected forms.

We can see here then that today the binaries between capital, labour, the peasantry (see also Chapter 7) have unfolded and become far more malleable and interactive. Critical here from a political ecology perspective is a focus upon re-embedded power relations, not just those emerging from capitals or the state, but also those being actively re-assembled by variable groups of actors in the more highly differentiated food systems. These also transcend different spatial and temporal scales (see Lamine et al. 2019; Rossi et al. 2019). Here, and in exploring these contingencies, we will begin to deepen this analysis by looking at two connected arena. First, what we call emerging the agri-food/energy nexus, whereby, with the onset of post-carbonism, renewable energy production once again becomes a more naturalized and land-based distributed activity, providing, we argue, significant opportunities for land-based groups of farmers to develop more multi-functional and sustainable systems (see Figure 5.1). Second, we focus on the more internalized transformations within agri-food systems and rural development *sensu strictu*, showing how political and social space can be found to 'carve-out' new and reconfigured power relations in embedded place-based networks.

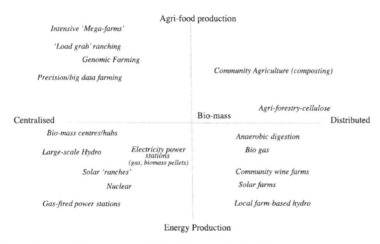

**Figure 5.1**   The new multi-functional agri-food/energy nexus

*Source:* Author's construction from Marsden (2018).

Contestations around land and the bio-sphere become a central rural dynamic as the world moves from its industrialized and carbonized regime. Rural property rights – who owns, occupies and uses these – comes to the fore as a critical area for rural development research. In what follows we look first at the shifting boundaries between common rights and private rights to land and the bio-sphere. We look at this in more empirical detail as to how these processes are playing out in the spatial and national context of the UK and Brazil. This is a continuing story of power and control, but now, unlike in Kautsky's day, it may not follow conventional industrial and capitalistic pathways. Maybe there are new opportunities in post-carbon rural development to create new opportunities.

## 4.  Land, shifting commons and sustainability

A key rural development dynamic represented in the above discussion and in need of further and deeper consideration here, is the contested and shifting boundaries which are created regarding 'common-pool' resources; of which land, and of course the wider bio-sphere and lithosphere, are clearly a central part. This is now a major area for further research. For as we have seen in earlier chapters (Governance, Chapter 2; and Financialization, Chapter 4) the rise of neo-liberalist and financialized policies both by the state and corporate capital have tended to attempt to re-appropriate what may have previously been public common rights to land and property. In addition now, as we see above with the rise of post-carbonist processes, especially in rural areas, the privatized and rentier capture not just of land, but water, air and sunlight become resources which can be attempted to be captured.

It is clear then that the social, legal and governance boundaries between what are defined as 'commons' and what are regarded as private rights, and indeed the combinations and 'bundles' thereof, become a key area for renewed rural development research. In the broader environmental field there has been considerable and variable efforts made to re-conceptualize 'the commons'. 'Commoning' is becoming again an important rural development strategy in a contemporary context of pressures for both privatized and corporate forms of control and enclosure of a wider range of bio-physical resources. It thus now contributes and, we can argue, is a potentially central part of the 'new agrarian' question, as indeed it was in Marx and Kautsky's day. This is so given, as we shall see in the sections below, the counter-tendencies of further intensive rounds of privatized 'rentier' rural-based capitalism whereby land rights are re-commodified for the benefits of landowners. It is worth reminding ourselves of the long-running nature of this process as a central part of the process of 'enclosure' and disempowerment which we elaborated on in Chapter 1.

In a widely cited passage, Adam Smith (1831) (Christophers 2019) realized that when the reduction of common rights occurs, at least to an extreme extent, it can create a growth in inequalities and 'morbid consequences':

> As soon as the land of any country has all become private property, the landlords, like all other men, love to reap where they never sowed, and demand a rent even for its natural produce. The wood of the forest, the grass of the field, and all the natural fruits of the earth, which, *when land was in common*, cost the labourer only the trouble of gathering them, come, even to him, to have an additional price fixed upon them. He must then pay for the license to gather them: an must give up to the land-lord a portion of what his labour either collects or produces. This portion, consti-

tutes the rent of land. (*The Wealth of Nations*, Inquiry, p21, quoted in Christophers 2019:57) [emphasis added]

As we argued in Chapter 1, this is by no means an exclusively rural phenomenon, with rentier appropriation now rife across most of the world's cities. But it is important here in re-considering the growth of rentier land-holding (indeed both by the state as well as private capital) as now a key process of re-appropriation and enclosure of rural land rights. For this provides a conceptual and material social location for 'commoner' struggle. Not least by new social movements to recreate 'commoning'; but also (as, for instance we see in Chapter 7 on family farming) for smallholders to protect against the monopolistic tendencies of rentier insurgency.

## 4.1    Mainstream and critical institutionalism: property-rights 'failures'

Despite Adam Smith's warnings and a host of other Marxist scholars demonstrating the rise and dysfunction of rentier capitalism (see most notably Harvey 1982) in the last two decades, 'Commons' research has been dominated by a mainstream institutional perspective led by the institutional economist Elinor Ostrom. For these researchers, commons systems are common-property rights regimes for organizing the management of common-pool resources (Table 1 in Romero 2018, see also Romero et al. 2019). The main arguments are that common-pool resources collapse and are unsustainable without the appropriate property rights' rules and enforcement mechanisms (property-rights failure). This body of work originated from rational choice theory, a theory portraying humans as seeking individual material benefits, yet bounded to their available information, and embedded in contexts shaping their cost–benefit individual calculus.

In these ways, 'commoners', it is assumed, need external incentives (institutions as rules or norms) to detract from their intrinsic willingness to overexploit. Significant efforts have been made to develop Institutional Design Principles that can guide institutional crafting in a way that improves the likelihood of spuring a sustainable management of an ecosystem. These Institutional Design Principles have been interpreted by policy makers, states or development agencies as top-down technocratic solutions for managing ecosystems, mainly in developing countries. The policy recommendations developing from this mainstream approach assume that human beings are rational and individualistic. Of course in the rural domain, as we have identified in earlier chapters this is not always the case. For instance farmers might be individual landholders, but corporate firms and large conglomerated estates often control large swathes of rural land. Also, groups of landholders are usually bound to a locality, and norms and rules are 'fixed' by customary or state rules. Also this perspective tends to limit the temporal dimension in not helping to explain why certain community norms emerge within a particular community or why the community itself changes through time.

Table 5.1      Commons definition within the three approaches on commons

|  | Mainstream Institutionalism | Critical Institutionalism | Community Economies Collective |
| --- | --- | --- | --- |
| Definition of common-pool resources | Common-pool resources are those resources that are difficult to bound, divide or exclude others of their enjoyment. But a good's de facto type may be affected by the way in which consumers use/regulate it. | | Non-existent, it is a social construct. A good's type depends totally on the way in which consumers use/regulate it. |
| Definition of 'Commons' | Commons are considered common-property rights regimes, understood as the institutions derived from law, custom, or convention that maintain a property system used in common with others, and where users are co-equal in their rights to use, manage and exchange their rights towards the resource. | | A social organization by which resources for the community are (re)produced (a community economy). It is a dynamic, evolving social activity, built through commoners engaging in negotiations for defining the rules for access and use of a shared resource – thus better to refer to it as commoning. |
| Relation between common pool and Commons | Common pool resources need common property right to hinder overexploitation. | Common pool resources need common property right regimes but it is not enough. | Any type of resource can be commoned independently of its nature or its property right regime (private, open access or common property right regime). |

*Note:* We acknowledge Marta Nieto Romero's framing here as part of the SUSPLACE ITN EU research programme.
*Source:* Romero (2018).

Critical institutionalism (CI) creates a modified perspective and refers to a varied group of researchers interested in commons' that criticized the mainstream neoclassical commons approach (Cleaver 2012). Particularly, they provide new (non-rational) theories on how humans build and shape institutions of the commons. Contrary to the mainstream approaches, CI claims that the commons dynamics are far from being just a problem of over-exploitation and property rights. Instead, social relations such as community relations are key (not as external factors affecting decisions but as main drivers of human behaviour). The CI researchers consider that dynamics of markets and states disturb communities and can create undesired outcomes in commons systems (e.g. over-exploitation, access inequalities, conflict, etc.). That is why, rather than property-right failures, critical scholars would rather agree to identify commons problems as community failures. Critical scholars do not aim at predicting outcomes, but at understanding why specific institutional arrangements come in place and why they deliver different outcomes for people and the environment.

Indeed, instead of rational-choice theory, CI's researchers use Practice Theory to explain action and social and institutional transformation. Practice theory aimed at transcending the rigid action-structure oppositions through a focus on practices: practices are the building blocks that constitute the social, humans are not rational but socially and practically driven. Action is not a matter of individual choice and preference but is inter-dependent on others or relational. Social relations and the subject's positions in these networks of relations shape the desires, opportunities and resources available to individuals. As a result, a commoner's agency involves conscious and unconscious actions guided by community norms of behaviour, moral worldviews, embodied practical experiences, social roles, taboos and emotions. Humans are not just rule followers but rule improvisers.

As such, a critical analysis of common-pool resources systems could follow in situ actors' practices to explore how the systems have evolved over time in relation to social, political and historical trends of society at large, so the analyst can place commoners as agents of struggles and cross-scale power dynamics over resource enclosures and development paradigms. Although rules are considered an important component to understand human actions, a critical approach would place more importance on how rules are used and shaped by actors in their daily practices.

These two approaches (Mainstream and Critical Institutionalism; see Table 5.1) are still limited conceptually, it can be argued, in that they still narrowly focus upon institutional dynamics in resource governance and narrow definitions of what constitute 'eco-systems', often as 'eco-system services'. Taking a broader definition of sustainability incorporates a wider understanding of the commons problem. This is advocated by the Communities Economies Collective approach (see Table 5.1) whereby more open-ended possibilities are constructed by local place-based communities to negotiate and re-organize commons and 'commoning'. Below we see this process as becoming all the more prevalent in the rural field both in the UK and in Brazil, as some place-based groups begin to re-establish community land rights, and where the state, as in the case of the Brazilian landless movement, and various indigenous movements, reclaim property rights around community-based sustainability principles. This represents a major contested dynamic in rural development; whereby the onset of privatized enclosures are resisted by collective and place-based forms of 'commoning' we can explore some of these cases below.

## 5.   The governance of rural land: a new bio-economic frontier in the UK

A major implication of the move towards a post-carbon economy, and the bio-economy more specifically, is a re-definition and new premium being placed upon the use and potential multi-functionality of rural land and property rights (as well as water and aquatic resources). As soon as it becomes unprofitable or unacceptable to mine for geologically deep, non-renewable resources (such as coal, oil and gas), the emerging post-carbon world has to face a renewed challenge of obtaining the bulk of its energy as well as its food needs from the land surface. This was ever the case in pre-industrial times when horse 'power' meant that draught animals had to be fed and catered for from the same land resource (as in early settler agricultures in North America and Australasia). The difference today, some two centuries later is that: (i) populations are of a significantly greater scale and urban complexity; and (ii) we have found during the carbon period all sorts of other things and amenity functions for the exclusive use of land, such that it is now no longer an extendable but very limited resource; coming with high social and economic costs. Hence the onset of the bio-economy, continued urbanization, and growing land-based demands for food, fibre and energy are now creating more intensity of land use. This is being expressed in the speculative 'land grabbing' experienced in Africa, but as we shall see here it is also occurring closer to home.

In the UK, particularly after the food and fuel price hikes of 2007–8 and the ensuing financial and fiscal crisis, we have seen a renewed political and economic need to intensify the demand and use of rural land. This is reflected in the persistently high price values accorded to it, and, as in the economic crisis of the 1970s, the attractive option of rural land as an investors 'safe haven' for individual and institutional surpluses and bonuses. The British countryside, as the financial crisis has unfolded, has become a major location for surplus investment which has ratcheted up the positional good and market value of land and rural housing far beyond the reach of the majority of Britain's urban and especially rural populations. This has further rendered much of the British countryside as a positional and exclusive space – a 'consumption countryside' where the economy is dominated by ex-urban lifestyle spending.

One measure of this is the number of rural homes bought as 'cash purchases' without mortgage or loans. This was significantly higher in sparse rural areas (26.9 per cent) compared to urban areas (19.1 per cent) in 2007. This differential increased by 4 per cent as the recession in 2008 ensued, and despite an overall nationally slower housing market.[1] Similarly, agricultural land prices rose as the recession hit in 2008, the first time for a decade, rising by 28 per cent and fuelled not least by city bonuses. By 2013 prices were forecast to continue to rise both for agricultural and forestry land at 5 per cent per year.

Unlike the 1970s and 1980s rounds of this, however, when we lived through a period of food surpluses and generally decreasing household costs for food and energy, we now witness the need to again see the rural land base as an intensive production and consumption space.

Since the food crisis hit in 2007–8 we have also witnessed the not unrelated emergence of a new scientific and policy bio-economic paradigm around the concept of 'sustainable intensification'. That is farming the land base in such a way as to further intensify production and productivity, whilst also attempting to reduce environmental and ecological costs and externalities. 'Having more for less' goes the mantra. This bio-economic paradigm is now at the centre of the UK government's agri-food and green growth agenda. In England and Wales this is re-opening the door for the development of 'mega farms' (especially in the dairy, pig and poultry sectors); and the less dramatic intensification process in the conventional agricultural sector. The latter is taking many forms including the reduction in the actual number of family run farms; the amalgamation of holdings with some 'farmers' only keeping their registered status for tax purposes; and the growth of contract farming of amalgamated parcels of land. In Wales over 250 dairy holdings were lost between 2009 and 2012, yet the average head size increased from 76 to 84.

This allows both agri-business interests and the cash-rich ex-urban incomers to create a new Faustian bargain, whereby whole farmsteads can become converted for residence, whilst the surrounding farmland becomes further intensified for production purposes. This dislocation of farms and farmland is further polarizing the rural communities across England and Wales; allowing a particularly more intensified model of the bio-economy to develop on the one hand, whilst furthering the more exclusive gentrification of the rural housing and estates on the other.

Against this backcloth of both sustainable intensification and the increasingly exclusive ex-urban colonization of much of the countryside, it is important to recognize the more fledgling development of the growth of urban-based food movements and alternative food networks over the past decade. Indeed, as partly a consumer response to the intensification processes, and the growing disenchantment of sizable proportions of the British urban population about the provenance and adulteration of their foods, there has been a growth in alternative and community-based food growing and consumption (farmers markets, food hubs, community land trusts etc.).[2] Whilst these have been so far mainly urban-based, and they have largely been ignored by rural residents and farmers, they are posed to play a more significant role not least in demanding land and property rights in rural areas, as demand for short-supply chains proliferate, but the supply of productive land to meet these demands remains restricted. For instance, the Community Land Advisory Service is a collaborative brokering service aiming to increase community access to land across the UK; and it liaises with community groups, local authorities, private landowners and other institutional landowners about providing more land for community-based food and energy initiatives. In the US and Canada, these 'back to the land' movements are proliferating through such mechanisms as Community-Supported Agriculture (CSA) schemes and city-based food councils.

We can witness then three highly varied but nonetheless significant trends all leading to the current and future intensity of demands being placed upon UK rural land and its existing property rights: ex-urban cash-rich investment opportunities, ongoing sustainable intensification of agri-food; and the proliferation of alternative, more eco-economic community-led food and energy developments. As land, food and energy resources get tighter and urban and suburban populations grow, so will these multiple demands upon the UK rural land base. We need a national level policy debate about how to capture and indeed spread the sustainable value and opportunities these trends provide.

## 6.    New enclosures in urban and rural Britain

Since the Thatcher governments of the 1980s and succeeding governments which have deepened the process of neo-liberalism in the UK, a somewhat hidden feature has been a process of privatization of former public land rights (see Christophers 2019). This started with the explicit Thatcherite policy of selling publicly owned council housing in the 1980s, at a publicly subsidized rate. By 1979, indeed a peak year with a third of all of Britain's housing stock was socially rented, a proportion only exceeded in Scotland, for instance, by up to 50 per cent. Devine noted that, by the 1970s Scotland (and indeed Wales) had 'probably the largest share of public housing of any advanced economy outside the Communist bloc' (see Jack 2019:21). An overwhelmingly domesticated urban population had largely lost its connection to the land under these state processes.

Whilst the selling off of these assets, mainly to sitting tenants, was a flagship ideological strategy for the successive governments from the 1980s, this was only the start of a wider process of both privatization and financialization of UK land, both in urban and rural settings. Since 1979 – the highpoint of publicly owned land in the UK when 20 per cent of all UK land was publicly owned – the state has sold over 2 million hectares, or about 10 per cent of the UK's landmass. This has been prime quality and sought after land, ten times the value of the social housing component. Forests, national defence sites and municipally owned farms have been privatized and bought up by the financial institutions and housing development firms. Public land stocks now represent 10 per cent, down by half since the 1980s. The devaluation of the public estate – forests, farms, moors, royal dockyards, military airfields, railway arches and sidings, museums, theatres, playgrounds, parks, bowling greens, allotments, children's centres, leisure centres, school playing fields – partly caused by the government squeeze on local authority spending, making them more likely to sell off assets at a devalued rate in order to attract private developer gain, have created the financialized conditions for massive private development profits through the planning development process. Relaxing public planning consent went hand in hand with local authority financial constraints, thus allowing private-sector development gain to proceed at a rapid rate. This has increased property prices and caused major housing affordability issues for low-income groups both in the countryside and especially in the cities.

The rise of the new *rentier class* whereby private landlords and a host of internationalized investors have sought to 'enclose' through freehold ownership of land and property, whist then letting these assets to needy tenants, have taken all political opportunities bestowed on them by neo-liberal governments. This process has intensified since the financial crisis of 2007–8, and its austerity policies thereafter. Financial institutions and property developers are the two largest donors to the Conservative Party, many members of which have directorships and investments in the sectors as well as large landowning portfolios. Land privatization shows no sign of abating, especially as its very regulation has been divested from the public civil service to outsourced private accountancy and land agents. This is 'the privatization of privatization', meanwhile, unlike other EU countries like Germany (manufacturing, cars) and Japan (manufacturing, electronics), the UK has become a rentier economy, with over half of all homes now privately rented, and rent as a proportion of household expenditure doubling since 2014. Rent is thus a major source of economic growth and uneven wealth accumulation in the UK.

So what lessons can we draw here about this mounting financialized land enclosure process operating inside one of the most advanced and economically wealthy parts of the north? There are at least three important points to draw out which link to our wider arguments in our introductory chapter which lays out some transversal conceptual themes.

First, this new enclosure of at least 10 per cent of the UK's former public 'commons' proceeds as largely a hidden and undisclosed process. Whilst Thatcher's 'right to buy' social housing policy was explicitly identified in a sequence of national elections, the rest of the privatizing enclosures have been conducted largely by undemocratic means and with a lack of public scrutiny. Whilst the public sector has been charged regularly with the need to be publicly accountable in all of its actions, the accounting, decisions and processes leading 'the great sell off of public assets' have been indeed a literally privatized process; and indeed either tacitly or explicitly endorsed by a sequence of national and local government bodies. Even the registers of land ownership are shrouded in off-shore tax havens.

Second, perhaps as no surprise to scholars of earlier enclosure processes, this process of 'appropriation by dispossession' is asymmetrical in the power geometries in which it occurs. The privatized development process is built upon the freedom to set and hoard land and property assets until high market prices for selling or developing can take place. Thus the private developers have been bestowed the freedom, once acquiring their new property rights, to sit on their assets until they judge maximum returns can be gained. Despite the land transfers involved, there is still, for instance, a need to build 2 million new homes to relieved housing shortages; yet land is 'banked' by the developers, especially once development rights have been permitted. Waiting usually expands the difference or 'development gain' between land with and without planning permission. This is the social and political construction of scarcity, which is so much a feature of neo-liberalized systems of enclosure, and runs completely counter to the bald assumptions that 'markets' can allocate goods and services far more rationally that slow moving and lazy state bureaucracies.

Third, and more broadly, these processes lead to a continuous process of disempowerment, especially for the low income urban residents and the young. Both groups have been excluded from the benefits of the devaluation of sales of council houses, and faced the loss of public commons in the 2000s. Urban as well as rural living goes through a re-domestication, this is a process of restricting access to formerly common and well-resourced public facilities. As Adam Smith in the *Wealth of Nations* argued (as quoted above): 'the landlords, like all other men, love to reap where they never sowed, and demand a rent even for its natural products'. As Hammond and Hammond (1913) well documented when exploring the effects of privatized land enclosure upon the rural poor in 19th-century England, those excluded in these enclosure processes not only stand to lose previous common right of land access, procurement, food security and so on, they are provided with only one real alternative. This is to face the spectre of further commodification and dependence upon marketized rights of consumption, rather than socialized rights of consumption. The 18th- and 19th-century peasant or 'cottager', having lost their cows for milk, needed to buy it from shops and urban processors; having lost their grazier rights and rights to forage, they were forced to buy oats rather than plant wheat for making bread. In the modern-day urban setting the low income groups and many of the young face parallel 'Hobson's choices' faced with the eradication of former common rights. They are forced to pay higher and higher housing, energy and food costs, and have less 'green space' in which to rear their children. This re-domestication only exacerbates their impoverishment, and their landlord's asset wealth.

More specifically in the rural domain one significant feature of this process of privatized enclosure has concerned the selling of former county council farm holdings. Since the First World War, and the onset of domestic food security concerns during the Lloyd George governments (see Marsden 2017), local authorities across the UK bought land for new agricultural smallholders so as to promoted small family farms entering the 'farming ladder' and giving formerly non-farming groups access to land. By 1926 about 1.5 per cent of British land was indeed owned by local governments for agricultural use and occupancy. This was a major entry point for the development of new farm families, or aspirant farm worker families who previously had no access to land of their own. This again, following the macro-political trends identified above, reached a high point by the late 1970s. Since then, with severe pressure on local authorities to sell off these landed assets so as to make their books balance and stave off their own fiscal crises created not by themselves but by the national governments of the day, the County Farms Estate has halved from 426,000 acres in 1977, to 215,000 today (2019). Fewer members of the public are aware of this transformation, with most of the land being sold to larger independent farmers and landholders. Needless to say this has reduced the operation of the farming ladder and made access to land and property in the countryside all that more difficult. In addition, of course, private farm land had become far more concentrated and owned with the number of fixed tenancies being reduced. There are now only 217,000 farms in the UK, and this is probably an over-estimate given there is evidence of many family farmers leasing their land to larger conglomerates whilst maintaining overall long-term land rights for taxation purposes.

This story of the decline of county farms follows the same logic as that occurring in urban landed Britain. At the time of writing there is the start of a new debate being re-ignited on the political left about these processes (see Christophers 2019). There is a growing realization that the processes of enclosure since the 1980s, which have been exacerbated since 2010 with the onset of a Conservative-led austerity government, are both a major engine for the growth of social and spatial inequality in the UK, and increasingly polit-ically unacceptable. This is mirroring early post-War Labour debates about restoring public authorities with the powers to repurchase land, re-nationalize for public assets and create new community land trusts. Scotland, with always a heightened political consciousness about the land question given the history of brutal land 'clearances' in the 18th and 19th centuries and the persistence of the crofting movements, is very much leading the ways in this regard, making fuller use of its devolved powers to intervene in these matters. In England, the political climate is both still anti-public sector, and strongly influenced by the relatively new landed interests (the development sector and financial institu-tions). Nevertheless, with a change in national governments a re-definition and a new debate about property rights seems long overdue. Community land ownership and rights is gaining ground also in Wales (e.g. Project Skyline 2019), and being linked to environmental sustainability goals like: protect-ing and re-wilding local habitats, addressing climate change, encouraging tourism and supporting a new generation of family farmers and foresters (see Community Land Scotland 2017).

The enclosure/empowerment dialectic is a vibrant and critical field in which to study rural development processes. We see here that in a new era of global resource scarcity, and a crisis in neo-liberalized systems of governance, we may be witnessing transformations in these balances, as people – both urban and rural – expect state authorities to empower and represent them rather than assume that by releasing 'market' mechanisms through asymmetrical systems of distorted privatization, public goods can be delivered. The growing ecological crisis is re-defining politically the need for a re-attribution of the public realm, as indeed it is recognized that this is critical to longer-term and intergenerational equity. Without changes in the 'law of the land', however, it is very difficult, indeed impossible, for local authorities to gain the financial means to redefine and open up the vast UK privatized enclosure process which has taken place since the 1980s. Without further financial and governance devolution of powers to the nations and regions of the UK, such a shift is unlikely to succeed.

## 7. Struggles for collective land rights: the case of Brazil

The enclosure versus commoning/empowerment dialectic has, and is, today a key site of parallel social struggle in modern Brazil, where the controversies over the longstanding monopolization of land rights, first by the colonists and latifundists, and now even just as vibrantly, by corporate agri-business interests. Whilst these monopolistic tendencies are challenged by landless workers' movements, most notably by the MST. At the same time this is a dual process of agrarianization and de-agrarianizition as landless workers and small farmers struggle for land rights, whilst agri-business interests force peasants and indigenous peoples off of their land (see Hebinck 2018). These parallel confrontations and dialectics are a fundamental part of the rural–urban dynamic in Brazil.

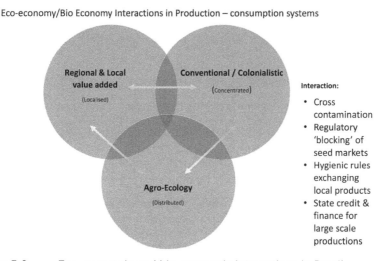

**Figure 5.2**    Eco-economic and bio-economic interactions in Brazil

*Source:* Author's analysis.

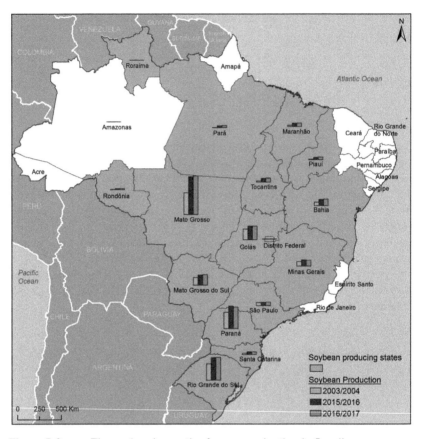

**Figure 5.3**     The regional growth of soya production in Brazil

*Source:* Author's construction from Pauli and Marsden (2018).

## 7.1    Struggles 1: the competing geographies between agri-business, family farming and agroecology (see Figures 5.2 and 5.3)

Figure 5.2 represents three different competing interests in agricultural land taken from the northern region of Rio Grande do Sul (Passo Fundo). It is indicative of many regions. Recent rapid rises in soya production for export has been shifting land-use patterns in many regions, either controlled by large agri-businesses or large-scale family farmers. We discover smaller niches of agroecological production, often linked to cooperative and solidarity movements working in the interstices of these production systems. Also, networks of family-based diversified agriculture exist and are indeed developing which are both producing and processing value-added food products like cheeses and meat products.

These different farming systems are developing side by side and have important geographical effects upon each other in the same regional settings. For instance, agroecological practices such as the growing of traditional seed varieties struggle to maintain their organic integrity when located by contiguous GM and pesticide-dependent soya production land uses (see Figure 5.3). Different state support for credit finance tend to favour the larger soya producers. And diversifying and value-adding producers and processors face often insurmountable regulatory burdens placed upon them by the local and federal state relating to food standards and hygienic regulations. This often means that smaller producers cannot afford to enter value added and regional markets.

## 7.2    Struggles 2: the changing character of the Landless Workers Movement (MST)

Born out of a waning military regime and societal pressure for political democratization (1979-89), the formation of the Landless Workers movement in Brazil represented popular and then more formalized struggle for land occupation for small family producers. This included direct land occupation as a way of reducing the lack of access to land, and political pressures on the state to open up land rights for landless workers and poor urban dwellers. Fernandes (2015) traces the development of the MST as a vibrant social movement, arguing that even under the more explicitly supportive Lula government of the 2000s the redistribution programme which aimed at altering the extremes of unequal land tenure, it was not pursued in a decisive or proactive way. Rather the state – which is crucial – has consistently followed 'on the coat-tails' of widespread peasant mobilizations. The evolution of these mobilizations shows different phases and geographies.

Over the past half century, Brazil's land struggles have been mainly undertaken by squatters (*posseiros*) and landless peasants (*sem terra*). The former tend to work around the agricultural frontier, resisting the progress of former landlords and latifundists, but now corporate agri-business, who often 'grab' land illegally (*grilagem*). Landless peasants mostly organized take-overs of large rural properties. Whereas the Brazilian state originally prioritized land re-distribution in the Amazon region and parts of the poor north east, in fact the larger number of peasant land occupations took place in the south, south east and north east regions. This was an important quid pro quo, for the state and agri-business interests. The latter are allowed to colonize and take over former peasant land in the more fertile and productive regions where capitalist agriculture is already dominant. Whilst successive governments have encouraged peasant movements to settle in areas where commercial agriculture is less advanced and often marginal. Even in these regions, peasants and agri-business firms have engaged in intense and violent disputes over existing farm land. Between 1988 and 2005, 903 people were assassinated over rural conflicts in Brazil. Fewer than 10 landlords responsible for hiring the killers were put on trial (Fernandes 2015).

Agri-business had experienced rapid expansion and territorialization since the 1990s, despite more supportive government policies for landless and peasant land redistribution. From 1992 to 2003, the area controlled by corporate agriculture grew by 52 million hectares, while the area under family farms increased by 37 million hectares. In this sense, Brazilian land reform has been partial, and not altered unequal agrarian structures in fundamental ways. It has reduced the pace of, rather than reversing, the pattern and process of land concentration and accumulation and disparities whilst also continuing to spatially fragment peasant land rights. Fernandes (2015) estimates that without the hundreds of land acquisitions, and the forced pressure on the state to redistribute land, agri-business landholding would have increased further than it did between 1992 and 2003, by 77 million hectares, whilst peasant farms would have dropped from 3.4 million to 1.1 million. As Fernandes concludes (2015:126):

> from the late 1970s to the mid 2000's – despite unprecedented levels of popular mobilisation and wide recognition as the best-organized peasant movement in the nation's history – this popular organisation has not been able to change Brazil's agrarian structure. All this substantiates the complex and indeterminate nature of Brazil's agrarian question. The territorialisation process driven by peasant movements and agribusiness forces are creating new conflicts that will re-fashion the agrarian question in years to come. The new internationalized context, shaped by agri-business corporations and trans-national peasant networks (like Via Campasina) and their allies, will become a critical reference for understanding the new conflicts in the cities and countryside of Brazil.

## 7.3   Struggles 3: the new frontiers and fragmentation of indigenous land rights

Indigenous land rights have become a particularly contentious area in Brazil as the agri-business and bio-economic interests continue to pressure for land rights for intensive forms of agricultural, energy and timber production. Out of a total of 1,119 murders of indigenous people in Brazil between 2003 and 2017, over 40 per cent of these were in the state of Mato Grosso do Sul. The state has been at the frontier of new agri-business occupation for productive lands, especially for soya and sugar cane production. The indigenous Kaiowa-Guarani, have faced the brunt of these incursions (Ioris 2019a). Disruption and aggression are long-established processes in these highly fertile and productive lands. This has, however, recently intensified as Brazil has continued to nationally prioritize export-oriented agriculture as a main national macro-economic goal. This is leading to renewed, forced and illegal appropriation of indigenous land rights, over-crowded indigenous reserves, chronic indigenous malnutrition, occupation of ancestral lands and a disregard or attacks from agri-business farmers, mainstream politicians, authorities and the business community. Kaiowa-Guarani practices, based upon common land, managed by large families and free regular mobility around the vast region is being substituted by the commodification of labour, land rights and increasingly by creeping unplanned urbanization, drug trafficking and cross-border contraband.

This is an active and vibrant form of 'frontier making' (Ioris 2019b; Moore 2015). It is 21st-century forms of enclosure. Instead of legal rights over their land the Kaiowa-Guarani have been offered only marginal spaces and reserves. The recurrent violence against their land rights is in direct breach of the principles of the Brazilian constitution. Out of 4 million hectares originally occupied by the Kaiowa in the region, they were left with 40,000 hectares of regularized land which is spread across various fragmented reserves and resettlements. Some of these are very small and over-crowded, but despite this they have struggled to maintain their identity, culture and knowledge systems. They are struggling to engage with the new frontier, and where they can they re-occupy some marginal lands on the edges of the agri-business lands and farms. These are spatially and socially expressed as indigenous reserves, roadside encampments, *Retomada* (re-occupation of original lands), where local judges and privately hired security guards hired by the agri-business farmers allow, and in participation in international networks which struggles to re-represent their traditional sense of place, identity and language. As Ioris (2019a:140) concludes:

> The political influence of agri-business is bad enough in the rest of Brazil, but in areas of agricultural frontier it gives rise to even higher levels of speculation, dispossession of common lands and wide-ranging brutality. Frontier making creates favourable conditions for the arrival of unscrupulous individuals in search of rapid enrichment and prepared to accept spurious economic and political practices. The recipe for serious politico-ecological conflict is surely there: on the one hand, agri-business farmers and a range of agro-industrial and financial groups (all with only recent experience of the region), and on the other, native peoples who have been living in the region for many generations and have a different relation to the land, nature and life, beyond the reductionist treatment of land as commodity and

agriculture as business. Their identity and social experience is directly influenced by the place where the family lived and where relatives were laid to rest.

## 8.     Conclusions: the new agrarian question

This chapter has re-addressed, in a contemporary sense, many of the original and guiding principles which emerged amongst critical scholars of the 19th century in the fields of rural sociology and geography, as well as more generally within the social sciences. For some peculiar reason, over the past two decades at least, the focus upon land rights, and their relationships with wider rural social, political and economic processes (with the significant exception of Brazilian scholars) have been unfashionable and rare. Indeed the 'land question', until very recently, has been something of a non-question in rural social science, despite – as we have seen in the UK – with vast quantities of common rights being transformed by rentier classes.

The growing crisis we have witnessed in neo-liberalism since 2007-8, however, seems to have sparked a renewed interest among scholars, not least in tracking the implications of what we might term 'new enclosure' movements, and the resistances and commoner struggles which surround them. Here in this chapter we have attempted to re-locate property and land rights at the centre of the new rural research agenda, and more specifically, as we outline in historical terms in the first part of the chapter, the ways in which it contributed significantly to 'the new agrarian question'. That is a question much broader now than in its original (Marxist) conception in the mid- to late-19th century.

Today, struggles and battles over land and bio-sphere rights are increasingly endemic across the world because of the increasingly recognized 'limits' placed on these finite resources, yet there are equally recognized growing and insatiable demands for them. This means that the balances between 'common pool resources' and privatized resources become all the more in contention, and that these contentions need to engage state agencies' operations in different ways to protect and enhance these common-pool resources. However, as we see with our cases of the UK and Brazil, here national states have been reluctant or unwilling in many ways to grasp these public challenges. This has led, in both countries among many others, to the increasing privatized managements of land and property rights, and indeed the concessions by the state to further allow increasing amounts of privatized enclosure.

In a world which is needing more land for urbanization, agricultural intensification and to varying degrees ecological amenity, this privatization process is unsustainable in social, ecological and economic terms. In many ecological and sustainability debates, and not least in global climate, bio diversity and sustainability debates, this new agrarian question is largely overlooked in favour of often assuming that land enclosures and their destructive tendencies can be offset by developing common pool resources elsewhere. This denies the very spatiality and place-based nature of land and property rights, that is, rights that are often quite unique and novel to those places. This, as we propose in the first part of the chapter, demands that scholars research and articulate the novel, endogenous and uniqueness of place-based land and property rights; and indeed increasingly feed these into political debates about where state actions are need to protect or re-invent common rights over private rights.

## Notes

1.  See Commission for Rural Communities (2010) and Murdoch et al. (2003).
2.  It is difficult to put a figure on how large the alternative and community-based food sector is in the UK in relation to the conventional food system given the lack of systematic data. But see Marsden and Sonnino (2012), and Marsden and Morley (2014).

# 6. Agroecology: a new paradigm for rural development?

The ecological and social unsustainability of the global food system is widely acknowledged by scientists, as well as by citizens and governments around the world. We know that the world has already lost 75 per cent of farming plant genetic diversity in favour of high-yielding varieties; that only four crops provide over 60 per cent of the calories we eat; that approximately 3 billion people have low-quality diets; and that land grabbing, ecosystem degradation and market pressures are ravaging traditional farming communities worldwide (HLPE 2017) while climate change is profoundly although diversely affecting agriculture in all parts of the world. Combined, these circumstances demand the urgent reorientation of global agri-food systems, and the identification of ecologically sound and socially inclusive transition pathways that lead to more sustainable agricultures and healthier diets in diverse contexts. Agroecology, as an agricultural (encompassing) model which not only valorizes ecological processes but also promotes systemic, multi-dimensional and multiscale approaches to agricultural changes, is advocated by many scientists, agricultural networks and social movements as a means to support such sustainability transitions not only at the scale of agricultural systems but in food systems (Altieri and Toledo 2011; Anderson et al. 2018; Sanderson Bellamy and Ioris 2017; Wezel et al. 2009). Since the early 2010s, agroecology is also being used as the organizing principle in public policies at a national level, such as in Brazil and in France (Lamine 2017; Schmitt 2016).

These institutionalization processes give rise to controversies between different visions of agroecology (Giraldo and Rosset 2018). Indeed, agroecology has given way to diverse processes of definition, appropriation and implementation. It has emerged – or rather been revived – in contexts where, both at the international and national scales (and below), diverse narratives were already circulating in the agricultural world, in the academia and in civil society, and had already been institutionalized and translated into public policies to support the necessary greening of agricultural practices. Thus, while many authors adopt the triangular framework proposed by Wezel et al. (2009), which distinguishes three meanings of agroecology as science, practice or social movement (Levidow et al. 2014), it seems necessary to add a fourth pillar, that of public policies.

In this chapter, we will articulate different perspectives inspired by the sociology of controversies and the sociology of public action in order to address agroecology as an object of confrontation and controversy between the agricultural worlds, civil society, public policy and science (Bellon and Ollivier 2018; Lamine 2015) and contextualize its legitimation and institutionalization processes. The first section will discuss the different 'narratives' built around the ecologization of agricultural and food systems, based on an analysis of discourses, debates and controversies that forge these narratives in different contexts. The second section will address the trajectory and processes of politicization of agroecology in the French and Brazilian contexts and the concrete public policy mechanisms put in place and the processes of appropriation they generate. The last section will discuss how agroecology might be a relevant paradigm for rural development in that it allows reconnecting agriculture, the environment, food and health and discusses the scales and approaches of such a reconnection.

## 1.   Agroecology within a diversity of competing agricultural models and narratives

### 1.1   A long sequence of models and narratives aiming at ecologizing agriculture

Almost any scientific or institutional publication on the future of agriculture starts with a relatively similar argumentation about the current challenges; these have, however slightly changed over time:

- Until the 1980s, food security and hunger in a context of a rising world population in the poorest countries were the key challenges that agriculture needed to address.
- In the 1980s and 1990s, bio-diversity loss and environmental impacts in general started to be mentioned more prominently, within the affirmation of the 'sustainable development' framework.
- From the late 2000s on, climate change, health and social justice started to appear in the first lines of these types of publications with an increasing place of the notion of 'transition' and ecological transition in the debates,

and an increasing diversity of paradigms and models claiming to address these challenges (see Figure 6.1).

| Post war auto sufficiency discourses | Agricultural modernisation | | Rise of environmental issues | | Rise of climate change, health and social justice issues |
|---|---|---|---|---|---|
| 1945 | 1960 | 1980 | 1990 | 2000 | 2012 |
| Marshall Plan | Modernisation laws / first CAP | | Agri-environmental schemes | | Agroecology enters public policies... along with many rival models |
| *Food security, productivity* | | | *Sustainable development* | | *? Ecological transition* |

**Figure 6.1**    Evolution of challenges, policies, and key paradigms regarding agriculture since WW2

*Source:* The authors.

The ways the global context is described are of course strongly dependent on the authors and institutions, hence the need to also contextualize and 'sociologize' this reading of the challenges. For example, social justice issues are more present – and earlier, that is, already in the 1970s and 1980s – in the publications of international social movements and social scientists (Friedmann and McMichael 1989) as well as more recently, of some expert groups emanating from international institutions that are in close interactions with social movements (such as CFS or IPES-Food/HLPE for example) than in the discourses of agricultural ministries.

Along with these changes in prevailing challenges, the type and range of agricultural models that are claimed to be relevant solutions to these challenges have also been redefined, with competing arguments over productivity and environmental impacts but also social aspects (employment, farmers' quality of life, etc.) and increasingly, health aspects (in both sanitary and nutritional terms). This is, of course, linked to diverse interpretations of the causes of the current state of agricultural and food systems, and to diverse perspectives on their desirable future; in other words to diverse framings of the public problem at stake. For example, and among a diversity of possible and circulating visions, while some (scientists, policy makers or other involved actors) would consider that we need to find ways to feed 9 billion people which, considering the current dietary trends, means to increase productivity and maintain a 'productionist' vision (Fouilleux et al. 2017); others would consider the need to profoundly change our dietary patterns towards vegetarianism (Clark and

Tilman 2017), regardless of other aspects such as rural landscapes, cultural and social dimensions of livestock breeding and so on. Finally, many contend we should redesign both our production and consumption patterns in ways that take also into account these social and cultural dimensions.

Reflecting this diversity of interpretations and framings, many encompassing concepts and models have been defined in the scientific and institutional arenas and/or in the social movements in order to induce changes in agricultural systems; such as sustainable agriculture (in the 1980s and 1990s), or sustainable intensification and agroecology more recently. Organic farming has a significantly different and longer trajectory that led to an earlier and more stable institutionalization through labels, proper networks and institutions and public policies and thus deserves a specific focus.

## 1.2    Organic farming, a tested although contested ecological model

In the 'northern' world, organic farming was the main constituted and institutionalized alternative model for ecological agriculture in many national contexts until the late 2000s, when agroecological networks started to forge their decisive alliance with peasant farming ones at the international scale, and despite – or within – the actual diversity of alternative agricultural movements.

Organic agriculture has diverse historical roots that are reflected in the diversity of its contemporary currents. One of the most famous ones is biodynamic agriculture, defined in the 1920s by the Austrian philosopher Rudolph Steiner, founder of anthroposophy, based on, among many other principles, taking into account the influence of the moon and stars in agricultural practices, and still present in devoted networks and labels, such as Demeter in Europe (the international collective network and brand of biodynamic agriculture, created in 1932). Other historical sources of inspiration are the works of Sir Albert Howard on Indian agriculture in the early decades of the 20th century which valorized the principle of peasant agriculture and subsistence, and of the American Rodale, based mainly on the concept of soil fertility – which led to the notion of 'organic' agriculture. Finally, in Switzerland, Rusch and Muller developed the concept of 'biological' farming, based on the use of renewable resources, in order to preserve a nature that has ceased to be inexhaustible.

Of course, organic agriculture took different pathways from one country to another. The majority of works on the institutionalization of organic agriculture concern, logically, countries where it has been institutionalized quite early, such as European countries (Smith 2006; Piriou 2002; Michelsen 2001;

Darnhofer et al. 2018), the USA (Guthman 2004), Australia and New Zealand (Lockie and Halpin 2005). In France, the first organic farming networks appeared in the 1950s, mainly with anthroposophical inspirations, at the cross-roads of three perspectives, the first mainly led by physicians and rooted in health concerns (with the AFRAN, French Research Association for a Natural Food), the second much more technical (with work of Raoul Lemaire, started in the 1910s, on improving the baking value of wheat and the use of organic fertilizers), and the third perspective more anchored in a spiritual view of agriculture. In 1958, a first Organic Farmers' Group was created in the west of France, initially influenced by Howard's work on organic manure. In 1961, the French Association for Organic Farming was created at the national level, but soon split into two movements, one more focused on the commercial exploitation of organic inputs and techniques as well as bakery products and influenced by the technical perspective mentioned above (Lemaire-Boucher company), the other one, Nature et Progrès, refusing on the contrary any commercial and industrial dependence and also distinguishing itself from the traditionalist and Christian current then dominant in the organic movements while being much closer to the ecologist political movement.

Organic farming is therefore represented by various movements since the early 1960s, but it is only twenty years later that it was officially recognized in France with an Agricultural Orientation Law edicted in 1980 (one of the first organic regulations worldwide) that defined it as an 'agriculture that does not use synthetic chemicals'. Between these two moments – the structuring of organic farming in different movements and its legal recognition – extends a period of almost twenty years in which organic farming is ignored or even strongly criticized in agricultural, scientific and institutional circles, although some sci-entific works attempted to demonstrate its interest and legitimacy. Moreover, the recognition of organic farming by the law may also have contributed to the legitimization of the continuation of an agricultural productivist policy, since it is also a means of defusing a radical criticism charge against agricultural policy (César 1999).

While the French law of 1980 put in place a certification system based on guidelines that had to be validated by a national committee bringing together farmers, consumers, providers and industries, the European regulation estab-lished in 1991 (CE 2092/91) appeared to many actors of the French organic movement as a step backwards both in terms of ecological ambition and of multi-actors involvement, due to its focus on third-party certification (Lamine 2020). This led to intense controversies between organic movements and the French administration (and among organic networks themselves). A key issue was then how the previous framing of organic practices set up in the French law of 1980 – that appeared stricter and more 'demanding' than the European regulation – could be taken into account. The national organic farmers organization launched a consultation with its farmer members and carried out an analysis of the diverse guidelines that then existed in France, which led to the introduction in the French translation of the European regulation, key elements that were not imposed in the latter, such as feeding autonomy or prohibition of enclosed breeding. However, as some previously existing guidelines were much stricter, some organic actors felt unsatisfied and maintained their own guidelines and brands, such as the Nature et Progrès one. The new forms of third-party certification were strongly criticized for being purely formal and technical and not involving consumers/citizens any more – in the years 1999–2000, the main argument in favour of third-party certification was to avoid the frauds that were quite important at that time, especially with imported products. Some indeed maintained more participatory certification processes, and later on, played a key role in their diffusion in alternative food networks such as the AMAPs. Along with the type of certification, many actors criticized the fact that this supported a vision of organic agriculture that was coined by some as 'substitution organic agriculture', whereby organic input would replace chemical ones without any systemic change. These actors would in these years, and still today, promote a conception of organic agriculture that they consider more ethical and more systemic, a situation which echoes the debates that took place in the USA in the 1990s (Goodman 1999).

These debates and controversies and the increasing demand of consumers for both healthy products and more ecological forms of agriculture led to a profound change in the way organic agriculture was defined in the European regulation that was revised in the mid 2000s. Whereas in the first European regulation of 1991 (CEE/2092/91), organic agriculture was defined as an agricultural and market segment, in line with consumers' demand, in the next regulation established in 2007 (CE834/2007), it was defined as a public good, with the environmental and rural development dimensions put at the forefront (Lamine 2020). Whereas organic *products* (and the organic market) were first in the 1991 regulation, it is organic *production* which was mentioned first in the 2007 regulation. Organic agriculture is viewed in this revised regulation as an encompassing system that plays a double societal role: answer to consumers' demand but also provide public goods through ecological practices, preservation of natural resources and of bio-diversity, animal welfare rules, and rural development. This inversion in the priorities from the first regulation to the second one is the sign of an increasing legitimation of organic agriculture which in turn is the result of a long trajectory of negotiations at the European scale and of the involvement of organic networks in diverse arenas of debate and collective action.

From 2015 on, a new sequence of debates and controversies started in the context of a new revision of the European regulation, where new concepts arose such as that of ecosystemic services (Lamine 2020). The organic farming organizations claimed that the environmental services rendered by organic agriculture (such as water quality, bio-diversity preservation, development of ecological infrastructures, employment, and the production of healthy products)[1] have to be acknowledged and paid for. Through such arguments, these actors also claimed a reframing of the costs and benefits of organic farming, which gave way to a lasting controversy over the performance of organic farming within the academic world and beyond (Lamine 2017), leading to a growing acknowledgement of the 'positive externalities' of organic farming (Dalcin et al. 2014).

At the European level, the new regulation was eventually adopted in May 2018 (CE 2018/848) for an application starting in 2021. While the preamble has been extended from four pages in the 2007 regulation to 17 in the 2018 one, with new aspects included such as the notion of fair return for organic farmers, one of its main advances has been to open the way to group certification, as was advocated by the IFOAM and most European organic organizations, and had already been integrated in Brazil's law (see below).

## 1.3   Agroecology: A diversity of definitions and principles

Whereas organic farming, despite its actual diversity, has a clear stabilized 'minimal' definition translated into national and international regulations, agroecology is a much more heterogeneous concept, and not an object of international regulation, even though it is defined, debated and tested in many networks.

Agroecology in 'northern' contexts is most often presented as an importation of a southern social movements concept (Sanderson Bellamy and Ioris 2017; Ajates Gonzalez et al. 2018). Agroecological practices are often described as having been widely used for a long time and rooted in local traditional knowledge of peasant and indigenous cultures in southern contexts (Rivera-Ferre 2018; Altieri 2004), despite the fact that some scientists and agricultural actors claim to develop 'radical' agroecological innovations and many farmers in northern contexts would claim to actually mix ancient and radically new techniques.

Indeed, agroecology has emerged and is continuously transformed by a complex mix of influences and alliances. Tracing academic works allows us to identify agroecology as a concept emerging as early as the 1920s, when the term seems to have appeared in the scientific literature to qualify the application of ecological concepts to agriculture (Wezel et al. 2009). It is mainly from the 1980s on and by researchers[2] working in tropical and southern countries that the notion of agroecology was 'remobilized', with some mentions in the decades in between such as a 'tropical agroecology course' published in the late 1940s in the stream of French colonial agronomy (Bellon and Ollivier 2018). Agroecology came back to the foreground with two American scientists who had both worked in central America, namely S. Gliessman, who established the first agroecology programme at the UC Santa Cruz, and M. Altieri who was one of the advisors of CLADES, Latin American Consortium on Agroecology and Development. In the same period, the ISEC (Institute of Sociology and Peasant Studies) was founded by E. Sevilla Guzman in Cordoba, Spain. A large part of the literature on agroecology has indeed come from the Latin American sphere where it has been most deployed both in the academic world and in public policies, and most often under the influence of social movements. Because of this historical context of emergence, agroecology appears, in this literature, strongly associated with a political criticism of agricultural modernization and 'green revolution'. The emancipatory aim is the foundation of much of this literature: for many authors, it is the coalitions of peasant organizations, NGOs and consumer groups that must drive social change and an 'agroecological revolution', which should be epistemological, technical and social at the same time (Altieri and Toledo 2011; Warner 2007). In this literature, some authors search for the roots of agroecology in Marxist and libertarian social thought (Guzmán and Woodgate 2013), and would, for example, label Chayanov, who in the early 20th century explained how the peasant economy would resist alongside capitalism and developed what he called social agronomy, as a 'proto-agroecologist', even though the concept of agroecology as such was not used at that time by Chayanov (see also discussion in Chapter 7 on Family Farming).

Agroecology has increasingly been adopted as a banner by international peasant social movements since the 2000s. The international peasant movement La Via Campesina, established in 1993, declared agroecology as its core model – able to feed the world and cool the planet – in 2011, and created a network of agro-ecological schools inspired by the pedagogy of the emancipation developed by Paulo Freire. In the French Confédération Paysanne's publications, it is also mainly from 2011 onwards that we find references to agroecology, for instance in a report on the future Common Agricultural Policy, which calls for a practical turn towards agroecology.[2] Agroecology has only gained importance in these organizations' discourses over the last few years: interestingly, it was not mentioned in the declaration of the 2007 Nyeleni forum, which gathers peasant movements and consumer ones, while ecologically sustainable management, peasant and family farms were mentioned in this declaration, but it was central to the later 2015 Nyeleni declaration. The affirmation of the ecological dimension of peasant agriculture is partly related to the alliances that have developed among social movements and between these movements and the academic world. For example, P. Rosset, a Mexican-American researcher who is a well-known specialist on ecological farming and agroecology (Altieri and Rosset 1996), is also the technical support of the Sustainable Peasant Agriculture Commission of La Via Campesina (Thivet 2014).

Increasingly in the international peasant social movements, agroecology is mentioned inseparably from food sovereignty, that has been defined as '*the Framework for Family Farm Resilience*'[3] in the context of the Year of Family Farming (2014).

The definitions in Table 6.1 below can be distinguished along three main lines: whether they carry a more technical or a more socio-political vision of agroecology; whether the vision on the ecological dimension is based on resource sufficiency or on functional integrity (Thompson 2007); whether the scope is limited to agricultural practices and the farm or extends to the food system and/or the territory or community.

**Table 6.1**    A series of definitions by diverse scientists, social movements and institutions

| Definition | Source | Type |
| --- | --- | --- |
| The science of applying ecological concepts and principles to the design and management of sustainable 'agro-ecosystems' (replaced by 'food systems' in 2007) | Gliessman (2007) | Academic |
| The integrative study of the ecology of entire food systems, encompassing ecological, economic and social dimensions, or more simply the ecology of food systems. | Francis et al. (2003:100) | Academic |
| A paradigm based on the revitalization of small farms and social processes that value community involvement and empowerment. | Altieri and Toledo (2011) | Academic |
| Respond to social and environmental challenges and preserve economic and technical efficiency | French Agricultural law from 2014 | Policy |

**Table 6.1**      A series of definitions by diverse scientists, social
**(continued)**     movements and institutions

| Definition | Source | Type |
| --- | --- | --- |
| Peasant agroecology is a social and ecological system encompassing a great diversity of technologies and practices that are culturally and geographically rooted. It removes dependencies on agro-toxins, rejects confined industrial animal production, uses renewable energies, and guarantees healthy food. It enhances dignity, honours traditional knowledge and restores the health and integrity of the land. Food production in the future must be based on a growing number of people producing food in more resilient and diverse ways.[a] | La Via Campesina (2013) | International social movements |
| Agroecology is a key element in the construction of Food Sovereignty. ... not a mere set of technologies or production practices. It cannot be implemented the same way in all territories. Rather it is based on principles that, while they may be similar across the diversity of our territories, can and are practiced in many different ways. | Nyeleni (2015)[b] | International social movements |
| Agroecology is much more than a simple agronomic alternative, it is linked to a profound dimension of respect for life and places the human being in his responsibility towards the living. | Pierre Rabhi | French philosopher and leader |

*Notes:* Elaborated by the authors with the support of G. Ollivier, INRA.
[a] LVC, Jakarta call 2013. https://viacampesina.org/en/the-jakarta-call/, accessed on 7 July 2020.
[b] https://agroecology.co.uk/declaration-of-the-international-forum-for-agroecology/, accessed on 7 July 2020

Recent articles have explored agroecological narratives based on qualitative and/or lexicometric methods (Rivera-Ferre 2018; Ajates Gonzalez et al. 2018; Bellon and Ollivier 2018).

This leads, for example, M. Rivera-Ferre to identify five main narratives: agricultural development, performance, natural resources, climate change and food security, ecosystem's ecological management and people's and women solidarity. The first two characterize the French government texts and; according to the author, reduce agroecology to a set of practices, the third and fourth ones characterize the FAO discourse and the last one is that of the 2015 Nyeleni declaration – as well as the only one of the five to include a food system's approach. This approach allows to show the processes of 're-significa-tion' of agroecology in diverse narratives, even though the interpretative prin-ciple of these methods, which considers that word clusters represent relatively stable cognitive-perceptual frameworks, may be contested. Other analyses of the debates and controversies that have developed over agroecology have led to defining diverse categorizations and oppositions, such as reformist and radical agroecology (Holt-Giménez and Altieri 2013), strong and weak agroecology, agroecology that transforms or conforms the food system (Levidow et al. 2014), populist agroecology, green agromanagerialism and ecorational technology (Warner 2008), and so on.

Indeed, two competing visions of agroecology co-exist in many contexts: a vision of agroecology strongly linked to social movements, and which often leads to the claim that agroecology might rescue organic farming from an industrialization model (Altieri and Nicholls 2003) and that food issues and food systems should be included in the agroecological framework (Francis et al. 2003; Gliessman 2007), and a vision of agroecology which is more technical and closer to the notion of sustainable intensification. Although the boundary between the two visions is not that stable, certain key issues nevertheless define it, such as social and ethical issues (types of farms, types of certification, farmers' well-being etc.) and the consideration of food systems (Lamine and de Abreu 2009).

## 1.4    Legitimation, co-optation, re-differentiation

The processes of institutionalization of agroecology derive from the interactions and alliances across different social worlds, being the academic sphere, social movements, the agricultural sector and public policy. In the agronomic research, agroecology seems to be increasingly legitimized, despite a longer (and probably stronger) trend of 'molecularization' of agricultural technology and science (Buttel 2005) and unequal access to resources (Vanloqueren and Baret 2009). Like in agricultural circles, it gives way to a wide range of research programmes that rely on very diverse and sometimes contradictory interpretations and visions (Ollivier et al. 2019).

The processes of legitimation occur in different ways through diverse credibility tests, either in the scientific world, in policies, but also in practice and through civic validation (Wit and Iles 2016). They translate differently in different national contexts, as the cases of France and Brazil will later show. Agroecology is a model that can inspire both technocratic strategies and transformative transition. The agroecological principles as were defined, for example in the books of its most well-known theorists like M. Altieri, did not include social and political dimensions. This is the reason why many actors have redefined the key agroecological principles in order to include these dimensions (Dumont et al. 2016). What counts is therefore the broader political conception, with either the idea of a break with productivism (as in the narrative of the social movements but also of some more institutional circles such as the 2009 IAASTD or the 2011 SCAR reports), or a revival of capitalism as is the case with the European KBBE concept.[4] In public policies, agroecology may be articulated with legitimized models of ecological agriculture, such as organic farming, as well as with more controversial ones, such as conservation agriculture or more encompassing paradigms such as sustainable intensification (Lampkin et al. 2015). For example, in a recent document elaborated within the French national agroecology plan, titled 'Agricultural Innovations for 2025', agroecology is included in a general trend around prioritizing funding for precision farming, quantifiable agriculture, and research on the management of agronomic data.

Many authors (and actors) argue the institutionalization of agroecology generates a process whereby corporate and institutional actors are trying to take on a new green disguise (Giraldo and Rosset 2018), within 'co-optation' processes. Co-optation is increasingly mentioned by social movements, as in the 2015 Nyeleni declaration, that mentions climate smart agriculture or ecological intensification but also industrial monoproduction of organic food as such forms of co-optation. Agroecology indeed appears as a territory in dispute between social movements and institutions (Giraldo and Rosset 2018).

However, an ethnographic analysis of debates and controversies (and not just of texts such as official declarations) leads to more nuanced and also more complex interpretations, as direct interactions lead actors to adjust their argumentation (for example, to affirm or reaffirm their 'alternativeness') within permanent 're-differentiation' processes (Lamine 2017). Similarly, while agroecological policies are sometimes described as green disguise, a thorough analysis of their implementation and of what they perform and what the practitioners, such as agricultural advisors and farmers, make out of them also leads to more nuanced interpretations (see below).

## 2. When agroecology enters policies: diverse trajectories in different national contexts and at the international scale

### 2.1 Pioneer agroecological policies: Brazil and France

Brazil and France are two leading countries where agroecology has been translated into policies, as was also the case in other Latin American countries, starting with Cuba, Equador, Venezuela, and more recently Argentina and Uruguay. However, the French and Brazilian trajectories of politicization of agroecology (from the emergence of arenas and forums that try to influence policy makers until an actual translation in policies, and beyond) are very different and have to be contextualized. Agroecology emerged in Brazilian policy debates as a claim of alternative agriculture and social movements from the early 2000s onwards. During the 2000s and early 2010s, alliances with academics and policy makers as well as the favourable context of the Lula era that gave much wider room to civil society in governance bodies, led to a strong process of institutionalization of agroecology as a relevant framework for family agriculture, however threatened since the political changes that occurred in 2016 and then 2018. In France, it appeared more recently in 2012 as a new policy framework which aimed at encompassing and impacting the agricultural sector as a whole, and led to a combination of potential profound changes (such as in public agricultural education) and uncertain dynamics (in link with the heterogeneity of the agricultural models and networks that have been legitimized by this policy turn) as well as inertia (Lamine 2020).

In Brazil, the first emergence of agroecology can be dated back to the 1980s within networks linked to 'alternative agricultures' that defended family farming against the emerging 'agri-business' (industrial agri-food system), in the political context of the Brazilian dictatorship. This alternative agriculture movement constituted a counter movement to the modernization process then supported by the dictatorial state. It soon became organized through a national network of 'alternative projects in agriculture' (AS-PTA, created in the early 1980s) and was progressively institutionalized in the 1990s, still under the family farming banner. One of the main spaces of expression of these social movements was the EBAAs (Brazilian Encounters of Alternative Agriculture) that were held beginning in 1981, bringing together agronomists, students and rural workers' organizations.

These social struggles led to the creation in 1996 of the PRONAF (programme of differentiated credit for family agriculture) and then in 1999 of the MDA (Ministry of Agrarian Development), in a context of acute rural exodus and inflation, where family agriculture was seen as needing to be supported for its capacity of absorbing the rural labour force and provisioning the domestic market. This first generation of family agriculture policies stemmed from a distinctly agricultural frame of reference (Grisa and Schneider 2015). The MDA was indeed created to respond to the demands of family farming organizations, which, in contrast to the French case, institutionalized the coexistence of two 'frames of reference for the sector' (Muller 2000), since this new Ministry coexisted from that point onwards with the Ministry of Agriculture whose policies are dedicated to 'large-scale agriculture'. The MDA has counterbalanced – though with far fewer resources – the traditional Ministry of Agriculture which for decades implemented the successive phases of Brazilian agricultural modernization.

The election of Lula in 2002 led to the entry of individuals promoting the notion of agroecology in state agencies (both at a federal and state level), who were indeed situated at the interface between the academic world and social movements (Lamine and de Abreu 2009). As such, in the early 2000s, the alliance already established between peasant social movements (and sometimes environmentalists or consumers) and the academic world was extended to an alliance with public managers working towards the construction and establishment of policies dedicated to family agriculture, which led to the incorporation of agroecology into these policies. However, the institutionalization of agroecology started well before, as some key actors report that it was already discussed in the 1980s and that M. Altieri, probably the most cited author in Brazilian scientific literature about agroecology, had been invited in several Brazilian universities at that time.

This institutionalization of agroecology was the result of strong, lasting and organized interactions between social movements, scientific arenas and policy making, through specific arenas of debates and also within stakeholders' trajectories (Lamine and de Abreu 2009; de Abreu et al. 2011). The increasing influence of agroecology had a lot to do with the fact that from 2000 onwards, key members of Brazilian agroecological movements have occupied important positions in the government and public institutions (Ministry for Agrarian Development, extension services, research). Brazilian extension policy officially turned towards agroecology in 2010, and agroecology is also increasingly present in research and education as various universities developed doctoral and post-graduate programmes in this field.

It was only around 2010 that agroecology began to be institutionalized in France, later than in Brazil where the 2003 law on organic farming had already officially recognized it. This institutionalization process started within research, probably more under the influence of international academic and institutional debates (IAASTD, FAO, UN, etc.) than as a result of the influence of social movements (like in Brazil), and mostly as a framework combining agronomy and ecology. Soon afterwards, agroecology started to appear in national agricultural policies as a paradigm aimed at accelerating the greening of agricultural practices.

The Brazilian National Policy of Agroecology and Organic Production (PNAPO) was launched in 2012 and was to be rolled out into a national action plan and into regional policies at the state level. The first national action plan (PLANAPO – National Plan of Agroecology and Organic Production 2013-15) had four main lines of action: production, use and conservation of natural resources, knowledge and commercialization–consumption (Sambuichi et al. 2017). Despite the limited portion dedicated to actions of development and extension (the majority of the budget of 8.8 billion reals (€2.4 million) was dedicated to credit), some of these actions allowed for true progress, namely in regards to the access to seeds and traditional varieties for family agriculture, coordination of agroecological networks (*nucleos*), women's access to training, farmers' access to the food programmes PAA and PNAE, and finally through the programme Ecoforte, seeking to support regional collective initiatives (see below). The second plan (2016-19) innovated with the addition of two new themes: one seeking to guarantee access to land and the promotion of 'eth-nodevelopement' and sociobiodiversity, and the other focused on the recognition of socio-cultural identity, the reinforcement of social organization and the guarantee of the rights of indigenous peoples and traditional communities. However, it was dampened by the 2016-18 political events.

Announced in December 2012 – the same year as in Brazil – and presented in a national conference, the French agricultural programme called 'Produisons autrement' aimed to put agroecology back at the core of the system. These announcements have triggered critical reactions within many French rural networks, especially since some very large farmers, cooperatives and farmers' organizations in France have also recently adopted this paradigm. In January 2013, several CSOs joined forces to write an 'open letter' in which they claimed that the Ministry of Agriculture talked of agroecology while promoting industrial agriculture instead of an agroecology defined as a 'proximity agriculture' which allows numerous peasants to make a living, territories to remain lively and people to get fresh and diversified food products. Soon later, they would adopt the notion of 'peasant agroecology' to specify their own vision of agroecology. The Collective asserted: 'we also fear that the social project agroecology represents is in the process of being hijacked, in favour of an approach that would settled for prescribing more ecological agronomic techniques to an unegalitarian model that continues to be founded on capitalistic profit' (Collectif pour une Agroécologie Paysanne 2014[5]). They would thus denounce the usurpation of agroecology – that these stakeholders consider to have been forged precisely in their own *alternative* sphere – by the government, with the goal of reinforcing a *conventional* programme of 'ecological modernization', exemplified for them by conservation agriculture or ecologically intensive agriculture. The oppositional strategy would then be combined with a re-differentiation strategy. For these social movements, it is a matter of defining which agroecology they defend (Lamine 2020). Peasant agroecology is then pushed to the fore, 'in order to distinguish it from the communication campaign of the Ministry of Agriculture that brandishes the flag of agroecology with the sole goal of better camouflaging the offensive blitz of industrial agriculture towards the commodification of nature and a bioeconomy [...] Peasant agroecology is above all else a tool of societal transformation' (Collectif pour une Agroécologie Paysanne 2014[6]).

These significant differences between the processes of emergence and institutionalization of agroecology in France and Brazil are due to differences both in the historical process of social and political restructuring of the agricultural sector and in the interactions between the academic world, public policies and civil society. Family farming concerns the majority of Brazilian farmers (about 70 per cent of them, see Chapter 7), who have mostly remained outside the modernization process. In France, by contrast, most family farms have been transformed or excluded by the modernization process since the 1960s. These differences are also linked to the trajectory and place of organic farming in each country. In Brazil, the presence and organization of organic agriculture was rather weak until recently, except in a few richer regions like the state of São Paulo (Blanc 2009), whereas in France organic farming has been institutionalized for much longer, since the early 1980s. This may explain why agroecology in France was initially embedded in a counter-movement stemming from some of the most 'alternative' environmental and farmers' movements, all of which criticized and rejected the institutionalization and 'conventionalization' of organic farming. In fact, unlike the Brazilian case, French pioneers of agroecology in the 1980s came from social movements which had few interactions with the academic world (Bellon and Ollivier 2013). From the late 2000s onwards, we observe a process of differentiation within organic farming and within alternative and ecological agricultures, along with more interactions between these social movements and the academic world, that is partly leading, as could be foreseen a few years ago (Lamine 2015) to a sort of convergence between peasant organic farming and peasant agroecology that respectively emerged, in the French context, in opposition to 'conventionalized' organic agriculture and 'institutional(ized) agroecology'.

Regarding the place of food issues, the politicization of agroecology in Brazil supports a claim to articulate and reconnect agricultural, environmental, food (and health), and social issues. The case of the Brazilian public food procurement programmes (PAA, Food Procurement Program, set up in 2003, and PNAE, National School Food Programme, reformed in 2009), which have a strong focus on family farms, include price premiums for agroecological products, and are managed with a concern for families and school children's diets, in terms of both nutritional input and cultural and local meaning, illustrates a strong will to reconnect these issues (Grisa et al. 2011). In contrast, the analysis of French debates suggests that agroecology seems to be seen by most policy makers and many scientists in mainstream research institutions as a convincing version of the agriculture–environment connection rather than as a paradigm aiming at a wider reconnection with food, health and social issues. Even though food does seem to be more present in current debates on these issues, largely due to the influence of civil society on the academic world and on policy making, it is only recently with the 2014 agricultural law and its introduction of 'territorial food projects',[7] that food issues were more effectively included in agricultural policies (Lamine 2020).

## 2.2 From a stabilized convergence of claims to strong destabilization processes in times of political crises

In Brazil, the strong advances of the 2000s and 2010s are the result of the combined efforts of various social groups that forged alliances in order to articulate their respective claims, and found forums to express these converging claims in the new governance spaces that had been created or reactivated from the early 2000s on, mainly the CONDRAF for family agriculture and its equivalent the CONSEA for Food and Nutritional Security, two joint bodies that have been framed and structured through the key principle of parity between civil society and government. This principle underpinned all the public policies that deal with family agriculture, agroecology and access to food, at the three main levels of public action, from federal to municipal, through regional (state). It has allowed for civil society to play an increasing role in the implementation of these public policies.

These policies were elaborated and implemented under the pressure of the coalitions of three main advocacy groups and thanks to the progressive convergence of their claims and narratives. These three groups were, since the 1970s and 1980s respectively, involved in (i) family agriculture and access to land issues, (ii) alternative agriculture with a clear turn towards agroecology and since 2002 a common platform called the ANA (National Articulation of Agroecology) and (iii) the food and nutritional security debate. These groups could articulate their claims thanks to the new governance spaces that had been created in the Lula era (Lamine 2020). For example, family agriculture, a category politically and institutionally recognized in the 1990s, was progressively also recognized as a means to promote the access to food and a fairer agri-food system (Grisa and Schneider 2015). Food and nutritional security entered the family agriculture's narratives thanks to the progressive affirmation of the food sovereignty vision within the peasant movement La Via Campesina at the international scale (Wittman 2011). However, the process of convergence was long and by no means straightforward. For example, the MST had long maintained quite a productivist view of family farming (where access to technology, equipment and inputs was a key claim and a key process in the *assentamentos* settlements), until the early 2000s when it adopted agroecology as its new line.

The CONSEA appears as the key arena where this convergence of claims could concretely influence public policy making and be translated into laws and policy instruments (Pinton and Sencébé 2019). In the early period corresponding to the re-democratization phase following the dictatorship era (from the mid-1980s onwards), it was mainly a place where experiences at the regional or local levels were shared between participating actors. In a second phase, corresponding to the institutionalization of the national food and nutritional security policy (in the mid-2000s), whose main key steps are the *Fome Zero* (Zero Hunger) Project, the creation of the PAA (*Programa de Aquisição de Alimentos* or Food Acquisition Programme), the institution of the SISAN (National System for Food and Nutritional Security) in 2006, and the inclusion of the Human Right to Appropriate Food (DHAA) in the federal constitution in 2010, this council involved more civil society activists who succeeded in reframing the debate.

This capability of social movements to influence the political agenda relies on the existence of alliances between different social groups that both *represent* the different social worlds considered legitimate in the definition of public policies (i.e. civil society, family farmers movements, academia and of course the policy makers and institutions themselves), and *articulate* the different claims (food security, family agriculture and agroecology) (Lamine 2020). The articulation of these claims allows for a greater legitimacy than each (group and claim) would have achieved separately. Social justice appears as one of the cognitive operators of this convergence, as it is common to all three claims and areas and can be used to connect them (Lamine 2020). For example, favouring family agriculture and agroecology in policies devoted to food security allows for the inclusion of socially vulnerable farmers and their transition towards sustainable practices, both as providers of food products for the public programmes and as consumers of their own products.

Finally, another key feature of Brazilian governance, especially in comparison with the French case, and which is less commented, is the notion of *inter-sectoriality*. Besides the joint representation bodies described above, that articulate civil society and government, for the same three issues of food security, family agriculture, and agroecology (and organic agriculture), inter-ministerial organs have been provided for by the law, both at the national and at the regional scale. These inter-ministerial bodies also strongly contributed to the articulation of food security, family agriculture and agroecology in public policies.

With the political crisis that followed the destitution of President Dilma Roussef in 2016 and led to the election of Jair Bolsonaro in 2018, the situation described above has been subject to profound changes. In the first period of this crisis, these joint representation bodies became arenas of resistance to the conservative forces that were back in power, as described in the case of the CONSEA (Pinton and Sencébé 2019). However, soon after the election of Jair Bolsonaro, the CONSEA was simply closed down (like the Ministry for Agrarian Development had been in 2016) through a 'temporary measure' (January 2019). The robustness of the Brazilian innovative governance system is thus more fragile than could have been expected.

By contrast, the independence of an organization like the ANA, an independent organization that brings together various social movements and rural –agricultural organizations as well as academics, might appear as a strength in this new context, as there is hopefully no risk of it being abolished through an authoritarian measure by any government (Lamine 2020). The ANA could indeed become one of the key areas of resistance in the near future. Of course it is not the only one. Regarding food security, the PENSSAN network (Research Network in Food and Nutrition Security and Sovereignty) created in order to promote interdisciplinary debates about these issues throughout society, and the FBSSAN (Brazilian Forum of Food and Nutritional Sovereignty and Security) – created in 1998, after the participation of a delegation of Brazilian NGOs, government members and researchers in the World Food Summit in Rome in 1996 and which was instrumental in the revival of the CONSEA under the first Lula government – are another two of these resistance networks. Another key factor of resilience might be the proximity between state secretaries' staff and social movements within the state councils devoted to food and nutritional security, family agriculture, agroecology and organic agriculture. However, all these arenas also need to resist the pressures of the agro-industrial sector (in Brazil called *agronegocio* or agrobusiness) which, for example, oppose the publication of national food guides that denounce the negative effects of industrial food on health, in a context where obesity strongly increased in Brazil in the last decades and where the debate over the responsibility of 'ultra-processed food' in this situation has grown since the late 2000s (Louzada et al. 2015). It seems indeed that the *agronegocio* lobbies and actors are reinforcing their position, as was evidenced at the COP21 Paris conference where they supported the notion of an 'agri-business for the future' (Aubertin and Kalil 2017).

## 2.3 What do the actors make of agroecological policy instruments?

Agricultural public policies are defined to orientate the choices and actions of farmers and agri-food systems actors. It is thus necessary to look at the processes of appropriation of policy instruments and at the practical translations they give way to among these actors. While an analysis focused on the meanings of agroecology may rely on discourse analysis – whether these discourses are expressed in programmes, media, or in interviews, and the evaluation of policies' economic effects on quantitative assessment (of devoted funds, number of actors targeted etc.); understanding *what actors do with* agroecological policy instruments requires other methods, such as the collection of ethnographic data: meetings, commissions, scientific advice, conferences, and so on, in addition to comprehensive interviews and documentary analysis. Here we can see the need for a critical convergence between agroecological research, practice and policy developments.

This is what was done on two instruments respectively set up in France and Brazil, the MCAE programme and the Ecoforte one. In France, soon after the national agroecological policy was launched, a first policy instrument was set up: the Collective Mobilization for Agroecology call, launched in May 2013 and aimed at financing over three years, farmers or multi-actor groups that would develop collective agroecological approaches. This programme was considered as an experimentation for a larger recognition of collective dynamics, later on recognized as an Economic and Environmental Interest Group (GIEE), a new type of legal entity created in the 2014 agricultural law in order to promote collective agroecological dynamics through a prioritization of these groups in subsidies' allocation decisions.

With this call, the Ministry of Agriculture then aimed at opening the range of projects and organizations that could be supported, beyond the 'usual suspects', that is, the institutionalized actors of agricultural development (Lamine 2020). The call was thus open to more alternative organizations and even to non-agricultural ones (such as the AMAP movement), and the evaluation process was conceived in order to allow the concrete translation of this principle despite the fact that institutionalized organizations were much more used to setting up such projects, and, which was an institutional innovation, open to farmers' groups as such, while usually government funds would only be attributed to development and extension organizations. These farmers could be refunded for the time they would spend in training their colleagues or managing the projects.

This programme allowed the funding of 103 beneficiary groups of which part were traditional actors of agricultural development (chambers of agriculture and cooperatives), but many were other kinds of entities, such as farmers' groups, alternative agricultural and rural development organizations, original partnerships between farmers and municipalities, as well as newcomers in the landscape of agricultural development such as specialized consulting groups.

The diversity of the agricultural models that were claimed by these groups correspond to different visions of the agroecological transition. Some groups adopt a more technical vision (focused on a particular practice, a particular technical itinerary, on technical itineraries aimed at a defined sustainability objective) and emphasize the double environmental and economic performance, while others adopt a more procedural vision (exchanging on practices, accompanying new entrants, collective learning). Some groups would claim a 'natural' convergence with already legitimate models (such as organic farming, extensive livestock breeding or peasant agriculture), while for others, agroecology appeared as a support point for 'intermediate' models in search of legitimacy, such as soil conservation agriculture, that also have a more controversial 'ecological' dimension than more established and legitimate models like organic farming (Lamine 2020).

In Brazil, the Ecoforte programme, whose extensive title was 'Programme for Strengthening and Expansion of Agroecology, Extractivism and Organic Production Networks', was launched in 2013 within the National Plan for Agroecology and Organic Agriculture (Planapo I). Like the MCAE programme in France, it aimed at supporting collective dynamics such as the structuration of local and regional circuits, of seeds conservation and exchange, of women's groups, or of 'study groups in agroecology'. This programme funded 28 networks and allowed to strengthen promising collective initiatives in various regions of the country as well as the recognition of traditional knowledge and of the role of women in agroecological transitions. It also favoured synergies with other public policies such as the food procurement ones (PAA and PNAE), supporting combined transitions in production systems and in consumption practices. Finally, it supported strong territorialization processes, favouring agroecological transitions at different scales. The mobilization of the programme as well as the 'systematization' of its outcomes was carried out by the ANA, with the aim to foster a reflexive and collective assessment of the dynamics at play with and by the networks.

Both programmes shared a relative flexibility and openness in terms of how the beneficiary networks and groups could define their trajectory and possibly redefine it along the way (Lamine 2020). Their analysis, carried out by researchers and participating actors, led in both cases to structure an appropriate methodology in order to systematize and understand qualitatively and in a reflexive and participatory manner, the outcomes and difficulties of these programmes (rather than carrying out a classical policy evaluation). In the MCAE case this process led to structure a 'sociological observatory' composed of qualitative studies structured along shared themes and of workshops for reflection, learning and exchange of experiences.

### 2.4 United Kingdom: learning networks and partial/proto agroecological approaches despite state policies

Unlike in countries such as France and Brazil, agroecological approaches in the UK have until recently (the past 10 years) largely surrounded the emergence of organic farming as a formally certified practice administered by the UK Soil Association. This has reflected a growth in consumer demands for organics over recent years.

More recently though, as in other European countries, a diversity of innovative farmers and farmer networks in the UK are developing a range of agroecological approaches, often with a number of intentions, including improving soil quality, reducing their use of inputs and/or maintaining/increasing the profitability of small-scale farms. *Innovative Farmers* is an example of a recent action-research network of farmers, agronomists and scientists which aims to develop new approaches to growing good food, reduce waste and pollution and boost profit margins. The network uses 'field labs' to bring farmers and researchers together to experiment with practical solutions for both conventional and organic farms. Topics covered include managing weeds without herbicides; finding alternatives to glyphosate for terminating cover crops (especially approaches that are beneficial to farm profitability, soil structure and the environment); cultural alternatives for controlling black grass; and crop varieties that are suitable for low-input systems. *The Pasture-Fed Livestock Association, the Agroecology Network*, the *Permaculture Association* and the *Centre for Alternative Technologies* (of Harper Adams University) are other examples of the current emergence of agroecological networks in the UK. Against the current idea that agroecological or organic farms are less profitable, these networks show that by moving farming in an agroecological direction farmers can make a difference to their balance sheet and their sustainability (PFLA 2016).

These different initiatives are resulting in a range of hybridities: different farming systems are adopting agroecological principles and practices while still using some conventional practices, perhaps using chemical inputs in a reduced or more resource efficient way (e.g. conservation agriculture) and thus are coming to compose a kind of 'middle ground' (Morris and Winter 1999). However the shift towards a more agroecological farming system generally involves a change in emphasis from following an agronomical approach (focused on crop yields at the plot scale) to a more holistic, systems, approach (Lampkin et al. 2015).

Proto-agroecological networks are now proliferating in the UK, as these examples suggest. They are characterized by their diversity of approach and practice, and a notable absence of strong or even minimal support from government (again in contrast to Brazil and France). Indeed, with Brexit there are severe doubts about what sort of organic and/or conversion policies might or might not be put in place in the UK. The government in its preparations for a new 'Food Strategy' (as of January 2020) emphasized a new round of productivist technologies (including 'hands free' farming, automation, crisp GM technologies) rather than a strong agroecological set of principles.

Nevertheless, and despite this overriding policy narrative, the very crisis in the conventional farming sector, associated with falling farm incomes and subsidies, and attendant rises in farm debts, is likely, as we see above, to encourage farmers to move away from the conventional agri-food 'treadmill' and explore new, and in many cases retro-innovative farming practices around more mixed farming approaches. So far there is a strong need for more applied micro-economic and sociological research which can demonstrate to farmers the advantages of these conversions, and indeed the significant employment and sustainability gains that can be made in adopting these strategies even on relatively small farms. In addition, these conversions are being matched with the development of a diversity of new, shorter supply chains being created. The pasture-led farmers, for instance, are linked to their own local butchers shops; and a whole range of new 'distributed' and cooperative systems of supply-from-box schemes, food coops, farmers markets and so on, are developing, especially around the major UK cities (see Moragues Faus et al. in press).

## 2.5   Legitimation at the international and European scales

A first step of the recognition of ecological forms of agriculture at the international scale was, in 2007, the recognition by the FAO of organic agriculture as able to feed the world, based on the global survey by Badgley et al. (2007) and despite vivid controversies. Soon afterwards, the International Assessment of Agricultural Knowledge, Science and Technology for Development (IAASTD) report meant a turning point in the introduction of agroecology within the policy-making arena (Rivera-Ferre 2018). From 2010 on, and until now (2019), agroecology has been increasingly present in the FAO debates, with a series of devoted forums and encounters. During the First International Agroecology Symposium organized by and at the FAO in 2014, the FAO then Director General José Graziano da Silva even suggested that agroecology could be a potential model to replace the 'cathedral of the Green Revolution' (Ajates Gonzalez et al. 2018) and agroecology appears today as one of the possible alternatives to address the current challenges (Loconto and Fouilleux 2019). At the European scale (see van der Ploeg et al. 2019) debates over the possible role of agroecology in the future CAP reform are only starting, but some recent studies have started to consider the possibility of generalizing agroecology on a European scale, such as the TYFA project, which quantifies an agroecological scenario by 2050 by testing the implications of different hypotheses such as the adoption of healthier diets and radical changes in production methods, and concludes that a widespread adoption of agroecology could lead to a 40 per cent reduction in GHG emissions from the agricultural sector, reduce Europe's global food footprint and provide healthy food for Europeans while maintaining export capacity (Poux and Aubert 2018).

## 3.   Agroecological transitions: agroecology and the necessary reconnection of agriculture, environment, food and health

Agroecology is increasingly advocated, by social movements but also in public policies, as we have seen above, as a potential paradigm – not to say a model, which it is not – able to serve as a guidance or at least a narrative for the future of our food systems, at the confluence of climate, health, and social issues.

### 3.1   Agroecological transition: conform or transform?

The role agroecology as a guiding paradigm has to play in food systems and wider rural transitions, is a matter of contested views. There is an ideological split between those who think the current food production system could be reformed, and those who want to radically change it (and consider there is no other option as is the case in the 'collapsology' debates), as well as several interpretations of how to bring about change to the food system (Sanderson Bellamy and Ioris 2017). There are different and rival visions of agroecology itself: that of ecological modernization, a progressive trend, and a radical one (Levidow 2015). The progressive and radical trends can be related to eco-economy, which relates to 'complex networks or webs of new viable businesses and economic activities that utilise the varied and differentiated forms of environmental resources in more sustainable ways. These do not result in a net depletion of resources but provide cumulative net benefits that add value to the environment' (Kitchen and Marsden 2009:275).

## 3.2    Regeneration, holism, diversity, variability: renewed key principles for agroecological transitions

The agroecological principles have been amply debated and redefined in many ways in the last decades, mainly in order to better include social and political dimensions (Dumont et al. 2016), but also to clarify how the ecological processes should be addressed. In this second aim, much less discussed in the recent literature, regeneration, holism, diversity and variability appear as key principles that should be added to the core agroecological principles (recycling of biomass, enhancing soil biotic activity, minimizing losses, species and genetic diversification). Agroecology is valued for its capacity to generate and regenerate the ecosystem services – from soil nutrient cycling to bee pollination – that industrial farming disrupts. It is defined by some authors by its socio-ecological metabolic consistency, where human resource use and waste production are consistent with nature's capacity to replenish resources and assimilate wastes. Agroecology activates a conception of ecological understanding but also of knowledge that is alternative to the idea of decomposing processes in separate units and problems and thus also a paradigm of innovation associated with integration (Allaire and Wolf 2004). It also valorizes diversity, and some authors draw a parallel between the reforms needed to strengthen democratic accountability in society and to build more sustainable agro-food systems, both of which rely on increasing the diversity of ecosystems, structures, cultures and institutions (Stevenson 1998; Dahlberg 2001). While the agro-industrial paradigm is based on the principles of homogenization and stabilization, the agroecological one, on the contrary, is based on on heterogeneity and variability (Bell et al. 2008). This points out the need to design and validate a research model that does integrate local variability, based on networks of decentralized experimental farms (Wit and Iles 2016) as well as forge new transdisciplinary alliances between rural and urban food growers, and academic scientists and extension specialists. As an overarching principle, recent works claim an agroecology theory that would offer contextually sensitive principles of general relevance but not universal outcomes, thus 'generalizing without universalizing' (Bell and Bellon 2018).

## 3.3    Addressing the intricacy of ecological and social processes: towards a territorial approach

The modernization and industrialization processes within agricultural and food systems have led not only to increasing detrimental environmental impacts but also to increasing health problems all over the world, thus disconnecting agriculture, food, environment, and health. Integrated Food Systems approaches are increasingly advocated, developed, and applied by food and health scientists, often in interaction with other disciplines in order to address the necessary reconnections between agriculture, food, environment, and health. They are mostly designed at the global or national scale (Hammond and Dubé 2012) and most often based on life cycle assessment (Heller et al. 2013) and modelling (Verger et al. 2018). Most of these studies still overlook major aspects such as bio-diversity or eco-toxicity (Schader et al. 2014) and focus on environmental *impacts*, thus also overlooking the role of ecological *processes*. They adopt an *environmental* rather than an *ecological* perspective on the sustainability of agri-food systems (Lamine et al. 2019). The environmental perspective has been developed in direct links with a vision of natural resources as a finite stock and, therefore, a conception of sustainable management based on 'impact assessment'. With this approach, a lesser and/or more efficient use of natural resources in agricultural and food practices must lead to a reduction of the impact on these natural resources. An 'ecological' perspective allows introducing explicitly a fundamental change in the way we consider nature and its resources in order to explore functional interactions between agricultural practices and the 'non-human'. In reference to ecological sciences, the term 'ecological', as opposed to 'environmental', allows introducing the processual, dynamic, and evolutionary dimension, which is specific to natural systems and more largely to bio-physical systems.

Moreover, most food systems approaches overlook the social processes that can facilitate or impede actual changes in agricultural and food practices: actors' strategies, power relationships, coordination between actors, and public policies. They also ignore the complex transition mechanisms that involve ecological, social, and economic processes together, such as the consequences of diverse food production systems on rural landscape and quality of life as well as inertia due to cultural habits.

The meso-scale of territorial agri-food systems appears as an appropriate empirical scale in order to take into account these diverse processes (Lamine et al. 2019). The territorial scale is used in diverse approaches such as foodsheds (Kloppenburg et al. 1996), regional food systems (Clancy and Ruhf 2010; Kneafsey 2010) or territorialized food systems (Bowen and Mutersbaugh

2014). Yet, these do not centrally tackle ecological transition processes – save for a few exceptions (Clancy and Ruhf 2010; Vaarst et al. 2017) – nor the reconnection between agriculture, environment, food and health. The relevance of a territorial approach relies on two main arguments: (i) it is the scale of direct interactions between ecological and social processes, which may create functionalities for improving agri-food systems' sustainability, and (ii) it allows the identification, and possibly the involvement in the research process, of the agri-food systems' diverse actors (Lamine et al. 2012).

A territorial approach allows combining an analytical perspective on past or current transition processes, and a transformative perspective where the aim is to bring researchers and actors together in the process of thinking and possibly implementing transition pathways. Indeed, taking into account the ecological, social, and health processes together as active principles of the organization and transition mechanisms of agri-food systems should rely on the collective (trans-disciplinary) analysis of past, current, and future transitions at the territorial scale. This allows for a collective understanding of the biological (ecological and health) dimensions of possible changes in food practices and of the social processes of transition mechanisms. The challenge is to share an appropriation, by the different disciplines and actors, of the ecology of a territory and the interplay of ecological and social processes within the territorial agri-food system. This can rely on the extension of the notion of ecological literacy, which defines the ability to understand the organizing principles of ecological systems and their links to sustainable transition processes, to that of socio-ecological literacy. In contrast to studies carried out at the global or national scales, at the territorial scale, this is facilitated by the fact that people share a community of fate: the future of their landscape, of the local farms, and of the local and cultural food practices.

## 4.    Conclusion

The promises of agroecology as a relevant model for agri-food systems transitions and also for rural territories have generated vivid debates in diverse arenas, from civil society to academia and public policies. Agroecology is one of the paradigms that articulates interpretations about past and ongoing changes and visions of necessary future changes, and as such competes with rival paradigms, while it also encompasses diverse versions. These internal and external debates and the related controversies need to be analysed in diverse contexts, as well as their impact on public action and on policies at diverse levels, from the local to the international one. Thus internationally comparative research into the struggles and evolution of agroecology is, as we begin to see here in this chapter, a fruitful arena for future research. Also, as a paradigm 'in action', translated in policies, programmes, rules, practices, networks and so on, it also merits specific methodological approaches that combine analytical and transformative stances. In this regard, the territorial scale appears as a relevant scale, increasingly advocated in the academia, in social movements and in international organizations (IPES-Food 2018; OECD, FAO and UNCDF 2016), which should give way to conceptual and methodological innovation.

## Notes

1.  http://www.reporterre.net/Le-gouvernement-flanque-un-coup-de, accessed on 13 March 2020.
2.  http://www.confederationpaysanne.fr/rp_article.php?id=320, accessed on 13 March 2020.
3.  http://viacampesina.org/en/index.php/main-issues-mainmenu-27/sustainable -peasants-agriculture-mainmenu-42, accessed on 13 March 2020.
4.  The notion of bio-economy is here a reinterpretation of that which was suggested by René Passet in the 1980s (Levidow 2015).
5.  https://www.legrandsoir.info/communique-pour-une-agroecologie-paysanne .html, accessed on 7 July 2020.
6.  Ibid, quotation translated by authors.
7.  Their goal is to articulate agriculture and food within a food strategy at the local level (of a small region or an agglomeration), based on the involvement of a diversity of local actors.

# 7. Family farming in changing agricultural social structures

## 1.    Introduction

How will agriculture produce healthier and sufficient food to supply the urban population of the planet in the 21st century? Who will produce these foods, and which farmers and which production systems are the most appropriate to meet this challenge? Obviously, there is no ultimate answer to these questions yet, but this is undoubtedly one of this millennium's greatest issues (IFPRI 2010; *The Economist* 2011).

Considering the outcomes that have been published in recent years (Pretty et al. 2010; HLPE 2012; IAASTD 2009) by international think tanks and researchers, one can already point at least to one certainty: the small farmers in the world, those who live and work on small plots of land and manage restricted resources (waters, forests, pastures and other ecosystems), through the predominant use of the family workforce, will undoubtedly be part of the solution and the answers about who will feed the planet in the near future (Belieres et al. 2013; CIRAD 2013).

The role of peasants, small producers and family farmers – later we shall better assess these differences – in the production and the supply of food has become clearer and more evident since 2014, when the United Nations fixed the International Year of Family Farming (FAO 2013). The celebration of the year of the family farming created a favourable environment for several initiatives, political discussions and academic debates that shed light on the role of family farming in food security and rural development around the world.

The most important outcome of the international year was an increase in better understanding the size, feature and scope of family farming. The FAO, for instance, prepared a study in which it states:

> there are more than 570 million farms in the world. Although the notion of family farming is imprecise, most definitions refer to the type of management or ownership

and the labor supply on the farm. More than 90 per cent of farms are run by an
individual or a family and rely primarily on family labor. (FAO 2014a: x–xi)

Further, other scholars, such as Lowder et al. (2014, 2016; Gladek et al. 2016),
using another data base, deepened these statistics and stated that 'globally,
about 84 per cent of farms are smaller than 2 ha (74 per cent are in Asia; 9 per
cent in sub-Saharan Africa), and they operate about 12 per cent of world's agricultural land' (Lowder et al. 2016:16).[1] According to Graeub et al. (2016), by
using a larger range of international agricultural census data (which together
encompass a majority 85 per cent of the world's food production), family
farms constitute 98 per cent of all farms in the world and at least 53 per cent of
agricultural land, thus producing at least 53 per cent of the world's food. More
recently, Fanzo (2018) also stated that smallholders produce some of the major
commodities consumed in the world and provide more than 70 per cent of the
food calories to people living in Asia and sub-Saharan Africa; yet many of these
farmers are poor and somewhat neglected (Samberg et al. 2016).

These data started to be published from 2014 and became important references
and contributed significantly to show that small producers and family farmers
have a strategic role in rural development in the 21st century (Fanzo 2018).
In general, all studies indicate that the importance of family farming lies in its
role in supplying and feeding the world's population as well as in mitigating
the effects of climate change.

This information is of great relevance because it reaches wide academic and
political repercussions, demonstrating that family farming is not residual,
nor of little importance in the whole food system or that it would be in the
process of disappearing. The image of highly mechanized agriculture, based
on mega-properties, using precision technologies that produce gigantic quantities of fibre and food raw materials, which are transformed and processed in
industries and, finally, transported by large ships around the globe and sold
at low prices in large supermarkets does not correspond to reality. Studies
elaborated by D'Odorico et al. (2014) show that the amount of food sold on the
international market more than doubled between 1986 and 2009, registering
an increase from 15 per cent in 1986 to 23 per cent in 2009. But 77 per cent of
the total food produced in the world is still consumed in national markets and,
above all, local or place-based. Only about 23 per cent of food produced for
human consumption is traded internationally.

On the basis of these data and statistical evidence, myths and fallacies were
left aside and, finally, it became possible to argue that family farming will have
a central role in feeding the planet in the 21st century. The most up-to-date

scientific evidence available, such as the work of Reganold and Wachter (2016) and Ponisio et al. (2015), reinforce the conclusions of Godfray et al. (2010), who had already stated: it is possible to supply and feed the current and future population of the planet (the 9.5 billion mouths to be fed in 2050), based on production systems based on family work and without the use of agrochemicals.

Therefore, we can say that family farming is not a problem or an obstacle to the development of agriculture and the rural community as a whole in the 21st century (FAO 2014c). Quite on the contrary; strengthening family farming is vital for solving critical problems for sustainable development, such as over-coming hunger and poverty, producing healthy food and preserving natural resources and bio-diversity in rural areas.

Several international organizations have launched studies in recent years to highlight the strategic role of smallholder agriculture – family farming – in rural development and food security (HLPE 2013). FAO itself estimates that 'family farms are by far the most prevalent form of agriculture in the world. Estimates suggest that they occupy around 70–80 per cent of farm land and produce more than 80 per cent of the world's food in value terms' (FAO 2014a:11). The UNDP (2011) study suggests that family farming may be decisive for generating environmental resilience and strengthening rural ways of life in such a way that they are more sustainable and able to cope with the environmental changes generated by climate change. The IFAD/UNEP report (2013) highlighted the strategic role of small producers for food security and the environment.

Thus, a clear message pops out: worldwide small farmers – those who have small plots of land or handle limited amounts of productive resources (water, forests, grasslands and other ecosystems) – will undoubtedly be part of the solution to the key problems of the 21st century. Scholars like Wiggins et al. (2010 and Wiggins, 2009), Pretty et al. (2011), Larson et al. (2012) and De Schutter (2010, 2014) analyse the conditions and possibilities for the role of small-scale farming in the context of agriculture post-modernization and post-green revolution, and suggest a process of sustainable intensification to enable increased labour productivity and economic surplus.

Moreover, there is also a consensus that family farmers will play a critical role in reaching the Sustainable Development Goals, of the 2030 Agenda of United Nations (Fanzo 2018). This finding has several consequences, one of the most evident of which is the fact that the multilateral international organizations linked to the United Nations system will recognize and push the role and potentiality of family farming for the development of sustainable food systems. In this context, at its 72nd Session, the United Nations General Assembly proclaimed the Decade of Family Farming 2019-2028 (FAO and IFAD 2019).

Therefore, the moment seems to have come when small producers (owners) should not be treated as a synonym for poverty or backwardness anymore, or doomed to the inexorable disappearance (Buttel and LaRamee 1991). That is why it is important to change the terminology that has been used, stop referring them as small-scale producers or other terminologies and start to call them family farmers or family production units (Schneider 2014; Ramos 2014). It is, of course, not just a matter of changing the name, since there are conceptual and theoretical implications beyond this. But, and above all, this change might indicate that the social category of family farmers can play an active and strategic role in the processes of rural social change that will come.

## 2.    Expressions of family farming in the world – where and how much?

Although studies have indicated the majority presence of family forms in global agriculture, it is necessary to consider that there are a wide variety of types and forms as well as important regional differences, which need to be considered. The work of Graeub et al. (2016) brought an important contribution to the description of family farming at a world level. The authors sought to make a more accurate estimate than that presented in studies by FAO (2014a) as well as by Lowder et al. (2014), which had been published in 2014.

The data presented by Graeub et al. show that the distribution of family farming is not uniform in different regions of the world.The study indicates that the highest percentage of family farmers was in Asia (99 per cent) and the lowest – both statistically significant – were in Oceania (78 per cent) and South America (82 per cent). Compared to the global family farmers' share of 98 per cent, Europe (97 per cent), and Africa (97 per cent) were just below this average, with North and Central America (88 per cent) resting in between. Graeub et al. also disaggregate the data by country income group and this provides additional insights into existing differences across economic groupings. Not surprisingly, they point out, the percentage of family farms are highest in the lower income countries, with low-income to upper-middle-income ranging between 98 per cent and 99 per cent. High-income countries still hold, on average, 90 per cent of family farmers.

The conclusion of Graeub et al. clearly emphasizes the global importance of family farmers in terms of agricultural holdings as well as in terms of agricultural production. Though the importance of family farming – as a percentage of all farms and in terms of the percentage of land worked by family farmers – differs strongly in countries within similar income groups (2016:9).

Herrero et al. (2017) shed light on another important aspect of the contribution of the smallholder farmers to the quantity and quality of food supply. They found that most large farms (>50 ha) are found in North America and South America, Australia and New Zealand, and produce 75–100 per cent of all cereal, livestock, and fruit in these regions, whereas small farms (<20 ha) found in sub-Saharan Africa, South Asia, Southeast Asia and China produce 75 per cent of food commodities globally, and 50–65 per cent of the production volume of major food groups. Very small farms (<2 ha) in the same region produce approximately 30 per cent of most food commodities.

More recently, Fanzo (2017) explored a little different perspective on the value of the family farmers. Looking at the role that family farms play for the dietary diversity and the safety of the traditional food systems, she highlighted the food culture and the inheritages related to food knowledge that come from those farms. It is already well known that most of the commodities produced on small farms come from diverse landscapes, producing a variety of horticulture, roots, tubers, fish, and livestock, whereas most of the plantation-based crops, such as sugar and oil, are produced from less diverse landscapes, mainly large-scale farms. Fanzo points out that studies reveal (IPES-Food 2017; Popkin 2014; Global Panel 2016) that mixed production systems generate more diversity of key nutrients (zinc, iron, vitamins A and B12, and folate) essential for human health. According to Herrero et al. (2017), most global micronutrients (53–81 per cent) and protein (57 per cent) are produced on more diverse agricultural landscapes (H-index >1·5). One thing to note is that in farm landscapes with higher agricultural diversity and more nutrients generated from that diversity, farm size does not matter (IPES-Food 2016).

In 2014, at the request of FAO, we coordinated the preparation of studies on the characteristics and profile of family farming in the five regions where this international agency operates (Schneider 2014). The data presented here below are a summary of these studies, which were published in the book *Deep Roots* (FAO 2014c) and in more wider and bigger papers at the Working Papers Series published in collaboration between the Food and Agriculture Organization (FAO), the United Nations Development Program (UNDP) and the International Policy Center for Inclusive Growth (IPC-IG).

## 2.1    Family Farming in Latin America and the Caribbean

The discussion about the role and the place of family farming in the social and economic development of Latin American and Caribbean countries has become a key topic of interest since the mid-2000s (Bengoa 2003; Baumeister 2012). This process started in the mid-1990s in Brazil and slowly gained ground and spread from the 2000s to other countries in the region (Salcedo and Guzmán 2014). The creation of REAF (Specialized Network of Family Farming) among the countries that integrate MERCOSUR, in 2004, and the Plan of Family Agriculture (PAF) of El Salvador in the Central American region have been important to spread the concept of family agriculture and the understanding of its meaning (REAF 2011; Sabourin et al. 2014).

This conceptual shift has been crucial for changing the ideas and conceptions of policy makers and scholars on family farming (Schneider 2013, 2016). Such change has not only theoretical and conceptual effects, but also political and ideological ones. It is increasingly evident that family farming is not necessarily synonymous with small-scale farming. For a long time – and still today – small-scale farming has been considered poor, marginal and inept, and thus was always on the verge of disappearing. Many papers have made the case that peasants and all kinds of small farmers were poor because they were small and thus could not achieve great economic performance. Fortunately, current discussions on family farming are overcoming this bias. Family farming is increasingly seen less as synonymous of poverty or aversion to markets and technology (Schejtman 2008).

It is estimated (FAO and ECLAC) that the family farming sector in Latin America amounts to nearly 17 million units, comprising a population of about 60 million, and that 57 per cent of these units are located in South America (CEPAL/FAO/IICA 2013). According to Leporati et al. (2014:35), family farming accounts for about 81 per cent of agricultural activities in Latin America and the Caribbean; at the country level, it supplies between 27 per cent and 67 per cent of the total national production of food; it comprises between 12 per cent and 67 per cent of agricultural land and creates between 57 per cent and 77 per cent of agricultural jobs in the region (FAO 2011, 2012). Although these data lack statistical accuracy, they indicate that family farming plays an unquestionable role in primary production, food security and more generally in the economic development of the region.

Family farming has assumed a central role in the social and economic development of Latin America and the Caribbean in the last two decades (Grisa and Sabourin 2019). Family farming creates jobs and income in rural areas, and also accounts for a significant share of food supply, especially at local and regional levels. In most countries of the region, family farming provides a major contribution to agri-food production, both in the domestic market and in the export of commodities and other products (FAO 2014b).

But the contribution of family farming to the rural development is not only economic (De Janvry and Sadoulet 2000, 2001). With regard to social and demographic factors, family farming also contributes decisively to keep families in rural areas. Rural communities that count on family farming feature an active social life, which is often reflected in virtuous local dynamics. Moreover, family farming is also important for women and young people, as access to land and productive assets are key resources to guarantee their livelihoods when men migrate to work in non-agricultural activities (Reardon et al. 2001).

The contributions of family farming to development in rural areas of Latin America and the Caribbean could certainly be expanded. Studies and academic research on family farming and the training of human resources on the topic has increased and expanded in the last decade. However, there remain gaps and limitations that must be overcome, like the availability of data and information on family farming, since census updating is poor in many countries in the region. In what relates to policies, there are at least two foci in which public policies for family farming might have a particularly important role, which are the access to technical training and innovations and the support to create and work properly the markets under the increasing constraints of globalization on prices and access to trade (FIDA 2014).

## 2.2 Europe and Central Asia – Reshaping Family Farming

In Europe, as several scholars point out (van der Ploeg 2016a; van der Ploeg et al. 2002; Gasson et al. 1988; Marsden 1989; Marsden et al. 1986; Whatmore et al. 1987), there is a long tradition of studies on peasants and, more recently, family farming. In fact, as highlighted by Henry Mendras (1987), family farming is part of the civilization that was ground and shaped in the old continent since the Middle Ages, when peasants lived in conditions of serfdom and produced essential food not only for fiefdoms, but also to feed armies and towns. It is worth remembering that in addition to producing and cultivating the soil, peasants paid heavy taxes and had commitments of honour and fidelity to fulfil, given by the vassalage relations. Although they always existed as a subordinate and subordinate social group, it can be said that peasants were the essence of European society (Jollivet 2001).

Nowadays, out of a total of 12,248,000 farms in Europe (EU28), some 11,885,000 (i.e. 97 per cent), might be classified as family farms. In the remaining European countries, one encounters more or less the same situation. The notable exception is Russia where family farming and corporate agriculture co-exist. In Russia and Western CIS countries family farms only cover 34 per cent of all land (although they produce 62 per cent of all output).[2] In Central Asia family farming is stronger: family farms control 71 per cent of all agricultural land (on which they produce 88 per cent of total output) (Davidova and Thomson 2013; Davidova 2014; Davidova and Bailey 2014). In Central Asia, as a whole, family farms control 71 per cent of the land on which they produce 88 per cent of the total agricultural production.

In the perspective of van der Ploeg (2016a), over the last fifteen years the context in which family farming is embedded and the nature of the family farm as such have been changing in ways that increasingly threaten. There is growing awareness of the need to construct new sovereign forms of food and nutritional security. This will be a far from easy task and it will surely take many years. In the author's opinion, it is equally sure that in Europe family farms are to be at the basis of this new food model – simply because they are and remain the most productive, most sustainable, most resilient and most socially appropriate land-labour institution.

In Europe, many family farms are actively responding to the threats in different ways (Oostindie 2015; van der Ploeg 2017b; Brunori and Bartolini 2016; Darnhofer et al. 2016). These include engaging in pluriactivity (one or more family farm members having an off-farm job) and multi-functionality (creating new economic opportunities within the farm) (Marsden 1990). Women often play a decisive role in these activities. Multi-functionality allows farming families to meet a range of new societal demands that are being articulated from the cities towards the countryside. Family farmers are also building new intermediary organizations (such as territorial cooperatives that take care of the landscape, bio-diversity and sustainability) in order to respond to rigid regulatory schemes.

However, the capacity to meet new needs (whilst simultaneously strengthening farming and food production) and to respond to new problems is a reflection of the strength and resilience of family farms (Darnhofer et al. 2016). When it comes to meeting new challenges (reducing energy use, mitigating climate change, enlarging bio-diversity and water retention, etc.) this capacity will probably once again turn out to be decisive.

However, the panorama of family farming in Europe and Central Asia is complex. Family farming is omnipresent and is of strategic importance, both now and in the future of the two continents. But, in van der Ploeg's opinion, it is under threat. Whilst its presence, role and dynamics were once self-evident, we can no longer be certain that family farming will be with us in the decades to come. There is a widespread feeling that the disappearance of family farming would be an immense loss (van der Ploeg, 2017a).

In van der Ploeg's (2016a:24) sense, the transitional process that is needed to overcome the threats will require extending the definition of the family farm. And to rephrase these proposals in positive terms: the operation of the family farm needs to be aligned with the major societal demands, needs and requirements of Europe and Central Asia. New policies are definitely needed to institutionalize such a realignment.

## 2.3    The Presence of Family Farming in Africa

From all the five studies we conduct during the International Year of Family Farming, in 2014, the African case was the one that clearly indicates some uncomfortable feelings with the notion or concept of family farming (FF). After examining several authors, reports and discussing the matter with reputable scholars, it became undeniable that this concept was quite new and people still prefer to use and talk about small-scale farmers or smallholders, instead of family farming. In fact, as Moyo (2016) highlights, in Africa, small-scale farmers have generally been pejoratively perceived and labelled by many policy experts and scholars as 'traditional' or 'backward', 'subsistence farmers', inferior to technologically progressive profit-oriented farmers.

Moyo and other scholars (Mamdani 1996) state that regardless of no official or legal definition of family farming in sub-Saharan Africa (SSA), the term small-scale farmers (SSF) or smallholder famers, is commonly used by governments, civil society and scholars, while the term peasantry is mainly used in sections of the scholarly literature. In Africa, however, the same authors highlight that small-scale family farming is a relative term which differentiates them from large-scale commercial (capitalist) farming, which are businesses managed by family owners who hire most of their labour.

Nevertheless, the fact is that over 75 per cent of the SSA population is involved directly and indirectly in small-scale farming, and this is why family farmers are pervasive in the economic life of the whole region. Moyo (2016:20) estimates that there are over 100 million FFs in the 44 countries of SSA. Their numerical growth is largely in consonance with the changing density of the region's rural population, particularly those active in agriculture. While the proportion of SSA's rural population fell from 84.5 per cent in 1961 to 62.4 per cent in 2013, the absolute number rose substantially from 188.4 million to 562 million in 2013. This means that the number of families dependent on farming may have trebled since 1961.

A recent report by AGRA (2019) on Africa also shows that 64 per cent of food consumed in the region is handled by millions of small- and medium-sized enterprises (SMEs), creating vast opportunities for family and women farmers. The report indicates that only about 20 per cent of the volume of food consumed in Africa fits the conventional notion of subsistence agriculture – food consumed directly by the farming households that grow it. A full 80 per cent of food consumed in Africa is purchased from private sector value chains, about 64 per cent of total food consumption is sourced from SMEs and 16 per cent comes from larger enterprises. The report also identifies other pivotal changes in African rural economies by noting that although 70–80 per cent of people in rural Africa work on their own farms, they spent 60 per cent of labour time off the farm, and about 40 per cent of this non-farm labour time is in agri-food system work such as wholesale, logistics, processing and retail.

In the last decades, the scale and organizational forms as well as the production focus of family farming in SSA has mutated significantly. Structural changes, including rapid demographic growth and urbanization, snail-paced technical shifts in agriculture generate new forms of urban demand for food, and their increased market integration. Moyo (2016) states that family farming shapes the social organization of life in a largely rural SSA, and consequently plays a key role in social protection. The human development in SSA (e.g. poverty, food security and gender relations) largely reflects the socio-economic fortunes of FFs. Furthermore, family farming communities are a critical electoral constituency which shapes political organization in SSA, even if their socio-political importance is not reflected in public policy priorities.

Notwithstanding, family farming in SSA is facing several constraints imposed by increasing arable land scarcity. In several countries, the portion of the land that small-scale farmers might access in not enough to make a livelihood (Moyo et al. 2012). In this particular case, the access to equitable distribution of land and secure land tenure (not necessarily as private property) is a precondition for the reproduction of family farmers and reduces their vulnerability.

But, the problem is not just related to land access, because land and other forms of capital and labour are not spread evenly within the household, because it tends to be differentiated according to gender and generation. Generally, the patriarchs control the means of production, while women and children mainly provide largely unwaged labour, and the management of FFs is largely divided by gender, with men being dominant in decision making. Not surprisingly, the marginalization of women in access to and control of family land and farming resources within FFs remains an increasingly recognized impediment to the development of FFs.

In SSA the phenomena of deagrarianization and changing rural–urban relations is also an ongoing process, and this is why about 600 million rural people derive their main source of income (and food) directly from cultivating and/or grazing small family landholdings, while large sections of the urban population are fed by FFs. Although most FF members reside in the countryside, large sections of them straddle between urban and rural areas, and part-time urban family farming is common in SSA. Despite the high rate of urbanization and migration, due to the scarcity of non-farm employment and incomes, many SSA families struggle for access to land and to maintain stable food production at very low yield levels (Moyo and Yeros 2005).

The state and the international agencies (NGOs and international aid bodies like DFID, AGRA and others) have intervened quite strongly in recent decades by using policies to change the shape and position of family farming. Most of the initiatives encompass the support to improve and develop food markets to create incentives for investments which can improve the productivity and diversification of FF production and foster food sovereignty. These include promoting food supplies to local markets, including through public procurement programmes for various institutions, and by augmenting social welfare transfers, as well as building collective FF action to aggregate inputs and output marketing (Gelli et al. 2010; Sumberg and Sabates-Wheeler 2011; Sulemana 2016).

## 2.4　Family Farming in Asia and the Pacific Region

According to Ye and Lu (2016), the Asia and the Pacific region has the largest number of family farms in the world. It is home to 60 per cent of the world's population and to 74 per cent of the world's family farmers, with China alone representing 35 per cent and India 24 per cent of the estimated 570 million farms worldwide. It is undeniable that family farming has played a central role in the socio-economic development and well-being of the whole population in the region.

Throughout the history of Asia and the Pacific, family farming stands as a means of production, a cultural norm and an institutional arrangement. In the Asia and the Pacific region, which has the largest number of family farms in the world, irrigation-intensive agriculture and rice farming required small social groupings such as families or villages to be the basic unit of production. Small-scale family farming is well adapted to the high density of population and relatively scarce agricultural resources.

Family farming in Asia and the Pacific region is highly diverse, making it difficult to come up with a simple definition. Spanning from full-time family members farming with the support of wage labour, as in China, to small-scale and subsistence farmers as in Pakistan and the Pacific Islands, family farming can be characterized in a general sense as family-based and small-scale. Defining family farming implies an ongoing process of increased understanding of situations at the local and national levels. Family farming is a self-evident phenomenon in Asia. However, there is hardly a clear and comprehensive definition that spans all the different realities at national or at regional levels in Asia and the Pacific. Similarly, the term 'family farm' is not commonly used in the history of Asian agriculture.

Family farming has been an essential part of the folk custom and rural culture of Asian societies since it first appeared. This cultural aspect of family farming explains why research on Asian rural societies (for example, Japan and China) pays so much attention to 'family'. Family farming is seen as the comprehensive outcome of land legacy, ancestral rules, household rights to common agricultural resources and strong social bonds interwoven by individual families. Peasant agriculture and family farming has supported the orderly operation of traditional agrarian society due to its incomparable advantages in production organization and social stabilization. Many Asian countries formally institutionalize the family as the fundamental farming unit through land reform and legislation.

In Asia and the Pacific family farmers often develop farming systems and practices to adapt to different local conditions, marginal land endowments and climatic variability. Diversification is therefore an important farm strategy for managing production risk in small farming systems. Family farming cannot be perceived separately from the pluriactive role of rural households. However, family farming's contribution to non-commodified household production is largely underestimated in national economies. Despite the importance of family farming and its contributions to enhance local traditions, food heritage, community ecosystems and rural landscapes in Asia and the Pacific, the forces of globalization, deregulation and withdrawal of government from agriculture create an ambiguous environment for policy making and support to family farming.

In such a context, family farming faces dramatic challenges under global capitalization and agrarian transition. The transition from family farming to large-scale, capitalized farming that occurs in the developing countries of Asia and the Pacific are involved in capitalization through contract farming. Compared to the income increase brought by contract farming, the loss of social standing and political power over their own land and labour, the increased social differentiation and disintegration of rural communities, and the rising inequality and risks of landlessness represent immeasurable impacts for family farming and rural society as a whole. A second significant challenge comes from land grabbing, both by global players and domestic development. A third major challenge for family farming is the deagrarianization of rural youth in the trend of migration. Nonetheless, family farming has a critical role to play in food sovereignty and food safety in Asia and the Pacific region of the world.

## 2.5    Family Farmers in North America

In North America, family farms held positions of esteem in the dominant cultures led by Thomas Jefferson, who believed that the 'yeoman farmer' best exemplified the kind of 'independence and virtue' that should be respected and supported by government.

Ikerd (2016) described the origins of farm families by indicating that they migrated from Europe to the US and Canada and participated in a form of enclosures when indigenous peoples were forced off their land and the frontier was privatized. Homesteads gave farm families 160 acres in both the US and Canada. Prior to the mid-19th century, farming in North America was predominantly a 'way of life' and most farms were clearly family farms. Farm sizes began to increase during the 1800s, as farms on the US and Canadian prairies began to mechanize and expand production to provide food for growing populations in the East. In early 1900, farms continued to expand in acreage and productivity, with various setbacks associated with economic recessions. Following the Second World War, millions of US and Canadian farms were destined to become farm businesses rather than ways of life, and agriculture soon became an industry.

During the 1950s and 1960s, capital and technology replaced labour and management and farms were consolidated into larger and fewer farm businesses. By 1970, farm numbers in both countries had dropped by more than one-half from their peak. The global economic recession of the 1980s caused roughly one-quarter of the remaining farms to go out of business in the US. Since then, farm numbers have continued to decline and the average farm size is now 421 acres in the US and 778 acres in Canada.

Farming in Mexico has followed a quite different path from the US and Canada, but the tendency towards industrial consolidation has been much the same. One must remember the Mexican revolution of 1910 and the Constitution of 1917, which authorized agrarian land reform. By 1940 most of the country's arable land had been redistributed to peasant farmers. Since 1994, under the new North American Free Trade Agreement (NAFTA) between Mexico, the US, and Canada, family farming has been subordinate to a pattern that creates a toxic environment to the survival of the small-scale family farms in North America.

The US case is emblematic of those major changes. In 2017, the Agriculture Department (USDA 2018) released Agricultural Census which showed the hollowing out of the middle-range farmers.[3] The census show that in 2017 most of American farms were small (89 per cent) and operated 52 per cent of total farmland, even though they accounted for only for 26 per cent of production. In general, farmers' ages skewed older, leaving questions about what happens when they age out. The number of farm operations dropped 3.2 per cent to 2.04 million. Total acreage farmed nationwide dropped 1.6 per cent, while the average farm size increased by the same percentage, to 441 acres. The National Agricultural Statistics Service, which compiles the census, indicated that just 105,453 farms produced 75 per cent of all sales in 2017, down from 119,908 in 2012. While the number of male producers declined 1.7 per cent, the number of female producers increased nearly 27 per cent to about 1.23 million. Only two out of every five American farm producers (1.42 million) list farming as their primary job. Almost as many, 1.37 million, spend 200 days or more each year working outside of the farm.

In North America, family farming is constrained by the industrial model of agriculture, which determines not just a way to farm, produce and sell the food stuffs, but removes the room and the environment that those kind of farmers need to survive in a hostile context. The whole industrialization of the sector went too far and eroded the conditions of existence for family farmers. Another major challenge to family farmers in North America is the advancing age of farmers. Young people without farm backgrounds have begun to operate small farms in the US and Canada, but not enough to offset those leaving established farms.

According to Ikerd (2016), policies supporting multi-functional farming might be the way to further support and foster family farming. In his opinion, policies could provide basic health care to multi-functional farm families as well as workers' compensation and other 'fringe benefits'. This would be key to restore farmland to the commons and permanently zone enough farmland for food production to meet the food sovereignty needs. This should include developing land tenure policies that will support more farms, local markets, local control and food democracy, thus ensuring the use of farmland for the common good. And public research and education should be redirected to serve public interests, giving priority to on-farm research and with-farmer education.

## 3. Overcoming old controversies – from peasants and small-scale to family farming

After this broad review on the state-of-the-art of family farming alongside different regions in the world, one comes to the issue of definitions, categories and concepts. This might be seen as something marginal and less important, but it matters to talk, state and use different words to name, frame and refer to certain social groups. In social science, names and words have a meaning and, by consequence, this changes practical materialities as well as the cultural identity. This is of critical importance because individuals and social groups organize themselves on the basis of certain characteristics and upon them a common sense of sociability is built, which creates habits, values and norms. In short, the way that social groups are named is key to the way they shape the way in which they live and exist as human beings. Therefore, the name matters (van der Ploeg 2017b).

Fortunately, there is a growing consensus about the inadequacy of production scale indicators (productivity and income) to the understanding of small-scale agriculture (Hazell and Rahman 2014; Conway 2014; Lipton 2005, 2006; Hayami 2002). It is probably true to say that rural sociology has continued to struggle with locating and defining family farming within its wider categorizations and characterizations of modern societal structures and institutions.

The size of farmed land became an internationally accepted unit of measurement to define a small-scale producer (Nagayets 2005; Garner and de la O Campos 2014). FAO (Lowder et al. 2014) and the World Bank, for example, adopt the maximum size of 2 hectares to define a small-scale producer. As pointed out by Hazell and Rahman (2014), this criterion has become decisive for the development of comparative international statistics.

Despite the statistical advantages of using the concept of small-scale production, this term has become questionable, since land size says very little about the real social and economic conditions of production and reproduction of farmers. A small-scale producer with up to 2 hectares of land can be considered as either not economically viable or as appropriate, depending on how the land is used, the type of cultivation, technology, access to non-agricultural income and so on. It was often based on these criteria that, for a long time, small-scale production was associated with rural poverty and, therefore, economic non-viability.

Labelling family farming as small-scale agriculture is a mistake because even in small areas enterprises can reach high technical and productive scales. There is a vast literature on the inverse relationship between size and productivity in agriculture (Ellis 1988; Woodhouse 2010), which would explain the persistence of economic family units in agriculture. However, it is important to recognize that the factors that contribute to the endurance and reproduction of the farming units go far beyond technology and the way of use and optimal allocation of factors. Since Chayanov (1966 [1925]), we know that the optimal size of establishments depends on economic and demographic variables, related to both the management of the units and their relationship with social and economic contexts. More recently, many scholars have pointed out that family farmers are able to overcome size limitations and scale disadvantages through collective action and the organization of cooperatives, as well as through political mobilization towards more favourable public policies (van der Ploeg 2013b, 2017a).

What is then, after all, the fundamental distinction between family farming and the other two terms, small-scale production and peasantry? Although this controversy has already yielded a significant amount of literature, in the interest of brevity it can be said that the difference between family farming and smallholding lies in the fact that the former refers to a productive activity (farming) that is performed by a social group (family) connected by ties of consanguinity and kinship, whereas the latter refers to the scale of production related to a particular agricultural producer (since a small-scale producer will not necessarily either be an agricultural producer or live in a rural area). Very often the small scale is linked to the size of the available land (owned or not) or even just to the area that is usable for farming, but it can also refer to the intensity of use of other factors, especially technology and capital (Chayanov 1966 [1925]; Shanin 1973, 2009; Ellis 1988).

Family farming constitutes a particular form of organization of labour and production that exists and is reproduced within the social and economic contexts in which it is embedded (Schneider 2003). Its reproduction is determined by internal factors related to the way of managing productive resources (land, capital, technology etc.), making investment and expenditure decisions, allocating the work of family members and adhering to the cultural values of the group to which they belong (van der Ploeg 2010, 2013a). Yet, family farmers cannot elude the social and economic context in which they live and by which they are conditioned, and sometimes subject to (Marsden 1991; Gasson et al.1988). Among these determinants, there are the increasing urban demands for both healthy foods and the preservation of landscapes, soil, water and bio-diversity (Fanzo 2018). Technological innovations are also determinants that can reduce the role of both the land and the labour force in the production processes; thus, they can be decisive for greater competitiveness of the productive units (Sourisseau 2015; Darnhofer et al. 2016).[4]

Finally, the point about the relationships and integration of family farming into the economy and capitalist society (Friedmann 1978; Bernstein 1977, 2006). To avoid falling into a conceptual trap, here again it is better to use the workforce criteria instead of land size or production volume to categorize farm units. Thus, we can find family farmers either focused on on-farm consumption and/or subsistence (when very little of the production is sold) or devoted to commercial aspects (when a significant part of the production is for sale). We may find both family farmers whose production is based solely on the labour of family members and who do not commercialize their production – characterizing family farming for on-farm consumption – and specialized family farming units, fully integrated into markets (Schneider and Niederle 2010). Neither the use of family labour nor the final destination of the production – on-farm consumption or sale – allow for the identification of peasants or family farmers per se with this or that model of society and economic system (van der Ploeg 2013a). Both social forms can be found and achieve their social reproduction in different societies and economies, including the capitalist mode of production.

## 4. Challenges for family farming in a changing world

At the rural sociology world congress, held in 2016 in Toronto, Canada, a memorable panel was held in which some of the leading scholars on peasant studies of the 20th century were present (Bernstein et al. 2018). Henry Bernstein, Harriet Friedmann, Jan Douwe van der Ploeg, Teodor Shanin and Ben White each posed questions about the key challenges of peasant studies in the 21st century.

Among the challenges highlighted by the scholars is the critical importance of family farming for food production and supply. Ben White was particularly emphatic in pointing out that there is no doubt that, given the technological advances achieved today, agriculture is a strategic sector for macroeconomic stability, and small farmers can supply the food needs of any country and even of the total world population. In such a vein, he points out, the question about whether the smallholders can feed the world in the 21st century doesn't make sense. The question to be asked is about the conditions under which they can meet this challenge, whether they have access to land, markets and the technologies necessary for them to play this role.

There was consensus among the scholars that the issue is not about size and scale anymore, but about the context and conditions in which family farmers achieve their reproduction. Among sceptics and optimists present at the debate, scholars believe that the current great challenges for family farmers are linked to demographic and climate changes. Regarding demographic issues, the challenge is to understand that rural families in the 21st century have very different characteristics in comparison to the past: the number of members of rural families has decreased and is currently pretty similar to the urban families, there are no more surplus workers and cheap labour force in the rural areas. Furthermore, members of rural families are no longer engaged only in agricultural activities, since even in the less developed countries and regions, non-agricultural occupations, pluriactivity and deagrarianization processes are a reality. Henry Bernstein, for instance, correctly states that 'hardly any rural people in the world today reproduce themselves exclusively through farming' (Bernstein et al. 2018:712). As a result, young people and women have changed their social position in the structure of families.

In the context of climate change, family farmers continue to face recurrent processes of *expropriation by dispossession* of their assets, especially losing control over their land and water (Borras et al. 2011). According to Harriet Friedmann (Bernstein et al. 2018:697-698) this raises old questions about power and property, which had already been central to Eric Wolf's studies of peasant wars in the 20th century (1955, 1966). Therefore, the challenges of the 21st century remain the same as those of the past. In a context of growing climate-related restrictions and vulnerabilities, the future of millions of peasants and smallholders is dire and the risks to their survival are real in many parts of the world.

Another challenge is related to the identity and heterogeneity of family farming. After all, what does it mean to be a family farmer in the 21st century? In his presentation, Jan Douwe van der Ploeg highlighted that diversity will continue to be a fundamental feature of family farms simply because producing exchange value (food merchandise) through the use of the labour and traditional knowledge of the farmers essentially differs from the use of wage labour. But, according to Ben White, in the 21st century, peasants are likely to have at least three different characteristics, because it is increasingly common for new 'entrants' in the agricultural sector to have several backgrounds: they may be the children of farmers who decide to take over the property at a given time, but they also may be the children who migrate out of the rural areas and when their parents get older and can no longer work, they return and take over the property or, still, they may be young people born and raised in the urban areas that become 'real' new entrants (Bernstein et al. 2018:708). In one way or another, the challenge is to accept and admit that in the 21st century there will be 'new peasants', whether or not they are children or heirs of families who were previously farmers, whether or not they are identified with the seal of belonging to the peasant class.

The challenges mentioned so far that family farmers will face in the 21st century have already been discussed and analysed in previous chapters of this book. Demographic changes and deagrarization patterns, as well as impacts on young people and gender relations need to be understood in the context of globalization and financialization processes. The access to land and other productive resources, such as credit and technologies, are also critical. In this regard, it must be pointed out that the future of family farming will clearly depend on the ability of this social group (or class, if one prefers) to be able to mobilize politically, whether through cooperatives or associations, social movements or even unions to demand public policies and struggle for state support (Akram-Lodhi and Kay 2009).

## 5.    Family farming and rural development

As mentioned up to here, rural development in the 21st century involves balancing the nexus between food, the environment (especially water and climate) and energy. Family farming might play a critical role for humanity to find sustainable and lasting solutions to the issue of supply and food security for increasingly urbanized societies (Lang 2005; HLPE 2017). There are several studies and diagnoses that point to the relationship between demographic and food issues by stimulating family production, especially in regions of the planet where famine and the risks of hunger are more evident, such as in Africa and in some other regions of the world such as Asia, as well as in Central America, notably Haiti. The same goes for cities and metropolises, where there is no shortage of food, but the nutritional quality deteriorates due to the use of agro-chemicals and the number of consumers willing to buy fresh and organic food directly from producers is only increasing (van der Ploeg et al. 2012).

Something similar occurs with the environmental challenges and the energy transition. In the case of the environment, there are consistent indications that changes in agricultural production are crucial for agriculture to reduce greenhouse gas emissions and contribute to mitigating the effects of climate change. In Europe, as in other developed countries, there are increasing restrictions on the production of milk and livestock for meat, as well as cereals. Family farmers and organic and agroecological production systems have been identified as viable solutions to the environmental crisis without reducing the food supply. Finally, family farming can contribute to new technological formats of energy production, whether through energy cooperatives or even decentralized units of energy production from biomass or waste, as has been happening in Germany and China.

Whatever, public policies and the role of the state are strategic for family farmers. Analyses of rural development policies, such as those that have been implemented in Europe and Brazil in recent decades, showed great potential and highly positive results for family farming. Indeed, public policies for family farming are inscribed in broader rural development policies. Therefore, policies for family farming are rural development policies; each benefits from the other. In light of the evident and recognized diversity of family farming, it is reasonable to expect that public policies in this area should take such heterogeneity into account. Therefore, the set of actions, programmes and policies should be diversified, seeking to meet the specificities of each situation.

However, there is a guideline that might be applied for devising public policies aimed at family farming. It is based, on the one hand, on the principle of capacity-building and, on the other, on the mitigation of vulnerabilities. In short, good policies for family farming are those that strengthen their livelihoods and are able to generate resilience (UNDP 2011). It is useless to attempt to rank the best or most appropriate policies for family farming, since it always depends on the conditions of local ecosystems and the characteristics of the family farmers themselves.

However, there are some areas in which public policies for family farming have a particularly important role in the current social and economic scenario.

The first area relates to the strengthening of the assets of family farmers. One of the major problems that undermines these productive units lies in the fact of being small and having limited or inadequate access to assets and resources. Obviously this does not mean to be poor or doomed to remain in a vulnerable condition; as a matter of fact, the pessimistic predictions that proclaimed the disappearance of small farmers did not perceive the crucial role of the state in developing public policies for this large social group (which represents a significant proportion of rural voters) or its potential for social and economic organization through cooperatives. Therefore, overcoming fragmentation and individualism is a necessary condition for adequately structuring family farming to compete and endure in a capitalist society. There is a long roll of assets that could be listed as major elements for family farming, with land, water and seeds being the most important. It is not our purpose to make recommendations on which assets should be supported, but it is worth noting that public policies should prioritize the collective use of these resources to promote social capital.

The second refers to mechanisms aiming to reduce farmers' dependence on external resources, especially regarding the use of inputs such as seeds and agrochemicals that could gradually be replaced by organic fertilization, or less intensive techniques for the management of plants and animals, such as agroecology and direct planting in straw mulch. This is not just about encouraging more sustainable production and cropping systems to reduce costs, but above all it is about increasing the resilience of the production units. In most countries of Latin America and the Caribbean, there is currently a myriad of low-cost resources and technologies that are relatively well known and are disseminated by public agencies and non-governmental organizations. Thus, such options are feasible and practical, but their implementation must respect the local conditions and lore, so that a true interaction between the tacit knowledge of farmers and the expert/scientific knowledge of mediators can be established without overriding one another, since they are complementary in nature.

The third regards supporting increased production and the generation of surpluses. Many small-scale farmers are poor because they cannot produce enough to feed their own families, often requiring cash transfer policies to supplement their incomes. There are several limiting factors for this, particularly the lack of resources, the lack of adequate knowledge, or even exploitation by other agents. Public policies play a key role in fostering production for on-farm consumption and supply, especially among indigenous and traditional populations, by investing in training and storage. Furthermore, the generation of marketable surpluses by adding value and generating new products, by means of agro-industrialization, has been highlighted as a viable alternative. Public policies in support of production should not be restricted to increasing scale, but should especially address the transformation, processing and storage of production.

The fourth area for public policy intervention relates to markets and commercialization. In the context of agri-food globalization, it is essential for family farmers to have access to protection mechanisms against unfair competition (Pegler 2015; Medina et al. 2015). This does not mean to clamour for protectionist policies in relation to global markets but, rather, for public policies able to guarantee food and nutritional security, environmental preservation and actions to keep people in the rural space, and for farmers to be able to access markets and build new sales channels, whether through public procurement, local fairs or short supply chains for direct sales to consumers. Public policies need to focus on the organization of the suppliers, through either associations, cooperatives or private networks.

For all these reasons, rural development in the 21st century is part of a more general process of changing the foundations of the economy, which will necessarily move to more environmentally sustainable bases, promoting bio and eco-economies (Marsden 2011) or circular shapes (Marsden and Farioli 2015). There is a healthy and necessary connection between this process and the panorama set by the Sustainable Development Goals (SDGs). A look at the 2030 Agenda of the UN and its subsidiary organizations clearly shows that the 17 objectives and the Sustainable Development Goals can only be achieved if a new development base is established (HLPE 2016; IPES-Food 2017; Fanzo 2018).

## 6.   Conclusions: overcoming the contradictions and vulnerabilities in family farming

The interpretation and positioning of family farming in wider sociological and geographical debates has continued to suffer from the conceptual hangovers associated with early Marxist debates about the eventual disappearance of the peasantry with the growth of capitalist agriculture and urbanization, and/or the persistence debates (e.g. neo-Chayanov). Now, in the 21st century, it can be argued that we need conceptual headroom to reposition family farming more at the heart of post-carbonism and sustainable development and, indeed, as part of an alternative model of more distributed business development associated with networks of producers and consumers, rather than the dominant concentrated model of corporate control.

As stated by Fanzo (2018:16), many smallholder farmers struggle to make ends meet, and historically, in many regions (see Chapter 1) we have witnessed an urban bias and disinvestment in rural areas. It is crucial to invest in smallholder farmers and give support to the rural transformation process and changes (IFAD 2016). There are several ways how this might happen, to better-connect farmers to markets (see Chapter 8), empower and engage women and jumpstart entrepreneurship among smallholder farmers. Food security and nutrition strategies are needed to ensure that family farmers are healthy, produce in sustainable ways and are capable of continuing to make important contributions to the overall dietary diversity of the world's population.

Such a repositioning, however, will not occur without concerted actions by the state. History tells us, from the first white family farm settlers in the British colonies, to the emergence of the protection of family farmers as a key aspect of the development of the EU Common Agricultural policy, to Lula's food poverty programmes more recently, that concerted actions on the part of the state are critical for the renaissance and development of family farming today as we face significant new challenges of sustainability and the need for a new agricultural and agrarian transformation. Work needs doing on what levels of the state are important here. It may not be just at the national state level, but at the local and regional levels. In some regions of Europe (as highlighted in Chapter 3) local and regional procurement policies are linking food feeding programmes and stimulating local family farmers. Traditional plant breeding and local quality production systems are being state-supported in regions in Italy and Wales. Also environmental cooperatives led by family farmers are stimulating wider family farming practices in the Netherlands (van der Ploeg 2016b, 2017a).

What we begin to see then is the need for *the grounded re-conceptualization of family farming as part-and-parcel of sustainable rural development*, rather than being rendered a minor or marginalized (awkward) adjunct to it. We need to see the support for family farming as an empowering rural development strategy linked directly to a range of key Sustainable Development Goals (SDGs). In order to progress this challenge we also need to recognize the very continuing narrowly defined agro-industrial economics linked to narrow definitions of productivity, bulk commodity production, as well as big and privatized data, that market and state constructions are almost ever continually 'rigged' against these family farming emancipatory processes. It was an old adage in the UK, for instance, which some decades ago argued that the agricultural economists professions were unique in developing and progressing their economic models for the continuing destruction of one of its major constituents – the family farmers. This must be changed.

In this extent, we desperately need to reverse these narrow economistic logics by building broader and more integrated and grounded models of sustainable production and exchange which foster smaller networks of producers and markets. Here, as we shall see in the next chapter on nested markets, family farming production systems need to be connected with new and grounded nested markets, rather that becoming subsumed into wider and appropriating commodity markets from which they will always derive their vulnerability and marginalization.

## Notes

1.  Based on agricultural census data from FAO, Nagayets (2005) estimates that there are about 525 million farms of all sizes in the world, Hazell et al. (2010) used similar data to maintain that there are about 500 million small farms of less than 2 hectares.
2.  'Family farmers owned only 13 percent of agricultural land in Russia in 2005 and household plots accounted for less than 5 percent. All other land is controlled by LFEs [large farm enterprises] and agro-holdings, both national and international […] By mid-2008 […] 196 large agro-holdings controlled 11.5 million ha. Of these agro-holdings, 32 had landholdings of over 100,000 ha' (Visser et al. 2012:906). Nonetheless, the family farms and household plots (with less than 20 per cent of all agricultural land) produced more than 55 per cent of total agricultural output (Visser and Steggerda 2013:16) which shows that the technical and economic performance of LFEs and agro-holdings is very poor.
3.  USDA uses acres of crops and head of livestock to determine if a place with sales of less than $1,000 could normally produce and sell that amount. Farm size is measured by gross cash farm income (GCFI), a measure of the farm's revenue that includes sales of crops and livestock, government payments, and other farm-related income, including fees from production contracts. By this criteria, Small Family Farms are those who make less than $350,000 GCFI per year, Midsize Family Farms between $350,000 and $999,999 and Large-Scale Family Farms of $1,000,000 or more GCFI.
4.  This definition of family farming shares the insights of a group of authors and academic debates that occurred in the 1980s and 1990s on the subject. Internationally, the main authors who decisively contributed to these discussions were Friedmann (1978, 1986); Ellis (1988); Gasson and Errington (1993); Djurfeldt (1996); Borras (2009); and van der Ploeg (2010).

# 8. The power of the new markets

## 1. Introduction

The discussion on markets remained largely under-theorized among social scientists until a few decades ago. In the field of rural studies, this absence is even greater. In recent years some scholars realized that the study of markets is a relevant task in sociology, and the early appeals from Swedberg (1994), reinforced by Lie (1997) and Fligstein (1996) start to resonate. As a result, the study of markets open up room in economic sociology with strength and robustness, becoming a consensus on the need to better understand how they are organized, what are the social forces that govern them and, above all, how power and social relations are built, and the domination mechanisms that allow the existence of different forms of interaction in market spaces.

The research agenda currently underway is showing that markets are not just spaces between demand and supply, limited to the laws of formation of economic wealth, and how societies allocate and distribute it along time (Abramovay 2004; Niederle et al. 2014). Increasingly markets are perceived and understood as spaces of social interaction, shaped through signs and relationships that are not only material and tangible, but fundamentally activated through social, cultural and cognitive interactions (Bourdieu 2000).

It is not uncommon to find diffuse understandings that sometimes perceive the markets as an expression that refers to an abstract entity, with its own values and motivations, capable of even predicting social behaviour (Favereau et al. 2002). In this case, 'the market' appears as an otherworldly entity that needs to be heard, respected and, hence, calmed down; implicitly understood is the recurrent need to re-stabilize the relationships between agents who trade goods and shares in global circuits, quite well represented by the behaviour of the stock market performance. On other occasions, the notion of 'market' takes on a more concrete meaning, revealing a space for interaction where exchanges, dialogues, negotiation, conflict, buying and selling take place (Fligstein 2001). This is the case with fairs, grocery stores, supermarkets and commercial houses, and so on. Whatever the understanding, markets are of crucial importance in people's lives, helping to define broad spheres of social, political and cultural organization in societies.

Markets need to be redefined and better understood by both social scientists and policy makers. Social scientists, and particularly rural sociologists, for the most part, think that markets are the expression of the capitalist mode of organization of exchange relations and social interaction (Fourcade 2007). Therefore, markets are viewed negatively and depreciatively, from which it turns out that almost no one studies them and much less understands how they operate and are governed. The basic question, after all is: what are and how do markets work? This is very poorly answered. Therefore, we need to discuss agri-food markets and how markets more generally affect rural society; to analyse the role of agents, examine the power relations and, above all, better understand how to construct alternatives outside the capitalist march and framework. Policy makers, on the other hand, either do not believe that markets can be built and governed – after all because this would be the task of the markets themselves – or they are not prepared to design policies to build markets (Harriss-White 2005).

Some social scientists point out that the market(s) might be treated as a place, or as a synonym for trade or negotiation, or even an ideological perception about how a given society should be structured, which means a society governed by the market or, in short, a market society (Shanin 1973). As a place or a concrete space, the market is placed and shaped by somehow a site or spot where people go to trade, whether as sellers or buyers. There are many examples of market places, the most frequent being those places in the cities where the stores and commerce of various products come together (Braudel 1985; Swedberg 2005; van der Ploeg 2016). They are often spaces where you can buy food or even watch a cultural event. But the market can also be referred to as a synonym for trade or negotiation. In this case, the market becomes a destination for products that will be sold out, which identifies the market as the destination of the sales ('sell to the market'). But it is also possible to talk of the market in a third way, which implies defining the market by its ideological or political dimension, in which the market becomes a vision of how a given society should be organized and structured. Markets become the symbol of a specific social order, usually associated with capitalism or a market capitalist society, and the market becomes almost an adjective for everything.

But, the fundamental point is to expand these visions and start to see and define the markets from the social relations that they engender. Markets turn out to be understood as mechanisms for exchange of goods and merchandise in which a seller and a buyer come together and agree to make an exchange on the basis of a transfer of the property right of a good or its equivalent from one to the other (Callon 1988). Markets are, therefore, social relations established with the purpose of making exchanges (Polanyi et al. 1976). Thus, it is possible to say that markets are social constructions or, which is the same, that markets are socially constructed. In complex societies, with a large population of individuals and high mobility in a certain social division of labour, the interactions that seek to make exchanges are intermediated by the money or another device (credit card, etc.) and the prices of products and goods are the indicators of the value of the exchanged goods.

In order for markets to work properly and that social exchange relations might take place without risks and mishaps, rules and norms were created, which are the institutions that organize and govern markets (Cassol 2018). Thus, if markets are the result of social relations, there are no markets that do not suffer from some extent of coercion or regulation, whether formal or informal. Therefore, the existence of markets presupposes some type of regulation, which are the rules that govern the markets (Beckert 2002, 2009). The understanding of markets as social constructions is one of the centre points of attention of economic sociology, which studies how markets work and seeks to understand how economic exchanges are embedded in social rules that organize these interactions (Granovetter 1985).

In this chapter we will analyse markets as social constructions that function as institutions which order and shape the forms of interaction between producers and sellers in a given context and space (Schneider and Escher 2011). Defining markets as social constructions removes from them the aura of the unknown and enigmatic and makes them something concrete, real; which then can be situated in space and time and, above all, can be changed and/or transformed by the agents who participate in them (Ménard 1995; Wilkinson 2010). Markets are not synonymous of capitalism, nor are they summed up by the so-called 'law of supply and demand' and have even less to do with prices and the balance of perfect allocation of private desires.

## 2.   Markets and commoditization studies, there are still gaps

The commoditization processes of social and economic life are rapidly growing in the contemporary period. Currently, most farmers and families that live in rural areas, whether they are producers or just dwellers, are inserted in some kind of markets whether it is for products, services or information. But the insertion of farmers in the markets and the way in which exchanges take place is very diverse and there is no model or pattern, nor a single path or a predetermined direction. Thus, it becomes relevant to understand how commodification affects the rural environment and agri-food production and, above all, how farmers and rural inhabitants enter in those markets and stablish relations with them.

A snapshot of the sociological literature on the subject shows that the insertion of individuals in the markets was interpreted by the socological classics as part of the process of expanding the social division of labour, which results in increasingly complex social relations. Marxist political economy, for example, attributes to this process the transition of societies and the evolution of pro-duction modes based on the production of use value in exchange for values, in which markets are understood as an essential space for the circulation of goods. and the formation of societies based on class division. Durkheim's functionalist sociology, in turn, realized that the expansion of markets implied the formation of a new sociability, characterized by organic solidarity. Perhaps the compressive sociology proposed by Weber (2000) and Simmel (1978) took the effects of markets to a deeper level when the authors claim that they would be the vector for the implementation of a new rationality or a culture, which advocated the use of money as a *par excellence* mechanism for social interac-tion (Raud 2005, 2007).

Later, Karl Polanyi retakes the discussion on the autonomy of markets in rela-tion to other social structures and suggests that 'instead of the economy being rooted (embedded) in social relations, it is social relations that are embedded in the economic system' (Polanyi 1957/1980:77). Polanyi also warned that whenever markets reached the point of imposing their logic as a *deus ex machina*, society was at great risk of disintegrating, as occurred in the periods immediately before the two great world wars. For this reason, for Polanyi, cap-italist societies learned that it is necessary to have mechanisms to regulate and control the 'satanic mill' of the self-regulated market in such a way as to create space for the coexistence of different and diverse forms of social interaction. It is not surprising that the agenda of economic sociology has for a long time been focused on analysing the markets and the interfaces between society and the economy as suggested by Polanyi.

In rural sociology, the analysis of the insertion of farmers in markets has also been the subject of several studies, and the limited understanding of their *modus operandi* has also been almost generalized. Just to remember, it is worth noting that Lenin's pioneering work highlighted the erosive character of mercantilization for peasants, which would lead them to a process of social decomposition and differentiation (Bernstein 1986). Chayanov, for his part, showed that the peasants held relations with the markets for the sale of their surpluses, which allowed them to ensure their economic reproduction with relative autonomy. Later, in the second half of the 20th century, Henry Mendras (1978) and Teodor Shanin (1973, 1988) indicated that peasants' relations with markets were an important factor in changing their own social condition. For Mendras, commodification is actually a step forward to the 'end of the peasants' as local collectives; whereas for Shanin, markets promoted the subordination of peasants and asserted their 'oppression by external forces'.

Bernstein's (1979, 1986) analysis of small-holder production (petty/simple commodity production, as he defines it) performs in a context of the expansion of capitalist forms of production, and Friedmann's (1978) studies on family farmers and their insertion in global commodity markets, as well as the characterization of van der Ploeg (1992) on the different degrees and levels of insertion in the markets, represented a return to the theme of relations between farmers and markets. Van der Ploeg's studies (2008) are particularly important because he demonstrates that the process of commercialization in agriculture does not necessarily have a negative and deleterious meaning. On the contrary, van der Ploeg showed that commercialization can be beneficial for the social reproduction of small farmers in the extent it allows for an increase in the degree of autonomy and room for manoeuvre in the negotiations and construction of their own markets and strategies of marketing (van der Ploeg 2008; Long et al. 1986).

However, the markets as such have not been analysed in great detail in the contributions of these authors. In general, it is possible to state that rural scholars left the discussion of markets to the economists, who did not go into the subject as much, with the exception of the important contribution of Frank Ellis who affirms that

> the markets present both opportunities and pressures to peasants. Joining them can increase the level of well-being or diversify access to consumer goods, but at the same time it exposes them to the problems of price adversities or the unequal conditions of market power. This makes the relationship with the markets a continuous tension between the risks of the advantages in their participation or the maintenance of a non-market basis for survival. (Ellis 1988:6)

As can be seen, despite its importance, the study of commodification or, more precisely, of the social process of insertion of farmers in markets, still has several gaps. Much of the research has been carried out to understand issues that affect the analysis of the markets themselves, such as supply strategies, consumer preferences, price formation and competitiveness, among others. In summary, economic exchanges between production and consumption agents, mediated by relative prices, have been studied, but the peculiar nature of how markets are structured and function, largely based on relations of reciprocity and/or inter-knowledge, as well as power relations and the mechanisms of domination, still need further understanding. Therefore, there is a sociological issue that needs to be better explored by contemporary rural and agri-food studies.

## 3.    Socially constructed markets

In recent years, the literature on markets in the social sciences has converged on the assumption that every economic action of exchange is embedded in social and cultural mechanisms that give sense and meaning to the ways and shapes in which actors interact to transact their assets (Hebink et al. 2015a). Increasingly, the weight of social relations and cultural origins is recognized as guiding economic action and, therefore, their influence on the structuring of markets (Wilkinson 2019).

It is around this convergence that the central framework of the current debate on the understanding of markets as social constructions within the scope of economic sociology is established. This translates into the assertion that markets emerge from social interactions between the actors and the collective arrangements for managing and maintaining economic transactions and mercantile exchanges. Nevertheless, even if it is correct to say that all markets are embedded in social relations – such as rules, norms and conventions mobilized and shared collectively – it cannot be said that all markets are socially constructed (Niederle et al. 2014).

There is an important difference that needs to be clarified. Although the functioning of any and all markets is only possible insofar as the actors and agents share a set of rules, norms, values and social conventions, it must be emphasized that not all markets are socially constructed. There are several types of markets, such as food, clothing, financial credit and others that are characterized by supply and demand mediated by relative prices or other devices, such as formal contracts. These are, therefore, conventional or mainstream markets, here understood as those that represent the usual, ordinary, linear, dominant and hegemonic approach. These markets are not the result of social structures shared collectively and built through interactions in specific institutional contexts. They work and operate according to rules, norms and formal conventions that are ordered and coordinated mostly by the price mechanism (Bagnasco and Triglia 1993).

Socially constructed markets, on the contrary, are the direct and concrete result of social interaction between agents, with no prior convention, rule or norm that defines the path or ritual to be followed by those who participate in the process of their construction (van der Ploeg et al. 2015). Social construction is a dynamic process, moving in a spiral direction, sometimes retroacting before moving forwards, generating contradictions, demanding agreements, negotiations and consensus can be revised and reassessed. A social construction reflects, therefore, the way of being of humans when they interact with each other and seek to create meaning for their action. Socially constructed markets are, therefore, instances, spaces and moments in which social interaction occurs between individuals who seek to exchange goods, products and services in order to meet different interests.

Nevertheless, it is still under discussion whether socially constructed markets would be alternatives to conventional markets, in the sense of representing a different way of making and/or carrying out social interactions that aim at exchanges or exchanges, or would coexist, admitting in this case the coexistence of hybrid forms of markets. The most orthodox analysts, whether liberal or Marxist, simply prefer to characterize conventional markets as synonymous with capitalist markets and, ultimately, claim that markets are the essence of the capitalist mode of production (Bernstein and Oya 2014; Beckert 2007). The heterodox, on the other hand, maintain that the markets were not created by capitalism and are not even close to it, since exchanges and economic interactions are present in several other social formations in human history (Swedberg 1994, 2005; Polanyi 1977).

## 4.    Agri-food markets

The current situation of food production and consumption has been increasingly called into question (Niederle and Wez Jr. 2020; Oosterveer and Sonnenfeld 2012; Carolan 2012). On the one hand, the modern agri-food system – which is vertically integrated and controlled by large private corporations – has the merit of increasing food production and productivity (supply), and consequently decreasing their prices. On the other hand, such success was accompanied by a number of negative externalities, either social (inequality and exclusion of small farmers, food insecurity), or economic (increase of squeeze on farming) or environmental (climate change and deforestation).

A key issue within these debates refers to the role and place of agri-food markets. A wide range of interpretations are in place, ranging from the most resigned and tolerant stances on the so-called 'market failures' to harsher criticism about the power of concentration and the exclusion that the corporate and globalized food systems have been imposing. In response to these more structuralist perspectives, some contrasting views have emerged that seek to enhance the role of the agents in processes of markets' construction (Schneider 2016). In this perspective, the markets are seen as strategic spaces in which new services and products can emerge and practices that are distinct from those found in the conventional system can consolidate, thus becoming concrete expressions of new rural development processes.

Food markets are understood as places or spaces in which agents interact briefly for exchanging goods, products and services (Schneider 2016; van der Ploeg 2015). In such spaces, a set of values is mobilized as a mediator of the social interactions between actors. These are the values that will define and build the notions and conventions of quality, locality, origin and relationship with nature, all of which are central dimensions to distinguish foods that are exchanged in these spaces.

Existing literature on the new food markets and the emergence of alternative food networks is not negligible, especially in countries of Northern Europe and in the United States. This perspective focuses on the processes of localization of production (Hinrichs 2003; Eriksen 2013), and on the reconnection between producers and consumers (Kneafsey et al. 2008). The notion of an Alternative Food Network (AFN) has become widely used in the discussions on emerging networks involving producers, consumers and other actors, which constitute new and different forms of agri-food production, processing and distribution (Renting et al. 2003). According to AFN's exponents, these food networks may represent alternatives to the conventional production system, because they reflect both a 'quality turn' and a process of (re)localization of the agri-food system (Goodman 2003).

According to Blay-Palmer et al. (2018), there are at least six dominant conceptual (and empirical) approaches to the development and analysis of sustainable agro-food markets and systems: bio-region and food storage (Kremer and Schreuder 2012; Getz 1991), alternative agri-food networks (Goodman et al. 2012), short food supply chains, urban–rural connections (Guthman 2014), sustainable food systems (Feenstra 1997), territorial development (Lamine et al. 2012b) and the city-region agri-food system (Jennings et al. 2015). We could also include the nested markets approach as another example of contemporary analysis of food markets, which we will discuss in detail in the next section.

The two approaches that most propose to theorize about markets and the ways in which food chain actors trade and interact economically are alternative agri-food networks and short food supply chains.

In rural sociology, theoretical approaches such as short supply chains (Lamine 2005, 2008, 2015; Darolt et al. 2013), and alternative food networks (Goodman et al. 2012; Renting et al. 2003) are mobilized to discuss practices that go in the opposite direction of the globalization of agri-food markets based on the food commodities production. These are approaches that seek to analyse the insertion and performance of farmers in local markets and products of differentiated quality. This discussion addresses geographical and territorial aspects related to the physical distance between food production and consumption and sociological issues related to the proximity between the actors (Lamine et al. 2012a). In short, these approaches point to the valorization of the place of the production and commercialization practices, the social roots of commercial exchanges and the social construction of the concept of quality based on trust established between producers and consumers as well as the provenance and identity of the products.

There is increasing consensus that the development of better and more diversified marketing channels is crucial for small-scale farmers to improve their access to markets, and more broadly to enhance their role in rural development (van der Ploeg et al. 2010, 2012; van der Ploeg 2016). Conventional markets tend to shrink the options to sell merchandises and buy input stuffs, creating a kind of squeeze in which competition and access to information and better prices are restricted. In order to overcome such restrictions there has been a growing effort to look to improve the markets in which small-holders are participating, rather to support the isolation of the markets as in the past.[1]

## 5.    Nested markets

The nested market is part of an emerging and comprehensive array of approaches that try to tackle the matter of small-holder farmers connections and participation in markets. These findings regarding the significant role of the modes of food marketing and distribution, and their consequent social relations involving commercial exchanges, have urged scholars to propose a new theoretical and analytical framework.

Considering markets as central elements for promoting social inclusion of small farmers and as expressions of rural development, such a perspective has been called nested markets (van der Ploeg et al. 2010).[2] Nested markets originate from what van der Ploeg calls *structural gaps* (van der Ploeg 2015:17). These gaps result from the strategies put in place by the global food markets, based on their logic of action. The physical and relational distance between production and consumption is so significant that food loses its freshness, origin and dynamism, becoming homogeneous. The nested markets then originate from these gaps, based mainly on the geographical and relational approximation between producers and consumers. This relocation movement allows us to re-establish not only the qualities of the products, in terms of freshness and healthiness, but above all they are based on a different governance logic from that which permeates the market of standard commodities.

Generally, nested markets are deemed as spaces of social interaction within which transaction standards and flows are established, and products and services are structured within time and space dimensions. These standards are a direct result of market failures and of the transformations stemming from the rise of global production and consumption processes. According to van der Ploeg (2016), many traditional food markets are affected and transformed by processes of globalization and by the flows and patterns of interaction they impose. This implies a disruption of the local networks and social ties, as well as of the cultural and material frameworks that sustain these markets. Thus, certain modes of production and kinds of products end up being changed, thereby creating 'holes' in which such social relationships cannot be created and/or materialized (for example, in the geographical reference to a product, as in the case of lamb meat analysed by van der Ploeg (2015)).

Nested markets are a feature of contemporary capitalism. As the social division of labour expands, as economic interactions intensify, deepen and become more complex and diverse, in this extend vacant spaces or interstices emerge, characterized by exchanges between actors and agents that do not submit to the rules, norms and conventions of the capitalist way of being of markets (van der Ploeg et al. 2012). The nested markets exist within capitalism, interact with its institutions, legal framework, its material and ideological structure, but are not limited to it and they are not even entirely dominated by it. They coexist with and reproduce themselves in relation to conventional markets and, therefore, they are compelled to adapt (Sonnino and Marsden 2005). Although they often succeed in enduring and flourishing, sometimes they are dominated, constrained and may even disappear.

The analysis of nested markets is based on a heterodox understanding of markets that aims to approach the different ways in which social actors around the world have organized themselves to build new spaces for commercialization and food consumption (Schneider et al. 2016). Highlighting that these processes are neither linear nor standardized, this perspective innovates when analysing local agri-food markets in a way that relates to global/conventional markets, emphasizing the processes of social construction of markets through the analysis of governance standards (norms and rules) and the distinct characteristics that reproduce them.

In this sense, it is critical for the nested markets approach to inquire in what ways 'alternative' rules, norms and social conventions are constructed, negotiated, reproduced and legitimized for the structuring of a set of food marketing spaces that distinguish their practices and their food from those found in conventional/industrial markets and spaces for production and consumption.

Despite its theoretical origin related to an institutionalist perspective of K. Polanyi's economy – giving preference to the analysis of the emergence of the social rules and norms that build markets – the nested markets approach demands a heterodox understanding of sustainable food systems and their markets, using networks and culture precisely to explain the emergence of such rules (Burawoy 2010).

In general, nested markets are seen as food marketing mechanisms built on social rules and norms shared and appropriated collectively by local actors. Following the perspective pointed out by Ostrom (2010), the analysis of nested markets focuses on the different governance patterns constructed and reproduced by farmers and consumers in the development of sustainable practices and processes of food production, commercialization and consumption (Polman et al. 2010; Hebinck et al. 2015a; van der Ploeg 2016).

For a definition, a nested market might be described as:

> […] a segment of a wider market. It is a specific segment that typically displays different price levels, distributional patterns of the total value added and relations between producers, distributors and consumers than those seen in the wider market. This segment is nested in a wider market. It is part of this market, but at the same time it differs from it. (van der Ploeg 2016:23)

Furthermore, they are markets defined by particular boundaries that are quite permeable, so as to allow flexibility and innovation.

In this context, new markets are created, emerging from the mobilization of a set of norms, rules and social conventions that seek to reshape the flow of goods and rearrange the patterns and the nature of transactions (van der Ploeg 2016). That is, to the extent that global markets advance and impose certain standards and rules (production, quality and marketing standards; sanitary and packaging norms, etc.), they affect and transform local food markets and networks, imposing on these spaces the development of new socio-material structures, and producing new and distinct patterns of transaction and interaction.

When compared to conventional markets, nested markets will exhibit one or more of these features (Brasil 2019): (1) a clear final price differential for the product, (2) a different distribution of value added, resulting in a higher price for farmers (or in this case foragers), (3) a different infrastructure (or socio-material infrastructure), (4) a different location of transactions in time and space, and/or (5) a different governance pattern (van der Ploeg et al. 2012; Grivins and Tisenkopfs 2018). The properties of nested markets emerge from the fact that these markets are not anonymous – nested markets could rather be described as embedded in a set of goals and values out of which these markets emerge. The actors operating in nested markets are known and set the shape of processes in the market. In contrast, anonymous free trade, manifesting itself through lack of ownership is expected to regulate the relations between actors in global markets.

Nested markets are socially constructed markets that are organized around social interactions between concrete actors, who occupy concrete spaces. These markets do not comply with, nor follow the straightforward and strict conventions of capitalist markets (Hebinck et al. 2015b). In this sense, they constitute new organizational and economic mechanisms based on innovative standards and models of trade, which aim to develop alternative ways for food marketing.[3] In turn, these alternative ways and practices are based upon three main dimensions: the notion of quality attributed to food, the definition of local, and their relationship with nature.

The nested markets framework enables understanding the emergence of new food markets in respect of the development and operation of conventional (wider) markets. In a way, the very failures arising from the conventional markets (the social and economic harm produced, health problems, inequality for small farmers, environmental impacts) make room for the construction of new practices, processes, services and products that differ from those found in hegemonic or conventional markets. Although they develop relationally to the conventional markets, the nested markets do not comprise niches within these broader markets. Unlike niche markets, the nested markets are open to products and actors, which can enter and leave these market spaces according to the relationships that they are able to maintain within them. In other words, while niche markets are closed to certain products and certain product standards and rules, nested markets are open and flexible market spaces that allow the emergence of new relationships (Polman et al. 2010). According to the nested markets perspective, alternatives to the mainstream agri-food model emerge from interactions between the established local/cultural practices and processes (based on relocalization and reconnection) and the conventional mechanisms of governance.

Nested markets arise from these interactions, although differing in relation to wider markets, inasmuch as their operation rests on elements like 'distinctiveness', 'socio-material infrastructures' and 'common-pool resources'. Distinctiveness is deemed as a primary characteristic of nested markets, and can be built on different dimensions. These dimensions are: *price*, since the product may differ for being either cheaper or more expensive; product *quality*, which will be socially defined; *production mode*, since different production processes can create different products; *social organization of time and space*, allowing the distinction of both fresh produce and those of local origin; and *availability*, because the scarcer the product, the greater will be its distinctiveness (van der Ploeg 2016).

As stated by Grivins and Tisenkopfs (2018), nested markets can be a part of a global market that through unique operational principles manage to enable local level actors. *Nestedness* signifies an attempt to incorporate into the market some regulatory, distinctive, supportive aspect that can only be replicated in certain conditions – either by following certain production practices or by being in a specific region, for example. The embeddedness of nested markets has also been explained as mutual agreements between the actors involved when it comes to product properties (Schneider et al. 2015).

In general, what sets the borders that protect and separate nested markets is an interpretation of uniqueness manifested through historical practices, tacit knowledge, specific tastes or maybe already institutionalized social structures, such as trademarks, schemes of geographical indications, or historical specialities (Grivins and Tisenkopfs 2018). This demarcation of uniqueness can be seen as a common pool resource (publicly available to everybody, yet owned by no one) that sets the specific market apart from surrounding common market structures (Schneider et al. 2015; van der Ploeg et al. 2012).

Moreover, it is through the transactions and exchanges that *distinction* plays its key role. According to van der Ploeg (2016), distinction is a feature developed and consolidated throughout the production chain. By being produced in a different manner, food reaches specific consumers who are able to appreciate and recognize this characteristic, and eventually incorporate such distinction.

At the same time, processors and suppliers also incorporate the distinction, which ends up generating symbolic – and positive – relationships between all the actors involved. Such relationships reflect on the quality/distinctiveness of the products and the establishment of social interaction networks.

These relationship networks – and exchange processes – are embedded in a set of values, norms and social conventions. Van der Ploeg (2016) highlights three levels of exchange in which distinction plays a central role. The first one refers to social construction of quality, which results from interactions between agents participating in the supply chains, ascribing reputation to both products and producers, and generating trust. The second level comprises the material exchange itself and the distinguishing aspects: differentiated products for money and vice versa.

The second structuring element of nested markets is the development of socio-material infrastructure. As the products circulating in these markets are distinct from those found in mainstream markets, it is necessary to develop a specific and different set of rules, regulations and conventions, for certifying this distinctiveness. It is these socio-material structures (rules and regulations) that allow the goods to flow and be recognized as distinct from those found in conventional markets, thus enabling the creation of novelties and innovation (new products and services).

The third and final feature of nested markets refers to common-pool resources, which play a key role in this dynamics. As much the distinctiveness as the novelties and socio-material infrastructures are all built and function as a non-material common-pool resource, since they connect different stake-holders and enable collective actions aimed at generating mutual benefits (Hebinck et al. 2015b:13).

In nested markets, common-pool resources are resources, because they allow producers to obtain additional benefits such as good prices and access to particular groups of consumers (see Chapter 6). These benefits could not be obtained otherwise than collectively. This is why they are considered 'common', for they cannot be appropriated individually. Conversely, they are collective resources more or less accessible to the actors, but able to generate and sustain benefits to all (van der Ploeg et al. 2010).

Therefore, the creation and maintenance of these new markets are only possi-ble insofar as a set of socially shared rules and norms becomes institutionalized at the local level and is (re)created on a daily basis by actors and organizations. It is by means of these norms that products and services acquire distinctiveness and that a socio-material structure different from those of mainstream markets can be built. That is, common-pool resources are both a result of the creation of new markets and the elements that originate them.

In this sense, the definition of such structuring features of nested markets enables to relate such perspective to the general debate surrounding the alternative agri-food networks, which has pervaded sociological food studies. The nested markets framework gets closer to that of alternative food networks, insofar as both propose a relational analysis of the practices and processes that have been emerging in the contemporary rural environment. Although drawing on different theoretical references (nested markets follows institutionalist and actor-oriented approaches, Long (2001)), both perspectives focus their analyses on local markets and on curtailment of distances between producers and consumers, especially regarding trust relationships, processes for building product quality and distinctiveness, and sustainable consumption practices. Furthermore, they share the idea that local markets emerge from their interaction with the global/conventional market.

Two assertions or inferences arise. The first is the recognition of the hybrid and multiple nature of the markets, either food markets or others. In the perspective of alternative food networks, food markets are deemed as hybrid spaces whose mechanisms of governance are defined by both the conventional standards, norms and values (competitiveness, efficiency, power) and the alternative relationships and conventions (reciprocity, friendship, reputation; interknowledge) (Goodman 2002). As to the perspective of nested markets, it comprises a multitude of markets (and modes of trade and commercial exchange) that coexist – whether they be conventional or alternative – entailing a diversity of practices and social interactions that create specific mechanisms of marketing and distribution.

The second assertion arising from these perspectives relates to the fact that, despite emerging from their relations with conventional markets, alternative markets differ from the latter by allowing the development of more just and sustainable social and economic relations. In other words, the major difference – and contribution – of nested markets and alternative food networks perspectives lies in the notion that the alternativity of local food markets results from their ability to strengthen local mechanisms and forms of governance that are founded on non-conventional values and social codes (friendship, trust, reputation, reciprocity, otherness).

However, the nested markets framework goes beyond that of alternative food networks, because it places the construction of (local) markets on the direct relation that these maintain with the conventional markets. In this sense, the nested markets' framework helps to answer to the issue pointed out by Sonnino and Marsden (2005), that between conventional markets and alternative food networks there are interfaces and a confluence zone, and not necessarily an opposition. The transformative potential of nested markets lies in their ability to show how the contradictory general development processes, based on the consolidation of conventional markets, are themselves generating responses and alternative processes of development, exemplified in the emergence of a diversity of food supply and consumption practices.

## 6.  The contribution of nested markets to rural development

The construction of these nested markets is also considered as part of a broader strategy for spatially rethinking and redefining rural development as regards to the understanding of the relationships and interactions established by small farmers, who seek more accessible, sustainable and fair ways of marketing their products (Scoones 2009). According to van der Ploeg et al. (2012), nested markets emerge from processes of agricultural reterritorialization and from new forms of distribution, which aim to reconnect not only the actors (producers and consumers), but also the links between rural and urban.

The conventional agri-food system continues to promote processes of subordination via entry into long agri-food supply chains, in which producers are integrated as mere providers of cheap primary raw materials (Sabourin 2014; Gazolla and Schneider 2017). However, everywhere, increasing cases and experiences have been emerging, which are clearly grounded on another model of market interaction and exchanges, based on social and cultural values, and which are mobilized by the farmers themselves able to build alternative (and more autonomous) practices and processes of commercialization. These processes teach important lessons for (re)thinking the rural development itself, which is no longer related to just the improvement of physical infrastructure or creation of social assistance programmes, as it was in the 1970s, when it consisted basically of a programme aimed at those who did not afford technological modernization. Rural development now means, more and more, to build markets that value differentiated products and services, in order to, on the one hand, restrain the subordination by the dominant model, and, on the other hand, confer more autonomy and room for manoeuvre to farmers.

When van der Ploeg et al. (2010) developed the analytical framework of nested markets (see Table 8.1), they emphasized Bernstein's (2010) recommendation on the need to always question who is in control or command of the markets; that is, who are their owners and what power relations are in place. The key questions in this regard are: who builds the markets; what is the capacity of agency of the actors involved in this process; who gains and what is gained with the construction of these nested markets; what are the asymmetries created; and, finally, what is the destination of the generated surplus, who appropriates it? Based on this framework presented in Table 8.1, in a subsequent work, Schneider et al. (2015) explore other key issues highlighting the relevance of nested markets for the practices, processes and policies of contemporary rural development.

**Table 8.1**   Framework of analysis: a comparison of the general agricultural and food markets and the newly emerging markets

|  | General agricultural and food markets | Newly emerging markets |
| --- | --- | --- |
| Who owns what? | Most linkages between production, processing, distribution and the consumption of food are controlled by food empires. | Short circuits that interlink the consumption of food. These short circuits are owned or co-owned by farmers (and sometimes) consumers. |
| Who does what? | The role of farmers is limited to the delivery of raw materials for the food industry. | The role of farmers is extended to embrace on-farm processing, direct selling and the redesign of production processes that better meet consumer expectations. |
| Who gets what? | The distribution of value added is highly skewed: most wealth is accumulated in food empires. | Farmers get a higher share of the total value added. |
| What is done with the surpluses? | Accumulated wealth is used to finance the ongoing imperial conquest (take-over of other enterprises) | Extra income is used to increase the resilience of food production, to strengthen multi-functional farming and to improve livelihoods. |

*Source:* van der Ploeg et al. (2010).

The new nested markets also exist elsewhere and are generally supported by short circuits coordinated by farmers and, in some cases, customers (as in the case of the Solidarity Purchase Groups – GAS throughout Italy and the Agroecological Integration Group in Porto Alegre, Brazil). The connection between production, processing, distribution and consumption of food is a central aspect that distinguishes nested markets from conventional agri-food markets, whose socio-material infrastructure is controlled by large corporations. According to Schneider et al. (2015) this aspect remarkably distinguishes them, once, in nested markets, the socio-material infrastructure that enables processes to flow constitutes a common-pool resource, and, thus, it belongs to the producers and consumers who participate in these markets. Therefore, it is important to note that the nested markets remain under the ownership and control of the different agents involved in its constitution, from farmers to consumers. The increased autonomy and decision capacity retained by these actors, enable them to appropriate the generated economic surpluses and thus contribute to rural development practices and processes in general.

Another important contribution that nested markets bring to rural development lies in the role played by actors. In conventional markets, actors involved in the supply side play an accessory and complementary role by simply delivering raw materials to the industry according to the standards imposed by large processors and retailers. In nested markets, in turn, it is substantially different, as family farmers, in addition to agriculture activity per se, also participate in processing (on property), commercialization, restructuring and evaluation, and in the redesign of production processes that better meet consumer expectations.

In this sense, these actors are not socially restricted to the production process, but are continually in contact with consumers through direct sales. This social network allows both consumers and producers to exchange information, get feedback and voice their expectations. These can be important elements in the development of new products and services, such as the pecan nuts mentioned in this work in the case of the nested market of rural tourism (van der Ploeg and Ye 2016:46). Moreover, these 'new' roles played by farmers involved in nested markets are quite attractive to younger populations, what can help in reducing rural–urban migration (Schneider et al. 2015).

Another noteworthy contribution relates to the distribution of value added. Schneider et al. (2015) argue that in major agri-food markets this distribution is quite biased, so that much of the accumulated wealth remains in the hands of food empires, because the farmers operate only in the delivery of their products to intermediaries, their activities being restricted to just one 'link' of the food chain. In turn, in the nested markets, producers act at various stages of the agri-food chain (production, processing, sale), what results in a higher share of the value added appropriated by them. That is, the revenues stay largely in the hands of farmers themselves.

Finally, there remains the issue of the use and appropriation of the surplus produced at the rural space. In the case of conventional agriculture, the accumulated wealth is used to finance the maintenance of its domination, by taking control of other companies, expanding their operating areas and forms of governance, and incorporating markets, products and services. As to the case of nested markets, surpluses are used to strengthen the resilience of agriculture, processing and products marketing (such as the development of new products) and to improve the livelihoods of involved actors (Schneider et al. 2015).

These four issues, comprised in the framework developed by van der Ploeg et al. (2010), make it clear that the main contribution of nested markets to rural development practices, processes and policies is the fact that their control is much more in the hands of farmers than in those of the large agri-food chains. These nested markets are part of and are continually connected with the wider conventional markets. However, they have very different forms of governance, in the sense that the autonomy of farmers regarding food production, processing and commercialization strengthens their capacity of resilience, generates common-pool resources and, accordingly, enhances the possibilities for social and economic reproduction in the rural space.

Van der Ploeg (2016) points out that the major issue arising in connection to nested and conventional markets refers to the imposition of the global regulations that comprise the modes of governance of conventional markets on the alternative ones. So, the latter are subject to an extensive set of rules involving production, circulation and food consumption, which are often incompatible with local realities. This is the case with the requirements found in the food safety systems and the food sanitary standards in Brazil and worldwide, which ultimately generate exclusions, power relations, competition and inequalities in the agri-food system (Hebinck et al. 2015b; Radomsky et al. 2015). In this sense, we believe that there lies the great relevance and potential of nested markets for rural development practices; since they provide farmers with greater autonomy, security, decision-making capacity and distribution of income, freeing them from submission to the rules of global food markets.

Finally, and aware of the criticism directed to this perspective, such as the issue of scale (Boen and Purcell 2006) – increasingly demanded in today's agriculture – and the conventionalization processes (Tregear 2011; Guthman 2014), there are two major contributions resulting from the adoption of nested markets perspective. The first relates to the fact that such a perspective avoids falling into a defensive localism (Goodman et al. 2012) and attributing an exaggerated role to local markets in resolving current problems of food supply, especially in view of the growing process of urbanization.

With regard to this aspect, Goodman et al. (2012) warn about the risk of considering 'the local' as a space where ethical standards and values can flourish, as the source of the alternative and sustainable practices and, therefore, where the 'good' agri-food networks build up. The authors try to deconstruct the idea of a pure localism, exempt from conflict, by proposing the notion of reflexive localism. They argue that this ideal of perfection associated with localism can deny the politics of the locality, with potentially problematic consequences for social justice. Moreover, this can lead to solutions based on doubtful standards of purity and perfection, leaving these markets vulnerable to co-option by the corporate agri-food system, and carrying out 'elitist, undemocratic politics of perfection marked by problematic conceptions of social justice and civic tolerance' (Goodman et al. 2012:13). Therefore, it is necessary to understand that the 'local', per se, may imply both inclusion and exclusion of people, places and particular ways of life. Similarly, it is necessary to be aware of who sets these limits and standards and how they are defined, what can be deemed as both a challenge and a limitation of this concept.

However, there is no point in delegitimizing the concept of localism, but rather to promote a better understanding about the complexity and the traps of local politics, as well as about the long-term effects of movements controlled by particular groups of people. Thus, instead of focusing the analysis on food localization processes, the nested markets perspective expands the understanding of food markets towards a broader view, by means of the notion that nested markets are part of (operating together or even within) conventional agricultural markets.

A second important contribution of the nested markets framework lies in the fact that it does not take the stance or speech of food sovereignty and the need to build an autonomous global food model – as it has been advocated by some social movements, such as Via Campesina – capable of developing a new world food order, socially just and able to reconnect nature and society, person and food (Bernstein 2014; McMichael 2014).

Differently, the nested markets framework proposes a heterodox view of markets and development processes, arguing that nested (and local) markets coexist with other markets (conventional) and struggle with these for space and legitimacy. This is a clear reference to the idea of coexistence of various forms of commercial interaction as pointed out by Karl Polanyi (Schneider 2016). Thus, it is admitted that different markets and mechanisms for exchange and trade coexist simultaneously and that nested markets constitute concrete spaces of interaction between specific actors, which are constructed and reproduced within the conventional markets, that is, within the capitalist mode of production.

Therefore, the main question to be examined in future works is related to the reasons why these markets, which are based on often informal inter-personal relationships, continue to exist (and in some contexts to expand). In view of both the growing power of influence by large supermarkets and retail chains and the requirements for increasingly formalized processes of trade and exchange (Reardon and Timmer 2007) it remains open to inquire why the markets based on interpersonal relationships (still) endure; on what governance mechanisms and values, norms and social rules they are based for continuing to exist and grow stronger. Accordingly, it opens up a research agenda, and perhaps the nested markets framework can be considered a new stage within rural studies, especially in those focused on the analysis of markets and of the mechanisms for exchange and commercial interaction.

## 7.     Challenges towards a sociology of food markets

In this chapter we seek to connect the debates on sustainable agri-food markets with the prominent approaches of the new economic sociology. This attempt implies some considerations that deserve some highlights.

The first one refers to the need for rural studies to incorporate the analysis of the markets themselves. As we have argued, most studies on agri-food markets have focused on their apparent forms, through the analysis of exchanges and social interactions (networks) between producers and consumers that are established within these spaces. However, it is necessary to go further, to take a step forward towards a sociology of markets in rural and agri-food contexts, by questioning how these spaces emerge and develop and, above all, to interrogate which actors and organizations control them and how goes the social differentiation that the markets shape and produce. This step forward will allow us to move forward in the analysis of the social commodification of agriculture and the contemporary rurality more broadly.

The second point is related to the studies of economic sociology itself and the challenges posed to these approaches. As Wilkinson (2019) points out, sociological studies of economics have been facing some significant problems. Above all, a difficulty is identified in incorporating the recent transformations in the capitalist dynamics (and their markets), represented by the increasing digitization and fragmentation ('uberization') of the social relations of work and production. These transformations have impacted the forms of work and the use of money (financialization and commodification/marketization), which are central concepts for the new economic sociology that need to be more problematized (Wilkinson 2019). In this sense, it is necessary that rural studies make an effort to better theorize and analyse markets, as we suggest in this chapter. This means that it is necessary to develop new methodologies for market analysis, such as the construction of typologies that differentiate how these spaces are constructed and signified in different regions.

Finally, there remains an open question in the studies on agri-food markets regarding the development of indicators and variables. As highlighted by Sonnino and Marsden (2005), studies on agri-food markets and food systems lack the construction of more robust and cohesive methodologies that are connected to the various empirical analyses that have been made. In addition, the development of indicators to analyse the markets will allow the construction of public food procurement policies more and more based on sustainable production and consumption practices, which might be replicated as the methodological issues will further develop. This is a research agenda that opens up both for future analysis as well as scholars training.

The central point is to recognize that markets, as social constructions, do not obey a general/universal pattern or model, as indicated by classic sociology authors. As social constructions, they are the result of interactions, values, conventions and norms shared by the actors which build them. Thus, markets have different governance characteristics and patterns that change according to the historical, cultural, political and social contexts in which they emerge. They are thus a critical dimension and dynamic of rural development, despite their heretofore 'Cinderella' status. This calls into question some assumptions and views that directly associate markets with the capitalist system. As this chapter has shown, it is time to demystify that. In fact, to sociologically understand markets there is a need to go far beyond capitalism, both because they existed prior to this social system of ordering, and because even under current (more diverse) capitalism they are not restricted to its *modus operandi*. The wider rural development dynamics explored in this book all have implications for a far wider re-conceptualization of markets.

# Notes

1. It is also important to point out that the debate about markets and family farming is gaining international recognition. A recent discussion about Connecting Smallholders to Markets in the CSF (Committee of Food Security, a body linked to FAO), is focusing on territorial markets, which has a lot of similarity with nested markets, and it is highlighting the importance of requiring policies for the construction or connection of markets to small-holders.
2. This section reproduces some of the ideas published in Schneider et al. (2016).
3. In the specialized literature on the subject, nested markets appear under different designations, according to the discipline dealing with the debate on the local and regional food systems, such as alternative agri-food networks (Goodman et al. 2012), short food supply chains (Kneafsey et al. 2013) and values based food supply chains (Lyson et al. 2008).

# Conclusions

In the introduction to this book, we raised eight transversal themes that were, to varying degrees, embedded and further explored in the eight research agenda-setting chapters. In this conclusion, we suggest eight concluding and emerging issues that are distilled from the framework we have pursued (see Figure 0.1) for the research agenda on global rural development.

## 1.  Privatization, financialization, globalization: processes of continued appropriation and risks of uneven development

The continuing domination and hegemony of corporate control, the processes of financialization and profit abstraction, and the rise of concentrated land rights, bio-sphere rights and enclosures, that we have described especially in Chapters 4, 5 and 8, are all socio-economic dynamics that give stimulus to an increasing number of studies, and should remain central to the research agenda.

Agriculture and food production is one of the key sectors in which the globalization process has advanced more profoundly in recent decades. There is a broad consensus among scholars that to understand problems of production, supply and consumption of food, there is a need for analytical frameworks that must be suitable to analyse the processes of globalization of agricultural trade, financialization, and food consumption, which shaped a kind of 'global junk food' diet. There are several thresholds and hindrances that might be highlighted, but the increasing loss of power of the national states – as well as from global transnational organizations such as the WTO, FAO and WFP – and the erosion of the governance capacity are surely of most concern. The consequences of these processes are dramatic and their effects are not yet adequately studied nor understood. As examples, we could mention the case of the food problems generated by Brexit in the UK as well as the global environ-mental problematic in the Brazilian Amazon. In both cases, it seems as if the national states have simply given up their exercise of control and surveillance role under the 'mask' of rising populist politics. Hence, it is worth asking: in the absence of state regulation, will private agents and other stakeholders be able to create some type of governance committed with something that might resemble real forms and processes of sustainability?

The globalization and financialization processes can be analysed as processes of continued appropriation of not only land rights and natural resources, but also of knowledge and science. They also signal a sort of comeback of the problem of uneven development which is today framed differently than it was in the 1970s with its critical focus on the 'imperialism' of the USA and more generally of the northern world. Today, the conjunction of the two processes of 'appropriation by dispossession' described by D. Harvey and of 'metabolic rift' analysed by J. Moore drives us to another scene of uneven development which translates, for example, in the forms of new extractivism driven by China and India or in the dramatic migration and demographic displacements. This requires a much less dichotomous, more nuanced and fine-grained approach to uneven development, both between (and within) the cities and the country-side (Chapter 1) and inter-regionally.

## 2.    Power for transformations: empowerment by association

Against these processes of 'accumulation by dispossession', concentration and enclosure, many social movements and experiences across the world stress the re-attribution of new common pool resources and sustainable place-making which should rely on processes of 'empowerment by association' (Chapters 1 and 5) that allow the sharing and preservations of 'common pool resources'; whether these are seeds, water, land, air and sunlight, or also knowledge and innovation.

Beyond and in relation to these struggles for democratization and participa-tion over natural resources, the ecological transition calls for new distributions of power, and new systems of governance. We have shown in the chapters (especially Chapters 3, 5 and 6) how new experimental associational and insti-tutional arrangements were emerging in the interstices of established systems of governance and governance practices; which should draw the attention of social scientists. The specificities of rural areas call for polycentric and distributed forms of governance instead of the concentric and concentrated modes that still often prevail; and rural sociologists and geographers have a key role to play in exploring the new forms of connected rural hubs that should be core arenas for the construction of innovative forms of contextualized and democratized public action.

On the other hand, contemporary rurality also faces changes and dilemmas in interpersonal relationships, especially those related to gender, ethnicity, sex and age. The issues of micropower and intersectional power relations appear as increasingly relevant with regard to the mobilization and political action. Demonstrations and protests in and arising from the rural 'space' of the 21st century are thus not just to claim more machines, access to land, credit or assets for production, but also encompass demands like those around the expansion of the emancipation of women in the management of agricultural enterprises and in the division of labour in the domestic space. Also the defence and promotion of certain types of agricultural and environmental practice becomes increasingly expressed and worthy are far more systematic research.

Regarding ethnic and identity issues, the changes are related to the new relations between natives and traditional inhabitants of the countryside with the continuous arrival of new dwellers. These can include: migrants who do temporary work on crop harvests, provide general services, like care and retail services, as well as actors like foreign investors, who simply are acquiring land, old houses (castles), vineyards and/or nature reserves in order to make this space a place for private use; and often isolating these places from the local communitarian life and the rural territory. The issue of sexuality also appears as a matter in the rural, either through a greater loosening of traditional values or even through the more dynamic interaction between rural and urban residents. The claim of new gender identities and the exposure of subjective options is expanding and the general profile of rural households is also changing. Finally, generational issues both related to the aging of the rural population, and the increase in some areas of the number of returning young people from the cities who start agricultural activities without ever being producers, is also a trend. Hence, at the individual and family level, power relations are increasingly diffuse, and for that reason new micro-political ways of action can be expected in the near future.

### 3.   A 21st-century rural renaissance: contrasted accounts

In parts of Western Europe and after decades of rural exodus and depopulation, the 1990s saw a kind of 'rural renaissance' (the title of a famous book published by B. Kayser in France in 1990), that was characterized by new demographic trends that actually benefited only some rural areas – and much more of course the peri-urban ones (see Chapter 3). Today, rural areas are confronted with even more difficulties due to the increasing abandonment by public services and infrastructures and the increasing costs of transport, exacerbated by the further concentration of these services. Moreover, rural areas are in fact highly diverse and their attractiveness is still very contrasting and uneven. We can observe, for instance, the emergence of new kinds of rural community leaders and communities of practices in some areas; but also the lack of such collective initiatives and social capital in many others, as well as, in the most attractive ones, processes of exclusion of some categories of the population in favour of those who can afford increasing property and estate prices. Against our own attraction as social scientists to focus upon 'successful' rural development pathways, this new divergent context, and this uneven attractiveness raises issues of territorial inequalities and justice that should be urgently tackled.

One of the aspects that will certainly deserve further studies and research relates to the influence of the internet and new information technologies in rural areas; especially with regard to a sort of new renaissance (to remind once more B. Kayser, now based on the mobility of communications instead of demography). Throughout the chapters of this book we explored several cases and examples in which the processes of social, economic and cultural interaction between the rural and the urban indicate renewed dynamics and characteristics. It is possible that the revival of rural social mobility could indeed reframe the scepticism generated by the 'deagrarianization' in Global North and South.

Scholars like Marc Mormont, Phillip Lowe and Fred Buttel had foresightfully already suggested that the decrease of the rural population occupied in agricultural activities would counter-intuitively not mean that the rural space would lose its importance or attractiveness for other purposes, especially tourism, renewables, traditional gastronomy, urban 'flight', and other non-agricultural activities. In the 21st century, it is possible that these new rural activities will be enhanced by the mobility and utility of new information technologies; and physical distances will no longer be hindrances. The rural renaissance depends not only on the development of tangible activities, but also on cultural, symbolic and, above all, landscape enhancement. This may be where new assets come from, which will then convert into comparative advantages and positive externalities to foster new rural development dynamics.

There is no doubt that contemporary rurality, as we knew it, studied it and defined it throughout the 20th century has changed profoundly in recent decades. On the one hand, there are processes that bring in increasing risks, such as the deagrarianization and extractivism promoted especially by the hegemonic food, energy and bio-economic system. But, on the other hand, there are certainly reasons for hope, ranging from the impressive potential of agroecological movements (Chapter 6), the new socially built markets, rural tourism, eco-living and de-growth movements among others, under which a new rurality that has been constructed and widely inserted in a different globalization in which high mobility accelerated by TICs behave like a Polanyian countermovement.

## 4.   Rural areas as sites for 're-coupling': the emergence of nexus-based eco-systems of rural relations

Among the optimistic accounts on rural development pathways are those that see rural areas as sites for the experimentation of more sustainable forms of production and circulation and thus of a 're-coupling' of humans and nature and of a reconnection of agriculture, food, environment and health (see Chapters 3 and 6). Whether this trend tends to counter the deagrarianization processes that have long been assessed across the world remains to be investigated and debated. The analysis of the diversity of these pathways and of the visions of re-coupling they embody, from self-sufficiency to inter-regionally chosen inter-dependencies within a gradient of visions of autonomy, is a key task for rural scientists, that should rely on internationally comparative research.

In this context, there is a key priority for rural development researchers to critically and normatively examine how concepts like the eco-economy and the circular economy may help to understand how new 're-coupled' economic relationships could indeed be fostered in rural spaces and places. Clearly we face a time when the world is searching for new forms of embedded social and economic practices – such as agroecology – which can progress more sustainable transitions (Chapter 6). We are only on the conceptual and empirical 'foothills' of fully and comparatively examining these new practice-based assemblages, taking a much more heterodox socio-ecological perspective. Indeed, one might postulate that in these new times of socio-ecological transformation – a time when established approaches to 'economic growth' are increasingly challenged or indeed completely rejected – it will be in the rural domain where creative and disruptive forms of innovative sustainable place-making can and are taking hold (see Special Issue of *Sustainability Science*, March 2020, as an example).

## 5. Urban–rural linkages: towards new emancipatory urban–rural relations

The notion of choosing rather than imposing inter-dependencies also applies to the spatial ecological dependencies and implied functionalities between cities and rural areas. The still dominating concentric visions which tend to define rural areas mainly as provisioning areas for cities in terms of workforce and food and other natural resources (a kind of domestication of the rural by the urban, see Chapters 1 and 2), should shift to more distributed, open-ended and symmetrical perspectives. These could rely on new emancipatory urban–rural relations which disrupt the earlier domestication–enclosure dialectic; and once again also postulate and design a shift towards a perspective of 'empowerment by association' (here of cities and mutually dependent rural areas). Food appears to be a potential key driver of this emancipatory reconnection between urban and rural; as is shown by many networks, experiences and studies across the world. Yet, the emancipatory and symmetrical nature of this re-definition of urban/rural linkages is still to be analysed. For instance, not only in the food sector but in the areas of energy, amenity, planetary and mental health, and more broadly relating to sustainable place-making, we can argue there are major experiments being unleashed which are based upon empowerment of creative urban–rural relations.

It is no longer surprising that in many rural regions there are new inhabitants and dwellers who were born in urban spaces and ended up choosing the countryside as a place to live and create new ventures for their livelihoods. For many of these newcomers to the countryside, the city and the urban are not strange or contradictory. On the contrary, the interactive flows between rural and urban are dynamic and constant, representing much more complementarity than antagonism or dichotomy. Thus, from a totally unexpected bias, it seems that the urban/rural linkages we are witnessing retake up the ideas of the classic founders of rural sociology, such as Pitrin Sorokin and above all Robert Redfield's notion of a rural–urban continuum.

## 6.     The need for a re-politicized rural social science

The contrasted trends mentioned above and the contested nature of the post-carbon transition raise the need for a re-politicized rural development sociology and social science, in three different meanings. First, we need to address the politicization processes of nature, food, and contested transitions as a core object. For example, in the current context of a New (globalized) Climate Regime (Chapter 2), climate-smart agriculture and agroecology (see Chapter 6) appear as two contrasted options (among a larger diversity): how do they give way to controversies, power reconfigurations, and alliances is a key object for rural social scientists. Second, we need to address rural politics, which in many countries is characterized by contradictory dynamics such as the rise of counter-nationalist and populist movements on the one hand, and the experimentation of new participatory forms of politics on the other, as well as the development of initiatives that allow for the integration of impoverished population and migrants. Finally, we need to re-politicize our conceptual frameworks (hence the suggestion of a new politicized political ecology raised in Chapter 5) and our ways of practicing research.

## 7.     Deep 'place-based' research to foster the 'great transformation'

Indeed, and this is a tribute to Philip Lowe's invitation to define rural sociology as an 'engaged' science, rural research practice is facing today a multi-faceted need of engagement. Engagement with place, with new epistemologies which are sensitized to place-based agency and endogenous and indigenous forms of rural development, and 'place-based' research allowing for including the ecological and the bio-physical into our analysis of transitions. Engagement with other disciplines in order to precisely include these dimensions and understand processes that favour ecological transitions (rather than 'only' assessing impacts) and thus contribute to the definition of pathways of rural development (see Chapter 6). Engagement with actors and in the needed transformations themselves. While transdisciplinarity literature is mainly anchored in sustainability sciences and partly dominated by engineering and management sciences, the challenge for social scientists is to bring in critical and pragmatist perspectives (i.e. taking into account power dynamics, actors' visions, controversies, analysing transformational ontologies), both within analytical and transformational postures. Social experimentation and rural communities of practices are here necessary to address situated problems through analysis and action together.

## 8.     Assessing and accompanying the converging hopes for rural futures

Despite the critical and necessary accounts of the processes and difficulties faced by rural actors and areas, there is of course a room for hope. This comes from the convergence and mixing of urban people and rural ones in their very social consciousness of the value of good and real food, of more sustainable diets, of the potentiality of rural areas for multi-functionality, as well as of preserved landscapes, restoring bio-diversity, and more equitably sharing the (shrinking) world's natures. In the urban world, the recognition of the role of rural areas is driven by the increasing support for local and low-carbon agriculture and food. In the rural world, interactions between young farmers – some of whom are originally urban people – and other rural actors open the way to new alliances where economic targets and non-monetary, socio-ecological and welfare objectives may be collectively targeted.

Indeed, the systemic and structural crises of the urban and cosmopolitan societies might look back (and forwards!) to the rural as a place for fertile and innovative solutions for the future. Energy, bio-diversity and amenities – which in other words we might say mean economy, nature and culture – are key aspects for sustainable humanity to resolve some of our most serious current troubles, which, as we have shown, interconnect with planetary health, climate change and (less acknowledged) the problems of high density, domesticated, con-urban living.

Not even during the time when the 'Spanish flu' haunted the western world has there been such a deep concern about how societies could redefine the relations among nature and humans. As we conclude this book a virulent and contagious pandemic (COVID19) raises new questions about high levels of urban density living, the increasing hyper-mobility of humans, plants and animals; and how fragile many of our cosmopolitan lives have become as they are increasingly dependent upon long, complex and environmentally damaging supply chains and markets.

But how do we become re-territorialized as well as globalized in the ways which encourage more widespread empowerment and association? We cannot simply re-construct old barriers and boundaries, or indeed 'turn the clock back' into forms of defensive localism or nationalism. We need to embrace and engage a global as well as local and practical 'politics and ethics of care'. The current moment is also showing that the industrial food system is not the answer for a sustainable, safe and healthy food system. A myriad set of actions and local initiatives arising everywhere are showing the great potential of territorialized food systems in terms of both capacity to feed people and inno- vativeness to deal with the tough moment. But this, as central as food is, is not just about food, it is about designing ways of caring and equitable living within and between the urban and the rural. In the past the modernist euphoria sur- rounding globalization seemed to be a success; now we are realizing it holds a poison for collective human well-being for existing and future generations. The ways we socially re-design our rural–urban interactions is a key to solving this anthropocentric dilemma.

So now we can say that not least we need to foster and cultivate a revised and critical rural development politics and sociology of hope for existing and future generations. This will, it seems need to be built upon re-drawing many of the assumptions about not taking either the social or natural world for granted.

The late Erik Olin Wright spent the second part of his career developing new sociological frameworks to outline 'real utopias' (see Buraway 2020); moving his own earlier work as well as much of established social science away from either a class-based Marxist and a more objectivist and positivist discipline towards a more engaged and emancipatory science of practical 'hope'. This took a lot of confidence on his part and that of his close colleagues. In *Envisaging Real Utopias* (Wright 2010) he proposed three parallel strategies of societal transformation: (i) ruptural transformation, (ii) interstitial trans- formations involving the development, not least as we see in the rural domain (see Chapter 3), of autonomous institutions developed within capitalism; and finally, (iii) symbiotic transformation, which returns us to the ways in which the state can be used to promote transformative struggles against itself in many cases. These ideas and developments have profound implications for rural social science today, and are of much relevance to the ways we have organized this book. Michael Buraway, in reviewing Wright's significant contributions and echoing a revisionist approach to Polanyi, comments (2020:93):

> Real Utopias cannot stop the expansion and deepening of the market, but they can provide the basis of a counter-movement to the commodification of everything – a commodification that is neither conjunctural nor contingent but systematically

generated by capitalism, so as to contain the crises of accumulation. (Erik's) real Utopias thus signify something organic to capitalism, namely the reaction to commodification. If capitalism depends upon deepening commodification, a move towards de-commodification conducted across all fictitious commodities has the potential to be anti-capitalist – but there are no guarantees. First a counter-movement to commodification is as likely to save capitalism from itself as to abolish it. Second a Polanyian counter-movement can easily assume an authoritarian form, as in the right-wing populism of today and the fascism of yesterday. That's the rub – how to turn a Polanyian 'counter-movement' into a Gramscian 'counter-hegemony'; for decommodification can only lead beyond capitalism if it inspires a socialist movement. Hence the importance of Erik's engagement with particular real Utopias and their practitioners, linking them together in an anti-capitalist movement that gives direction to the democratic-socialist project.

From a rural development perspective Buraway and Wright are not the only scholars to portend the idea of new counter movements, as many of the chapters in this book testify and explain. The rural development agenda we propose here indeed needs to be a central location and fertile place for the generation of both normative and pragmatic 'utopias' for wider social and environmental sciences more generally; ones which recast and challenge the power relations between nature and people in new ways and, at the same time, re-valorize social agency beyond narrow conceptions of commodification and appropriation. Indeed, as the substantive chapters here explain, these competing dialectics are as much a scientific venture as they are questions of politics and power.

We set ourselves as authors in the introduction to this volume the challenge of asking the question: 'What is the new research agenda for rural development studies?' Of course we have not completely answered this question; merely made a start. But in the course of attempting to address it we have realized that in a world where global rural development is both precarious and uneven, the connections between urban and rural living have never been more intense and stronger, yet their dichotomies and their potential transformational pathways are even more profound. Indeed, this is a new dilemma and conundrum – that our intellectual journey here has exposed and hopefully articulated.

# References

## Introduction

Marsden, T.K (ed) (2018) *The Sage Handbook of Nature*, 3 volumes. London: Sage.

## Chapter 1

Andersson, K, Sjoblom, S, Granberg,L, Ehrstrom, P and Marsden, T.K (2016) Metropolitan Ruralities. Research in *Rural Sociology and Development, Vol 23*. Bingley, UK: Emerald.

Bai, X, Nath, I, Capon, A, Hasan, N and Jaron, D (2012) Health and wellbeing in the changing urban environment. *Current Opinion in Environmental Sustainability*, 4(4), 465–470.

Byres, T.J (2012) *The Agrarian Question and the Peasantry. The Elgar Companion of Marxist Economics*. Cheltenham, UK and Northampton, MA, USA: Edward Elgar Publishing.

Carlson, C (2017) Re-thinking the agrarian question: agriculture and underdevelopment in the global south. *Journal of Agrarian Change*, 18, 703–721.

Clark, N (2011) *Inhuman Nature: Sociable Life on a Dynamic Planet*. London: Sage.

Gardener, B (2019) *Choked: Life and Breadth in the Age of Air Pollution*. Chicago, IL: University of Chicago Press.

Granberg, L (2018) Pitirim Sorokin between East and West: Russian traces of rural sociology. *вестник удмуртского университета*, Т.2(вып, 3), 324–335.

Harvey, D (2003) *The New Imperialism*. Oxford, UK: Oxford University Press.

Institute of Public Health (1996) *Second national health morbidity survey*. Kuala Lumpur, Malaysia: Ministry of Health.

Lanchester, J (2018) After the fall. *London Review of Books*, 40(13). https://www.lrb.co.uk/the-paper/v40/n13/john-lanchester/after-the-fall (accessed 30 June 2020).

Lanchester, J (2019) Document number nine. *London Review of Books*, 41(19). https://www.lrb.co.uk/the-paper/v41/n19/john-lanchester/document-number-nine (accessed 10 October 2019).

Latour, B (2018) *Down to Earth: Politics in the New Climatic Regime*. Cambridge, UK: Polity Press.

Lee, Y (2020) Exploring Malaysia's expanding waistlines: the role of dietary public health messages and guidelines tackling overweight and obesity issues. *Journal of Malaysian Nutrition*, 26(1), 31–50.

Li, Y, Westlund, H and Liu, Y (2019) Why some rural areas decline while others not: an overview of rural evolution in the world. *Journal of Rural Studies*, 68, 135-143.

Marsden, T.K and Rucinska , K (2019) After COP21: contested transformations in the energy–agri-food nexus. *Sustainability*, 11(1695), 2-17.

Milone, P, Ventura, F and Ye, J (eds) (2015) *Constructing a New Framework for Rural Development. Research in Rural Sociology and Development, volume 22*. Bingley, UK: Emerald.

Ministry of Public Health (2016) *National Strategic Plan for Non-communicable Diseases (NSPNCD) 2016–2025*. Kuala Lumpur, Malaysia: Malaysia Ministry of Health.

Murdoch, J and Marsden, T.K (1995) *Reconstituting Rurality: Class, Community and Power in the Development Process*. London: University College London (UCL) Press.

Ng, M et al. (2014) Global, regional and national prevalence of overweight and obesity in children and adults 1980–2013. *The Lancet*, 384(9945), 766–781.

Overseas Development Institute (ODI) (2016) *Population Change in the Rural Developing World: Making the Transition*. ODI briefing paper, Keats, S and Wiggins, S. April, 2016. London: ODI.

Schema (2018) Schema case studies: applying systems thinking to urban health and wellbeing. UNU Kuala Lumpur and Cardiff University research report.

Scott, J.C. (2017) *Against The Grain: A Deep History of the Earliest States*. London: Yale University Press.

Sorokin, P and Zimmerman, C (1929) *Principles of Rural–Urban Sociology*. New York: Holt.

Strittmatter, K (2019). *We Have Been Harmonised: Life in China's Surveillance State*. London: Old Street Publishing.

Tilzey, M (2019) Food regimes, capital, state and class: Friedmann and McMichael revisited. *Sociologia Ruralis*, 59, 230–254.

UN Habitat (2019) Framework for action to advance integrated territorial development. Urban–rural linkages guiding principles. Kenya: UN Habitat.

Wirth, L (1938) Urbanism as a way of life. *American Journal of Sociology*, 44(1) 1–24.

Woods M (2018) Re-imagining the global village. In Stringer, B (ed) *Rurality Re-imagined*. New York: Oro Editions, pp. 14–23.

## Chapter 2

Blay-Palmer, A (2014) Editorial introduction: sustainable food spaces: constructing community food. *Journal of Local Environment*, 18(5), 521-641.

Blitz J (2018) 'Why Chris Grayling's flotilla plan will sink', Financial Times Daily Brexit Briefing, 1 October, www.ft.com.

Environmental Protections and the EU Bill (2018) Department of Exiting the EU, Factsheet 8: Environmental Principles, May 2018. London: UK Government.

Friedmann, H (2005) From colonialism to green capitalism: social movements and the emergence of food regimes. *Research in Rural Sociology and Development*, 11, 227–264.

Friedmann, H and McMichael, P (1989) Agriculture and the state system: the rise and decline of national agricultures. *Sociologia Ruralis*, 29(2), 93–117.

HM Government (2018) How to prepare if the UK leaves the EU with no deal: Guidance on how to prepare for Brexit if there's no deal. London: UK Government https://www.gov.uk/government/collections/how-to-prepare-if-the-uk-leaves-the-eu-with-no-deal (accessed May 2018).

IPCC (2018) Summary for policymakers of IPCC special report on global warming of 1.5°C approved by governments, 8 October. Geneva: IPCC. http://www.ipcc.ch/pdf/session48/pr_181008_P48_spm_en.pdf (accessed October 2018).

Lang T, Millstone, E and Marsden, T.K (2017) A food Brexit: time to get real – a Brexit briefing. Brighton: SPRU, University of Sussex, Cardiff University and City University of London. July.

Lanchester, J (2018) After the fall. *London Review of Books*, 40(13). https://www.lrb.co.uk/the-paper/v40/n13/john-lanchester/after-the-fall (accessed 30 June 2020).

Latour, B (2017) *Facing Gaia: Eight Lectures on the New Climate Regime*. Cambridge, UK: Polity Press.

Latour, B (2018) *Down to Earth: Politics in the New Climatic Regime*. Cambridge, UK: Polity Press.

Marsden. T.K and Morley, A (eds) (2014) *Sustainable Food Systems: Towards a New Paradigm*. Abingdon, Oxford: Earthscan.

Marsden, T.K and Rucinska, K (2019) After COP21: contested transformations in the energy–agri-food nexus. *Sustainability*, 11(1695), 2–17.

Marsden, T.K, Hebinck, P and Mathias, E (2019). Re-building food systems: embedding assemblages, infrastructures and reflexive governance for food systems transformation in Europe. *Journal of Food Security*, 10(6), 1301–1309.

Marsden, T.K, Lee, R, Flynn, A and Thankappan, S (2010) *The New Regulation and Governance of Food: Beyond the Food Crisis?* London: Routledge.

Marsden T.K, Moragues Faus, A and Sonnino, R (2018) Reproducing vulnerabilities in agri-food systems: Tracing the links between governance, financialization, and vulnerability in Europe post 2007–2008. *Journal of Agrarian Change*, 19(1), 82–100.

Moore, J.W (2015) *Capitalism in the Web of Life: Ecology and the Accumulation of Capital*. New York: Verso Books.

Moragues-Faus, A, Marsden, T.K, Adlerová, B, and Hausmanová, T (2020) Building diverse, distributive and territorialised agri-food economies to deliver sustainability and food security. *Economic Geography*, 96(3), 219–243.

Morgan, K and Sonnino, R (2011) *The School Revolution*. London: Earthscan.

Parker, G and Blitz, J (2018) 'UK readies flotilla plan for supplies in no-deal Brexit', *Financial Times*, 24 October, p. 1.

Purdy. J (2015) *After Nature: The Politics of the Anthropocene*. Cambridge, MA: Harvard University Press.

Rodden, J (2019) *Why Cities Lose: The Deep Roots of the Urban–Rural Political Divide*. New York: Basic Books.

Rossi, A, Marsden, T.K and Bui, S (2019) Re-defining power relations in agri-food systems. *Journal of Rural Studies*, 8, 147–158.

Royal Society of Arts (RSA) (2018). Food, Farming and Countryside Commission, First Report. London: The Strand.

Self, P and Storing, H.J (1962) *Agriculture and the State*. London: Methuen.

Sjoblom, S et al. (eds) (2012) *Sustainability and Short-term Policies: Improving Governance in Spatial Policy Interventions*. London: Ashgate.

Starr, P (2019) The battle for the suburbs. *New York Review of Books*. Online: https://www.nybooks.com/articles/2019/09/26/cities-lose-battle-for-the-suburbs/.

Swyngedouw, E (2014) Insurgent architects, radical cities and the promise of the political. In Wilson, J and Swyngedouw, E (eds) *The Post-political and its Discontents*. Edinburgh: Edinburgh University Press, pp 169-188.

TRANSMANGO EU Research programme on Food Security in Europe (2015-2019). http://www.transmango.eu/ (accessed January 2019).

## Chapter 3

Alphandéry, P and Billaud, J-P (2009) *Retour sur la sociologie rurale*. Vol. 183. Éditions de l'EHESS. http://journals.openedition.org/etudesrurales/8895; https://doi.org/10.4000/etudesrurales.8895 (accessed 29 July 2020).

Alphandéry, P and Sencébé, Y (2009) L'émergence de la sociologie rurale en France (1945-1967). *Etudes rurales*, 183(1), 23–40.

Ambrose, P (1975) *The Quiet Revolution: Social Change in a Sussex village 1871–1971*. Brighton: Sussex University Press.

Avelino, F and Wittmayer, J.M (2016) Shifting power relations in sustainability transitions: a multi-actor perspective. *Journal of Environmental Policy & Planning*, 18(5), 628–649. https://doi.org/10.1080/1523908X.2015.1112259.

Barbier, M and Elzen, B (2012) *System Innovations, Knowledge Regimes, and Design Practices towards Transitions for Sustainable Agriculture*. Paris: INRA.

Billaud, J.-P (2012), *Sociologie rurale et environnement: renouveau ou dépassement?*, in Barbier, R, Bourdes, P, Bozonnet, J.-P, Candau, J, Dobré, M, Lewis, N, Rudolf, F (eds) *Manuel de sociologie de l'environnement*. Québec: Presses de l'Université Laval, pp. 99–112.

Bock, B.B (2016) Rural marginalisation and the role of social innovation; a turn towards nexogenous development and rural reconnection. *Sociologia Ruralis*, 56(4), 552–573. https://doi.org/10.1111/soru.12119.

Boltanski, L and Chiapello, E (1999) *Le Nouvel Esprit Du Capitalisme*. Paris: Gallimard.

Bruckmeier, Karl (2000). Leader in Germany and the discourse of autonomous regional development. *Sociologia Ruralis*, 40(2), 219-27. https://doi.org/10.1111/1467-9523.00144.

Bui, S (2015) *Transitions vers l'agroécologie : analyse de la pertinence de l'échelle territoriale pour impulser des changements au niveau du système sociotechnique*. Paris: Thèse de sociologie, INRA/AgroParisTech.

Bui, S, Cardona, A, Lamine, C, and Cerf, M (2016) Sustainability transitions: insights on processes of niche-regime interaction and regime reconfiguration in agri-food systems. *Journal of Rural Studies*, 48, 92–103. https://doi.org/10.1016/j.jrurstud.2016.10.003.

Buller, Henry (2000) Re-creating rural territories: LEADER in France., *Sociologia Ruralis*, 40(2) 190–199.

Campbell, H (2005) The rise and rise of EurepGAP: The European (re)invention of colonial food relations? *International Journal of Sociology of Agriculture and Food*, 13(2), 6–19.

Cañete, José Antonio, Navarro, Francisco and Cejudo, Eugenio (2018) Territorially Unequal Rural Development: The Cases of the LEADER Initiative and the PRODER Programme in Andalusia (Spain). *European Planning Studies*, 26(4), 726–44. https://doi.org/10.1080/09654313.2018.1424118.

Cash, D, Adger, W, Fikret Berkes, N, Garden, P, Lebel, L, Olsson, P, Pritchard, L and Young, O (2006) Scale and cross-scale dynamics: governance and information in a multilevel world. *Ecology and Society*, 11(2). https://doi.org/10.5751/ES-01759-110208.

Chevalier, P and Dedeire, M (2014) Application du programme leader selon les principes de base du développement local. *Économie rurale. Agricultures, alimentations, territoires*, 342(July), 9–25. https://doi.org/10.4000/economierurale.4382.

Clout, H (1972). *Rural Geography*. Routledge, London.

Diaz, M, Darnhofer, I, Darrot, C and Beuret, J.E (2013) Green tides in Brittany: what can we learn about niche-regime interactions? *Environmental Innovation and Societal Transitions*, 8, 62–75.

Dolowitz, D.P and Marsh, D (2000) Learning from abroad: the role of policy transfer in contemporary policy-making. *Governance*, 13(1), 5–23. https://doi.org/10.1111/0952-1895.00121.

El Bilali, Hamid (2019) Research on Agro-Food Sustainability Transitions: A Systematic Review of Research Themes and an Analysis of Research Gaps. *Journal of Cleaner Production*, 221, 353–64. https://doi.org/10.1016/j.jclepro.2019.02.232.

Eizner, N (1974) De la 'communauté rurale' à la 'collectivité locale. In Jollivet, M (ed) *Sociétés Paysannes Ou Lutte Des Classes Au Village, Problèmes Méthodologiques et Théoriques de L'étude Locale En Sociologie Rurale*, Paris: Armand Colin, pp, 129–154.

Escobar, A (2003) Displacement, development, and modernity in the Colombian Pacific. *International Social Science Journal*, 55(175), 157–167. https://doi.org/10.1111/1468-2451.5501015.

Friedmann, H and McMichael, P (1989) Agriculture and the state system: the rise and fall of national agricultures, 1870 to the present. *Sociologia Ruralis*, 29(2), 93–117.

Geels, F.W and Schot, J (2007) Typology of sociotechnical transition pathways. *Research Policy*, 36(3), 399–417. https://doi.org/10.1016/j.respol.2007.01.003.

Giddens, A. 1990. *The Consequences of Modernity*. Cambridge: Polity Press.

Gottlieb, Robert (2009) Where we live, work, play… and eat: expanding the environmental justice agenda. *Environmental Justice*, 2(1), 7–8. https://doi.org/10.1089/env.2009.0001.

Grisa, Catia and Schneider, Sergio (2014) Três gerações de políticas públicas para a agricultura familiar e formas de interação entre sociedade e estado no Brasil. *Revista de Economia E Sociologia Rural*, 52, 125–46. https://doi.org/10.1590/S0103-20032014000600007.

Guston, D.H (2001) Boundary organizations in environmental policy and science: an introduction. *Science, Technology, & Human Values*, 26(4), 399–408. https://doi.org/10.1177/016224390102600401.

Haesbaert, Rogério (2018) *Viver no limite: território e multi/transterritorialidade em tempos de in-segurança e contenção*. Rio De Janeiro, Brazil: Bertrand Brasil.

Hervieu, B and Viard, J (1998) *Au bonheur des campagnes et des provinces*. La Tour d'Aigues: Editions de l'Aube.

IPES-Food (2018) *Breaking away from industrial food and farming systems: seven case studies of agroecological transition*. http://www.ipes-food.org/pages/Seven-Case-Studies-of-Agroecological-Transition (accessed 29 July 2020).

Jollivet, M (2009) Un temps fort de la sociologie rurale française. *Etudes rurales*, 183(1), 67–82.

Jollivet, M and Mendras, H (1971) *Les Collectivités Rurales Françaises: Étude Comparative Du Changement Social*. A. Colin, Paris: Armand Colin,

Köhler, Jonathan, Geels, Frank W, Kern, Florian, Markard, Jochen, Onsongo, Elsie, Wieczorek, Anna, Alkemade, Floortje et al. (2019) An agenda for sustainability transitions research: state of the art and future directions. *Environmental Innovation and Societal Transitions*, 31,1–32. https://doi.org/10.1016/j.eist.2019.01.004.

Kovách, Imre and Kučerová, Eva. (2006) The project class in Central Europe: the Czech and Hungarian cases. *Sociologia Ruralis*, 46(1), 3–21. https://doi.org/10.1111/j.1467 -9523.2006.00403.x.

Lamine, C, Bui, S, and Ollivier, G (2015) Pour une approche systémique et pragmatique de la transition écologique des systèmes agri-alimentaires. *Cahiers de Recherche Sociologique*, 58, 95–117.

Lamine, C, Magda, D and Amiot, M-J (2019) Crossing sociological, ecological, and nutritional perspectives on agrifood systems transitions: towards a transdisciplinary territorial approach. *Sustainability*, 11(5), 1284. https://doi.org/10.3390/su11051284

Lindberg, M (2018) Promoting and sustaining rural social innovation. *European Public & Social Innovation Review*, 2(2), 30–41.

Lowe, P and Bodiguel, M (eds) (1989) *Rural Studies in Britain and France*. Belhaven, London: Pinter.

Marsden.T.K (2003) *The Condition of Rural Sustainability. European Perspectives on Rural Development*. Assen, The Netherlands: Royal Van Gorcum.

Marsden, T.K (2004) The quest for ecological modernisation: re-spacing rural development and agri-food studies. *Sociologia Ruralis*, 44, 129–146.

Marsden, T.K, Lee, R, Flynn, A and Thankappan, S (2010) *The new regulation and governance of food: beyond the food crisis?* London: Routledge.

Marsden, T.K, Murdoch. J, Lowe, P, Munton. R and Flynn, A (1993) *Constructing the Countryside. Restructuring Rural Areas, 1*. London: University College London Press.

Martínez-Alier, Joan (2003) *The Environmentalism of the Poor: A Study of Ecological Conflicts and Valuation*. Cheltenham, UK and Northampton, MA, USA: Edward Elgar Publishing.

Morin, Edgar (1967) *Commune en France, la métamorphose de Plodémet*. Paris: Fayard.

Mormont, M (2009) Globalisations et écologisations des campagnes. *Etudes rurales*, 183(1), 143–160.

Moulaert, F, Martinelli, F, Swyngedouw, E and Gonzalez, S (2005) Towards alternative model(s) of local innovation. *Urban Studies*, 42(11), 1969–1990. https://doi.org/10 .1080/00420980500279893.

Murdoch, J and Marsden, T.K (1995) *Reconstituting Rurality: Class, Community and Power in the Development Process. Restructuring Rural Areas, 2*. London: University College London Press.

Murdoch, J, Lowe, P, Ward, N and Marsden, T.K (2003) *The Differentiated Countryside*. London: Routledge.

Neumeier, S (2012) Why do social innovations in rural development matter and should they be considered more seriously in rural development research? Proposal for a stronger focus on social innovations in rural development research. *Sociologia Ruralis*, 52(1), 48–69. https://doi.org/10.1111/j.1467-9523.2011.00553.x.

Newby, H, Bell, C. Rose, D and Saunders, P (1978) *Property, Paternalism and Power: Class and Control in Rural England*. London: Hutchinson.

Noack, A and Federwisch, T (2019) Social innovation in rural regions: urban impulses and cross-border constellations of actors. *Sociologia Ruralis*, 59(1), 92–112. https://doi.org/10.1111/soru.12216.

Olsson, P, Folke, C and Berkes, F (2004) Adaptive comanagement for building resilience in social-ecological systems. *Environmental Management*, 34(1), 75–90. https://doi.org/10.1007/s00267-003-0101-7.

Osti, Giorgio (2000) Leader and partnerships: the case of Italy. *Sociologia Ruralis*, 40(2), 172–80. https://doi.org/10.1111/1467-9523.00139.

Ostrom, E (2012) Why do we need to protect institutional diversity? *European Political Science*, 11(1), 128–147. https://doi.org/10.1057/eps.2011.37.

Pahl, R (1965) *'Urbs in Rure': the metropolitan fringe of Heartfordshire*. London: Weidenfield and Nicholson.

Phillips, M and Smith, D (2018) Comparative approaches to gentrification: lessons from the rural. *Dialogues in Human Geography*, 8(1), 3–25.

Ray, C (2000) Endogenous socio-economic development in the European Union: issues of evaluation. *Journal of Rural Studies*, 16(4), 447–458. https://doi.org/10.1016/S0743-0167(00)00012-7.

Rey-Valette, Hélène, Chia, Eduardo, Mathé, Syndhia, Michel, Laura, Nougarèdes, Brigitte, Soulard, Christophe-Toussaint, Maurel, Pierre, Jarrige, Françoise, Barbe, Éric and Guiheneuf, Pierre-Yves (2014) Comment analyser la gouvernance territoriale ? Mise à l'épreuve d'une grille de lecture. *Geographie, economie, societe*, 16(1): 65–89.

Rhodes, R.A.W (2007) Understanding governance: Ten years on. *Organization Studies*, 28(8), 1243–1264. doi: 10.1177/0170840607076586

Rossi, A, Bui, S and Marsden, T.K (2019) Redefining power relations in agrifood systems. *Journal of Rural Studies*, 68, 147–158. https://doi.org/10.1016/j.jrurstud.2019.01.002.

RDR (2007) *Règlement de Développement Rural*. CE no 1698/2005.

Sjöblom, S and Godenhjelm, S (2009) Project proliferation and governance: implications for environmental management. *Journal of Environmental Policy & Planning*, 11(3), 169–185. https://doi.org/10.1080/15239080903033762.

Stotten, Rike, Bui, Sibylle, Pugliese, Patrizia, Schermer, Markus and Lamine, Claire (2017) Organic values-based supply chains as a tool for territorial development: a comparative analysis of three European organic regions. *International Journal of Sociology of Agriculture and Food*, 24(1), 135–54.

Termeer, C.J, Dewulf, A and van Lieshout, M (2010) Disentangling scale approaches in governance research: comparing monocentric, multilevel, and adaptive governance. *Ecology and Society*, 15(4), 29–29.

Vaarst, M, Escudero, A.G, Jahi Chappell, M, Brinkley, C, Nijbroek, R, Arraes, N, Andreasen, L et al. (2017) Exploring the concept of agroecological food systems in a city-region context. *Agroecology and Sustainable Food Systems*, 0(0), 1–26. https://doi.org/10.1080/21683565.2017.1365321.

van der Ploeg, J (1993) Rural sociology and the new agrarian question: a perspective from the Netherlands. *Sociologia Ruralis*, 33(2), 140–260.

van der Ploeg, J and Marsden, T.K (2008) *Unfolding Webs: The Dynamics of Regional Rural Development*. Assen, The Netherlands: Royal van Gorcum.

van der Ploeg, J, Renting, Brunori, G, Knickel, K, Mannion, J, Marsden, T.K, de Roest, K. Sevilla-Guzmán, E and Ventura, F (2000) Rural development: from practices and policies towards theory. *Sociologia Ruralis*, 40(4), 391–408.

Wezel, A, Brives, H, Casagrande, M, Clément, C, Dufour, A and Vandenbroucke, P (2016) Agroecology territories: places for sustainable agricultural and food systems and biodiversity conservation. *Agroecology and Sustainable Food Systems*, 40(2), 132–144. https://doi.org/10.1080/21683565.2015.1115799.

Whatmore, S, Little, J , Marsden, T.K and Munton, R (1986a) Towards a typology of farm businesses in contemporary British agriculture. *Sociologia Ruralis*, 27, 21–37.

Whatmore , S , Little, J, Marsden, T.K and Munton, R (1986b) Interpreting a relational typology of farm businesses in Southern England. *Sociologia Ruralis*, 27, 103–122.

Wiskerke, J.S (2009) On places lost and places regained: Reflections on the alternative food geography and sustainable regional development. *International Planning Studies*, 14(4), 369–387. doi: 10.1080/13563471003642803

Woods, M (2006) Redefining the 'rural question': the new 'politics of the rural' and social policy. *Social Policy & Administration*, 40(6), 579–595. https://doi.org/10.1111/j.1467-9515.2006.00521.x.

## Chapter 4

Adger, W.N (2006) Vulnerability. *Global Environnemental Change*, 16(3), 268–281. doi:10.1016/j.gloenvcha. 2006.02.006.

Anderson, P (2019) Situationism à l'envers? *New Left Review*, September–October, 47-95.

Bernstein, H (2004) Changing before our eyes: agrarian questions and the politics of land in capitalism today. *Journal of Agrarian Change*, 4 190-225.

Bernstein, H (2016) Agrarian political economy and modern world capitalism: the contributions of food regime analysis. *Journal of Peasant Studies*, 43, 611-647.

Birch, P and Lawrence, G (2009) Towards a third regime. *Agriculture and Human Values*, 26(4), 267-279.

Bonanno, A (2014) The legitimation crisis of neo-liberal globalisation: instances from agri-food. In Wolf, S and Bonanno, A (2104) *Agri-food Systems and Neo-liberalism*. London: Earthscan/Routledge, 13-31.

Borras, S and Franco, J (2013) Global land grabbing and political reactions 'from below'. *Third World Quarterly*, 34 1723-1747.

Borras, S, Franco, J, Isakson, S, Levidow, L and Vervest, P (2016) The rise of flex crops and commodities: implications for research. *Journal of Peasant Studies*, 1-23.

Clapp, J and Fuchs, D (2009) *Corporate Power in Global Agrifood Governance*. London: MIT Press.

Cousins B, Borras, Sauer, S and Ye, J (2018) BRICS, middle income countries and global agrarian transformations: internal dynamics, regional trends and international implications. *Globalisations*, 15, 1-11.

Durand, C (2017) *Fictitious Capital*. London and New York: Verso Books.

Edelman, M, Oya, C, Borras Jr., S.M (2015) *Global Land Grabs: History, Theory and Method*. London: Routledge.

Fairburn, M (2014) 'Like gold with yield': evolving intersections between farmland and finance. *Journal of Peasant Studies*, 41(5), 777-795.

Feeding Britain Report (2014) Report of the Commission on Food Poverty. London: UK Government.

Fairhead, J, Leach, M, and Scoones, I (2012) Green grabbing: a new appropriation of nature? *Journal of Peasant Studies*, 39(2), 237-261.

Harvey, D (1982) *The Limits of Capital.* Oxford: Blackwell.

Harvey, D (2003) *The New Imperialism.* Oxford: Oxford University Press.

Hebinck. P (2018) Special Issue on de-agrarianisation/re-agarianisation of *Journal of Rural Studies*, 61, 227–235.

Hirsch, P (2012) Reviving agrarian studies in South East Asia: geography on the ascendancy. *Geographical Research*, 50, 393-403.

Isakson, S.R. (2014) Food and finance: the financial transformation of agro-food supply chains. *Journal of Peasant Studies*, 41(5), 749-775.

Marsden. T.K (2003) *The Condition of Rural Sustainability.* The Netherlands: Royal van Gorcum.

Marsden. T.K and Morley, A (eds) (2014) *Sustainable Food Systems: Towards a New Paradigm.* Abingdon, Oxford: Earthscan.

Marsden, T.K, Lee, R, Flynn, A and Thankappan, S (2010) *The New Regulation and governance of food: beyond the food crisis?* London: Routledge.

Marsden, T.K, Moragaus Fous, A and Sonnino, R (2018) Reproducing vulnerability in agri-food systems: tracing the links between governance, financialisation and vulnerability in Europe post 2007-8. *Journal of Agrarian Change*, January, 1-19.

Moore, J (2016) *Capitalism and the Web of Life: Ecology and the Accumulation of Capital.* New York: Verso Books.

Niederle, P and Ioris, A (2019) Agribusiness and the neoliberal food system in Brazil: frontiers and fissures of agro-neoliberalism. *Review of Agricultural, Food and Environmental Studies*, 99, 1-4.

Ostry, J, Loungani, P and Furceri, D (2016) Neo-liberalism: undersold. International Monetary Fund (IMF): finance and development paper, June 2016. Paris: IMF.

Ouma S (2016) From financialization to operations of capital: historicising and disentangling the finance–farmland-nexus. *Geoforum*, 72, 82–83.

Roep. D and van der Ploeg, J.D (2003) Mutilfunctionality and rural development: the actual situation in Europe. In Van Huylenbroeck, G and Durand, G (eds) *Multi-Functional Agriculture. A New Paradigm for European Agriculture and Rural Development.* New Hampshire: Ashgate, 37-54.

Sauer, S and Borras Jr, S (2016) 'Land grabbing' and 'green grabbing': una letura da 'corrida na produção acadêmica' sobre a apropriação global de terras. *Campo – Território: revista de geografia agrária*, 11(23). https://doi.org/10.14393/RCT112301.

Sauer, S and Leite, S.P (2012) Agrarian structure, foreign investment in land, and land prices in Brazil. *Journal of Peasant Studies*, 39(3–4), 873–898.

Sauer, S., Balestro, M.V and Schneider, S (2018) The ambiguous stance of Brazil as a regional power: piloting a course between commodity-based surpluses and national development. *Globalizations*, 15(1), 32–55. https://doi.org/10.1080/14747731.2017.1400232.

Sender, J and Johnston, D (2004) Searching for a weapon of mass production in rural Africa: unconvincing arguments for land reform. *Journal of Agrarian Change*, 4, 142-164.

Tooze, M (2018a) *Crashed: How a Decade of Financial Crises Changed the World.* London: Allen Lane.

Tooze, M (2018b) Tempestuous seasons. *London Review of Books*, 13 September.

UK National Report, Transmango Project (2015) Assessment of the impact of global drivers of change on Europe's food and nutrition security (FNS). European Commission.

van der Ploeg, J.D (2008) *The New Peasantries. Struggles for Autonomy and Sustainability in an Era of Empire and Globalization*. London: Earthscan.

van der Ploeg, J.D (2010a) The food crisis, industrialised farming and the imperial regime. *Journal of Agrarian Change*, 10, 98-106.

van der Ploeg, J.D (2010b) The peasantries of the 21st century: the commoditization debate revisited. *Journal of Peasant Studies*, 37, 1-30.

Veltmeyer, H. and Petras, J (2014) *The New Extractivism: A Post-neoliberal Development Model or Imperialism of the Twenty-first Century?* London: Zed Books.

Visser, O, Clapp, J and Isakson, S.R (2015) Introduction to symposium on global finance and the agri-food sector: risk and regulation. *Journal of Agrarian Change*, 15(4), 541-548.

Wolf, S and Bonnano, A (eds) (2014) *Agri-food Systems and Neo-liberalism*. London: Earthscan/Routledge.

Wolford, W. et al. (2013) *Governing Global Land Deals: The Role of the State in the Rush for Land*. London: Wiley Blackwell.

Ye, J, van der Ploeg, J.D, Schneider, S and Shanin, T (2019) The incursions of extractivism: moving from dispersed places to global capitalism. *Journal of Peasant Studies*, 47(1), 155–183.

## Chapter 5

Christophers, B (2018) *Land for the Many*. London: Labour Party.

Christophers, B (2019) *The New Enclosure: The Appropriation of Public Land in Neo-Liberal Britain*. London: Verso.

Cleaver, F (2012) *Development Through Bricolage. Rethinking Institutions for National Resource Management*. London: Routledge.

Commission for Rural Communities (2010) State of the countryside report. London: The Stationary Office.

Community Land Scotland (2017) Report on community land holding. Edinburgh: Scottish Government.

Davis, M (2018) *Old Gods: New Enigmas: Marx's Lost Theory*. London and New York: Verso Books.

EAT-Lancet Commission Report (2018) *Healthy diets for sustainable food systems. Summary report of the eat-lancet commission*. Stockholm, Oslo, London: Commission on Food Planet and Health.

Fernandes, B.M (2015) The formation and territorialisation of the MST in Brazil. In Carter, M (ed) *Challenging Social Inequality: The Landless Rural Workers Movement and Agrarian reform in Brazil*. Durham, NC and London: Duke University Press, 115-149.

Friedmann, H. (2018) Metabolism of global cities: London, Manchester and Chicago. In Marsden, T.K (ed) *The Sage Handbook of Nature*. London: Sage, Chapter 66.

Friedmann, H and McMichael, P (1989) Agriculture and the state system: the rise and fall of national agricultures, 1870 to the present. *Sociologia Ruralis*, 29(2), 93–117.

Goodman, D, Sorj, B and Wilkinson J (1987) *From Farming to Biotechnology: A Theory of Agro-industrial Development*. Oxford, Blackwell.

Greenberg. P (2018/19) In the valley of fear. *New York Review of Books*, December 2018-Jan 2019, 91-93.

Hammond, J.L and Hammond, B (1913) *The Rural Labourer*, Vols 1 and 2. London: LSE Press.

Harvey, D (1982) *The Limits of Capital*. Blackwell, Oxford.

Hebinck, P (2018) De-/re-agrarianisation: global perspectives. *Journal of Rural Studies*, 61, 227–235.

Ioris, A (2019a) Challenges and contributions of indigenous geography: learning with and for the Kaiowa-Guarani of South America. *Geoforum*, 1020137-141.

Ioris, A (2019b) Political agency of indigenous peoples: the Guarani-Kaiowa's fight for survival and recognition. *Vibrant*, 16, 3-28.

Jack, I (2019) Why did we not know. Review of Christophers op. cit. *London Review of Books*. 23 May.

Kautsky, K (1988) *The Agrarian Question*, 2 volumes London: Zwan.

Kropotkin P (1904) The desiccation of Eur-Asia. *Geographical Journal*, 23(6), 722–734.

Lamine, C, Darnhofer, I and Marsden, T.K (2019) What enables just sustainability transitions in agri-food systems? An exploration of conceptual approaches using international comparative case studies. Editorial of the Special Issue in *Journal of Rural Studies*, April.

Levien, M, Watts, M and Hairong, Y (2018) Agrarian Marxism. *Journal of Peasant Studies*, 45(5-6), 853-883.

Marsden, T.K (2017) *Agri-food and Rural Development: Sustainable Place-Making*. London: Bloomsbury.

Marsden, T.K (ed) (2018) *The Sage Handbook of Nature*, 3 volumes. London: Sage.

Marsden, T.K and Morley, A (eds) (2014) *Sustainable Food Systems: Towards a New Paradigm*. Abingdon, Oxford: Earthscan.

Marsden, T.K and Rucinska, K (2019) After COP21: contested transformations in the energy–agri-food nexus. *Sustainability*, 11(1695), 2-17.

Marsden, T.K and Sonnino, R (2012) Human health and well-being and the sustainability of urban–regional food systems. *Current Opinion in Environmental Sustainability*, 4(4),427-431.

Marsden, T.K, Hebinck, P and Mathias, E (2019). Re-building food systems: embedding assemblages, infrastructures and reflexive governance for food systems transformation in Europe. *Journal of Food Security*, 10(6), 1301–1309.

McCarthy, J (2015) A socio-ecological fix to capitalist crisis and climate change? The possibilities and limits of renewable energy. *Environment and Planning*, A(47), 2485–2502.

Moragues Faus, A. and Marsden, T.K (2017) The political ecology of food: carving 'spaces of possibility' in a new research agenda. *Journal of Rural Studies*, 55, 275-288.

Moore, J (2015) *Capitalism in the Web of Life: Ecology and the Accumulation of Capital*. Brooklyn, NY: Verso Books.

Morgan, K, Marsden, T.K and Murdoch, J (2006) *Worlds of Food*. Oxford: Oxford University Press.

Murdoch, J, Marsden, T.K, Lowe, P and Ward, N (2003) *The Differentiated Countryside*. London: Routledge.

Pauli, R and Marsden, T.K (2018) Contested paradigms in the bio-economy and the eco-economy in agri-food in Rio Grande do Sul. RS Brazil. Sustainable Places Research Institute Working Paper. Cardiff University, UK.

Project Skyline (2019) Report of Pilot Project, by C. Blake. Cardiff Bay: Project Skyline.

Purdy, J (2015) *After Nature: A Politics of the Anthropocene*. Cambridge, MA: Harvard University Press.

Rasmussen, L.V, Coolsaet, B, Martin, A, Mertz, O, Pascual, U, Corbera, E, Dawson, N, Fisher, J.A, Phil Franks, P and Ryan, C.M (2018) Social-ecological outcomes of agricultural intensification. Review article. *Nature Sustainability* (June), 275‒282.

Romero, M.N (2018) Report on literature review of commons research. SUSPLACE Working Paper, Riga, Latvia.

Romero, M.N, Valente, S, Figueiredo, E and Parra, C (2019) Historical commons as sites of transformation: a critical research agenda to study human and 'more-than-human' communities. *Geoforum*, 10(107), 113‒123.

Rossi, A, Bui, S and Marsden, T.K (2019) Redefining power relations in agrifood systems. *Journal of Rural Studies*, 68, 147‒158. https://doi.org/10.1016/j.jrurstud.2019.01.002.

## Chapter 6

Abreu, L.S de, Lamine, C, Brandenburg, A, de Sa Mazarotto, A and Bellon, S (2011) Agroecologia, movimento social, ciência, práticas e políticas públicas: uma abordagem comparativa. *Congresso Brasileiro de Agroecologia, Fortaleza, December*.

Ajates Gonzalez, R, Thomas, J and Chang, M (2018) Translating agroecology into policy: the case of France and the United Kingdom. *Sustainability*, 10(8), 2930, 1‒19. https://doi.org/10.3390/su10082930.

Allaire, G and Wolf, S (2004) Cognitive representation and institutional hybridity in agrofood systems of innovation. *Sciences Technology and Human Value*, 29(4) 431‒458.

Altieri, M.A (2004) Linking ecologists and traditional farmers in the search for sustainable agriculture. *Frontiers in Ecology and the Environment*, 2(1), 35‒42. https://doi.org/10.1890/1540-9295(2004)002[0035:LEATFI]2.0.CO;2.

Altieri, M.A and Nicholls, C (2003) Agroecology: rescuing organic agriculture from a specialized industrial model of production and distribution. *Ecology and Farming*, 34, 24‒26.

Altieri, M.A and Rosset, P (1996) Agroecology and the conversion of large-scale conventional systems to sustainable management. *International Journal of Environmental Studies*, 50(3–4), 165‒185.

Altieri, M.A and Toledo, V.M (2011) The agroecological revolution in Latin America: rescuing nature, ensuring food sovereignty and empowering peasants. *Journal of Peasant Studies*, 38(3), 587‒612. https://doi.org/10.1080/03066150.2011.582947.

Anderson, C.R, Maughan, C and Pimbert, M.P (2018) Transformative agroecology learning in Europe: building consciousness, skills and collective capacity for food sovereignty. *Agriculture and Human Values*, 36, 531‒547.

Aubertin, C and Kalil, L (2017) La contribution du Brésil à la COP21: l'agrobusiness du futur. Brésil(s). *Sciences humaines et sociales*, 11(March). https://doi.org/10.4000/bresils.2154.

Badgley, C, Moghtader, J, Quintero, E, Zakem, E, Jahi Chappell, M, Avilés-Vázquez, K, Samulon, A and Perfecto, I (2007) Organic agriculture and the global food supply. *Renewable Agriculture and Food Systems*, 22(2), 86‒108.

Bell, M.M and Bellon, S (2018) Generalization without universalization: towards an agroecology theory. *Agroecology and Sustainable Food Systems*, 42(6), 605‒611. https://doi.org/10.1080/21683565.2018.1432003.

Bell, M.M, Lyon, A, Gratton, C and Jackson, R.D (2008) Commentary: The productivity of variability: an agroecological hypothesis. *International Journal of Agricultural Sustainability*, 6(4), 233–235. https://doi.org/10.3763/ijas.2008.c5004.

Bellon, S and Ollivier, G (2013) L'agroécologie en France: l'institutionnalisation d'utopies. In Goulet F, Magda, D, Girard, N, and Hernandez, V (eds) *L'agroécologie en Argentine et en France. Regards croisés*, Paris: L'Harmattan, 55–90.

Bellon, S and Ollivier, G (2018) Institutionalizing agroecology in France: social circulation changes the meaning of an idea. *Sustainability*, 10(5), 1380. https://doi.org/10.3390/su10051380.

Blanc, J (2009) Family farmers and major retail chains in the Brazilian organic sector: assessing new development pathways. A case study in a peri-urban district of São Paulo. *Journal of Rural Studies*, 25(3), 322–332.

Bowen, S and Mutersbaugh, T (2014) Local or localized? Exploring the contributions of Franco-Mediterranean agrifood theory to alternative food research. *Agriculture and Human Values*, 31(2), 201–213. https://doi.org/10.1007/s10460-013-9461-7.

Buttel, F.H (2005) Ever since Hightower: the politics of agricultural research activism in the molecular age. *Agriculture and Human Values*, 22(3), 275–283. https://doi.org/10.1007/s10460-005-6043-3.

César, C (1999) De La Conception Du Naturel, Les Catégories À L'œuvre Chez Les Consommateurs de Produits Biologiques. PhD in Sociology, University of Paris X, France

Clancy, K. and Ruhf, K (2010) Is local enough? Some arguments for regional food systems. *Choices*, 25(1). https://www.jstor.org/stable/pdf/choices.25.1.08.pdf?seq=1, (accessed 29 July 2020).

Clark, M and Tilman, D (2017) Comparative analysis of environmental impacts of agricultural production systems, agricultural input efficiency, and food choice. *Environmental Research Letters*, 1(6), 064016. https://doi.org/10.1088/1748-9326/aa6cd5.

Dahlberg, K (2001) Democratizing society and food systems: or how do we transform modern structures of power? *Agriculture and Human Values*, 18(2), 135–151.

Dalcin, D, Leal de Souza, A.R, de Freitas, J.B, Padula, A. D and Dewes, H (2014) Organic products in Brazil: from an ideological orientation to a market choice. *British Food Journal* 116(12), 1998–2015. https://doi.org/10.1108/BFJ-01-2013-0008.

Darnhofer, I, D'Amico, S and Fouilleux, E (2019) A relational perspective on the dynamics of the organic sector in Austria, Italy, and France. *Journal of Rural Studies*, 68, 200–212. https://doi.org/10.1016/j.jrurstud.2018.12.002.

Dumont, A.M, Vanloqueren, G, Stassart, P.M and Baret, P.V (2016) Clarifying the socioeconomic dimensions of agroecology: between principles and practices. *Agroecology and Sustainable Food Systems*, 40(1), 24–47. https://doi.org/10.1080/21683565.2015.1089967.

Fouilleux, E, Bricas, N and Alpha, A (2017) 'Feeding 9 billion people': global food security debates and the productionist trap. *Journal of European Public Policy*, 24(11), 1658–1677. https://doi.org/10.1080/13501763.2017.1334084.

Francis, C, Lieblein, G, Gliessman, S, Breland, T.A, Creamer, N, Harwood, R, Salomonsson, L, Helenius, J, Rickerl, D, Salvador, R, Wiedenhoeft, M, Simmons, S, Allen, P, Altieri, M, Flora, C and Poincelot, R (2003) Agroecology: the ecology of food systems. *Journal of Sustainable Agriculture*, 22(3), 99–118.

Friedmann, H and McMichael, P (1989) Agriculture and the state system: the rise and fall of national agricultures, 1870 to the present. *Sociologia Ruralis*, 29(2), 93–117.

Giraldo, O.F and Rosset, P.M (2018) Agroecology as a territory in dispute: between institutionality and social movements. *Journal of Peasant Studies*, 45(3), 545–564. https://doi.org/10.1080/03066150.2017.1353496.

Gliessman, S.R (2007) *Agroecology. The Ecology of Sustainable Food Systems*. Second Edition. London: CRC Press. Taylor & Francis Group.

Goodman, D (1999) Agro-food studies in the age of ecology nature, corporeality, biopolitics. *Sociologia Ruralis*, 39(1), 17–38.

Grisa, C., Schmitt, C, Mattei, L.F, Maluf, R and Leite S.P (2011) Brazil's PAA: policy-driven food systems. *Farming Matters*, 27(3), 34–36.

Grisa, C and Schneider, S (2015) *Políticas Públicas de Desenvolvimento Rural No Brasil*. Porto Alegre, Brazil: UFRGS.

Guthman, J (2004) The trouble with organic lite in California: a rejoinder to the conventionalisation debate. *Sociologia Ruralis*, 44(3), 301–316.

Guzmán, E.S and Woodgate, G (2013) Agroecology: foundations in agrarian social thought and sociological theory. *Agroecology and Sustainable Food Systems*, 37(1), 32–44. https://doi.org/10.1080/10440046.2012.695763.

Hammond, R.A and Dubé, L (2012) A systems science perspective and transdisciplinary models for food and nutrition security. *Proceedings of the National Academy of Sciences*, 109(31), 12356–12363. https://doi.org/10.1073/pnas.0913003109.

Heller, M.C, Keoleian, G.A and Willett, W.C (2013) Toward a life cycle-based, diet-level framework for food environmental impact and nutritional quality assessment: a critical review. *Environmental Science & Technology*, 47(22), 12632–12647. https://doi.org/10.1021/es4025113.

HLPE (2017) Nutrition and food systems: a report by the high level panel of experts on food security and nutrition of the committee on world food security. Rome: HLPE.

Holt-Giménez, Eric and Altieri, Miguel A. (2013) Agroecology, food sovereignty, and the new green revolution. *Agroecology and Sustainable Food Systems*, 37(1), 90–102 https://doi.org/10.1080/10440046.2012.716388.

IPES-Food (2018) Breaking away from industrial food and farming systems: seven case studies of agroecological transition. IPES-Food.

Kitchen, L and Marsden, T.K (2009) Creating sustainable rural development through stimulating the eco-economy: beyond the eco-economic paradox? *Sociologia Ruralis*, 49(3), 273–294. https://doi.org/10.1111/j.1467-9523.2009.00489.x.

Kloppenburg, J, Hendrickson, J and Stenvenson, G (1996) Coming into the foodshed. *Agriculture and Human Values*, 13, 33–42.

Kneafsey, M (2010) The region in food – important or irrelevant? *Cambridge Journal of Regions, Economy and Society*, 3(2), 177–190. https://doi.org/10.1093/cjres/rsq012.

Lamine, C (2015) Sustainability and resilience in agrifood systems: reconnecting agriculture, food and the environment. *Sociologia Ruralis*, 55(1), 41–61. https://doi.org/10.1111/soru.12061.

Lamine, C (2017) *La Fabrique Sociale de L'écologisation de L'agriculture*. Marseille: La Discussion.

Lamine, C (2020) *Sustainable Agri-food Systems. Case Studies in Transitions Towards Sustainability from France and Brazil*. London: Bloomsbury.

Lamine, C and de Abreu, L.S (2009) Compared trajectories of agro-ecology in Brazil and France: the role of scientists and social movements. *ESRS Congress*, 17–21 August, Vaasa, Finland.

Lamine, C, Magda, D and Amiot, M-J (2019) Crossing sociological, ecological, and nutritional perspectives on agrifood systems transitions: towards a transdisciplinary territorial approach. *Sustainability*, 11(5), 1284. https://doi.org/10.3390/su11051284.

Lamine C, Renting, H, Rossi, A, Wiskerke, H and Brunori, G (2012) Agri-food systems and territorial development: innovations, new dynamics and changing governance mechanisms. In Darnhofer I, Gibbon D and Dedieu, B (eds) *The Farming Systems Approaches into the 21st Century: The New Dynamics*, 229–256, Heidelberg, Germany: Springer Netherlands.

Lampkin, N, Pearce, B.D and Leeke, A.R (2015) The role of agro-ecology in sustainable intensification. Organic Research Centre, Elm Farm and the Game and Wildlife Conservation Trust, The Land Use Policy Group, UK.

Levidow, L (2015) European transitions towards a corporate-environmental food regime: agroecological incorporation or contestation? *Journal of Rural Studies*, 40, 76–89. https://doi.org/10.1016/j.jrurstud.2015.06.001.

Levidow, L, Pimbert, M and Vanloqueren, G (2014) Agroecological research: conforming – or transforming the dominant agro-food regime? *Agroecology and Sustainable Food Systems*, 38(10), 1127–1155. https://doi.org/10.1080/21683565.2014.951459.

Lockie, S and Halpin, D (2005) The conventionalisation thesis reconsidered: structural and ideological transformation of Australian organic agriculture. *Sociologia Ruralis*, 45(4), 284–307.

Loconto, A.M and Fouilleux, E (2019) Defining agroecology. *The International Journal of Sociology of Agriculture and Food*, 25(2), 116–137.

Louzada, M, da Costa, L, Galastri Baraldi, L, Martinez Steele, E, Bortoletto Martins, A.P, Silva Canella, D, Moubarac, J-C, Bertazzi Levy, R, Cannon, G, Afshin, A, Imamura, F, Mozaffarian, D and Monteiro C.A (2015) Consumption of ultra-processed foods and obesity in Brazilian adolescents and adults. *Preventive Medicine*, 81(December), 9–15. https://doi.org/10.1016/j.ypmed.2015.07.018.

Michelsen, J (2001) Recent development and political acceptance of organic farming in Europe. *Sociologia Ruralis*, 41(1), 3–20.

Moragues-Faus, A, Marsden, T.K, Alderova, B and Hausmanova, T (in press) Building diverse, distributed and territorialised agri-food economies to deliver sustainability and food security. *Economic Geography*.

Morris, C and Winter, M (1999) Integrated farming systems: the third way for European agriculture. *Land Use Policy*, 16, 193–205.

Muller, P (2000) La politique agricole Française: l'état et les organisations professionnelles. *Economie Rurale*, 255, 33–39.

OECD, FAO and UNCDF (2016) *Adopting a Territorial Approach to Food Security and Nutrition Policy*. Paris: OECD Publishing. https://www.oecd.org/regional/adopting-a-territorial-approach-to-food-security-and-nutrition-policy-9789264257108-en.htm (accessed 29 July 2020)

Ollivier, G, Bellon, S, de Abreu Sá, T.D and Magda, D (2019) Dossier: perspectives franco-brésiliennes autour de l'agroécologie – Aux frontières de l'agroécologie. Les politiques de recherche de deux instituts agronomiques publics français et brésilien. *Natures Sciences Sociétés*, 27(1), 20–38. https://doi.org/10.1051/nss/2019017.

PFLA (2016) The Pasture-led Livestock Association. Report 'Pasture for life': it can be done. The farm business case for feeding ruminants just on pasture. Grantham: PFLA.

Pinton, F and Sencébé, Y (2019) Soberania versus segurança alimentar no Brasil: tensões e oposições em torno da agroecologia como projeto. *Estudos Sociedade e Agricultura*, (January), 24–46.

Piriou, S (2002) L'institutionnalisation de L'agriculture biologique (1980–2000). Ecole Nationale Supérieure Agronomique de Rennes, PhD.

Poux, X and Aubert, P.-M (2018) An agro-ecological Europe in 2050: multifunctional agri-culture for healthy eating. Findings from the Ten Years For Agroecology (TYFA) modelling exercise, Iddri-AScA, Study no. 09/18, Paris, France.

Rivera-Ferre, M.G (2018) The resignification process of agroecology: competing narratives from governments, civil society and intergovernmental organizations. *Agroecology and Sustainable Food Systems*, 42(6), 666–685. https://doi.org/10.1080/ 21683565.2018.1437498.

Sambuichi, R.H.R, de Moura, I.F, de Mattos, L.M, de Avila, M.L, Spinola, P.A.C and da Silva, A.P.M (2017) *A política nacional de agroecologia e produção orgânica no Brasil: uma trajetória de luta pelo desenvolvimento rural sustentável*. Brasilia, Brazil: BDPA-Embrapa.

Sanderson Bellamy, A and Ioris, A.A.R (2017) Addressing the knowledge gaps in agro-ecology and identifying guiding principles for transforming conventional agri-food systems. *Sustainability*, 9(3), 330. https://doi.org/10.3390/su9030330.

Schader, C, Grenz, J, Meier, M and Stolze, M (2014) Scope and precision of sustainabil-ity assessment approaches to food systems. *Ecology and Society*,19(3), 42. https://doi .org/10.5751/ES-06866-190342.

Schmitt, C.J (2016) A transformação das 'Ideias Agroecológicas' em instrumentos de políticas públicas: dinâmicas de contestação e institucionalização de novas ideias nas políticas para a agricultura familiar. *Política & Sociedade* 15, 16–48. https://doi.org/ 10.5007/2175-7984.2016v15nesp1p16.

Smith, A (2006) Green niches in sustainable development: the case of organic food in the United Kingdom. *Environment and Planning C: Government and Policy*, 24(3), 439–458. https://doi.org/10.1068/c0514j.

Stevenson, G.W (1998) Agrifood systems for competent, ordinary people. *Food Policy*, 30(2), 199–207.

Thivet, D (2014) Peasants' transnational mobilisation for food sovereignty. In Counihan, C and Siniscalchi, V (eds) *Food Activism. Agency, Democracy and Economy*, London: Bloomsbury, 193–209.

Thompson, P.B (2007) Agricultural sustainability: what it is and what it is not. *International Journal of Agricultural Sustainability*, 5(1), 5–16. https://doi.org/10 .1080/14735903.2007.9684809.

Vaarst, M, Getz Escudero, A, Jahi Chappell, M, Brinkley, C, Nijbroek, R, Arraes, N.A.M, Andreasen, L, Gattinger, A, De Almeida, G.F, Bossio, D and Halberg, N (2017) Exploring the concept of agroecological food systems in a city-region context. *Agroecology and Sustainable Food Systems*, 42(6), 686–711.

van der Ploeg, J.D, Barjolle, D, Bruil, J, Brunori, G, Costa Madureira, L.M, Dessein, J, Drąg, Z, Fink-Kessler, A, Gasselin, P, Gonzalez de Molina, M, Gorlach, K, Jürgens, K, Kinsella, J, Kirwan, J, Karlheinz K, Lucas, V, Marsden, M, Maye, D, Migliorini, P, Milone P, Noe, E, Nowak, P, Parrott, N, Peeters, A, Rossi, A, Schermer, M, Ventura F, Visser, M, Wezel A (2019) The economic potential of agroecology: empirical evidence from Europe. *Journal of Rural Studies*, 71(October), 46–61. https://doi.org/ 10.1016/j.jrurstud.2019.09.003.

Vanloqueren, G and Baret, P.V (2009) How agricultural research systems shape a tech-nological regime that develops genetic engineering but locks out agroecological innovations. *Research Policy*, 38(6), 971–983. https://doi.org/10.1016/j.respol.2009 .02.008.

Verger, E.O, Perignon, M, El Ati, J, Darmon, N, Dop, M-C, Drogué, S, Dury, S, Gaillard, C, Sinfort, C and Amiot, M-J (2018) A 'fork-to-farm' multi-scale approach to promote sustainable food systems for nutrition and health: a perspective for the

Mediterranean region. *Frontiers in Nutrition*, 5(May). https://doi.org/10.3389/fnut
.2018.00030.

Warner, K.D (2007) The quality of sustainability: agroecological partnerships and
the geographic branding of California wine grapes. *Journal of Rural Studies*, 23(2),
142–55. https://doi.org/10.1016/j.jrurstud.2006.09.009.

Warner, K.D (2008) Agroecology as participatory science: emerging alternatives to
technology transfer extension practice. *Science, Technology, & Human Values*, 33(6),
754–777. https://doi.org/10.1177/0162243907309851.

Wezel, A., Bellon, S, Doré, T, Francis, C, Vallod, D and David, C (2009) Agroecology
as a science, a movement and a practice: a review. *Agronomy for Sustainable
Developmen*, 29, 503–515.

Wit, M.M de and Iles A (2016) Toward thick legitimacy: creating a web of legitimacy
for agroecology. *Elementa Science of the Anthropocene*, 4, 000115. https://doi.org/10
.12952/journal.elementa.000115.

Wittman, H (2011) Food sovereignty: a new rights framework for food and nature?
*Environment and Society*, 2(1), 87–105. https://doi.org/10.3167/ares.2011.020106.

## Chapter 7

AGRA (2019) Africa Agriculture Status Report: The hidden middle: a quiet revolution
in the private sector driving agricultural transformation (Issue 7). Nairobi, Kenya:
Alliance for a Green Revolution in Africa (AGRA).

Akram-Lodhi, A.H and Kay, C (2009) The agrarian question: peasants and rural
change. In Akram-Lodhi, A.H and Kay, C (eds) *Peasants and Globalization: Political
Economy, Rural Transformation and the Agrarian Question*. London: Routledge,
1–35.

Baumeister, E (2012) Construcción social del concepto de agricultura familiar con una
visión Centroamericana. Working Paper.

Belieres, J.F, Bonnal, P, Bosc, P.M, Losch, B, Marzin, J and Sourisseau, J.M (2013) *Les
agricultures familiales du monde: définitions, contributions et politiques publiques*.
Montpellier, France: CIRAD.

Bengoa, J (2003) 25 años de estudios rurales. *Sociologias*, 5(10), 36–99.

Bernstein, H (1977) Notes on capital and peasantry. *Review of African Political
Economy*, 4(10), 60–73.

Bernstein, H (2006) Is there an agrarian question in the 21st century? *Canadian Journal
of Development Studies*, 27(4), 449–460.

Bernstein, H, Friedmann, H, van der Ploeg, J.D, Shanin, T and White, B (2018) Forum:
fifty years of debate on peasantries, 1966–2016. *Journal of Peasant Studies*, 45(4),
689–714, doi:10.1080/03066150.2018.1439932.

Borras Jr, S.M (2009) Agrarian change and peasant studies: changes, continuities and
challenges – an introduction. *Journal of Peasant Studies*, 36(1, January), 5–31.

Borras, S.M, Hall, R, Scoones, I, White, B and Wolford, W (2011) Towards a better
understanding of global land grabbing: an editorial introduction. *Journal of Peasant
Studies*, 38(2), 209–216.

Brunori, G and Bartolini, F (2016) The Family Farm: Model for the Future or Relic of
the Past? In *Routledge International Handbook of Rural Studies*. London: Routledge,
222–234.

Buttel, F and LaRamee, P (1991) *The Disappearing Middle, A Sociological Perspective, Towards a New Political Economy of Agriculture*. Boulder, CO: Westview Press.

CEPAL/FAO/IICA (2013) Situación y perspectivas de la agricultura familiar en América Latina y el Caribe. In *Perspectivas de la agricultura y del desarrollo rural en las Américas: una Mirada hacia America Latina y el Caribe*. San Jose/Costa Rica: IICA, 173–223.

Chayanov, A.V. (1966 [1925]) *The Theory of the Peasant Economy*, ed. D. Thorner et al. Manchester: Manchester University Press.

CIRAD (2013) Les Agricultores familiales du monde – définitions, contributions et politiques publiques. Montepellier, France: CIRAD.

Conway, G (2014) On being a smallholder. In Hazell, P and Rahman, A (eds) *New Directions for Smallholder Agriculture*. Oxford: IFAD, Oxford University Press, 15–35.

Darnhofer, I, Lamine, C, Strauss, A and Navarrete, M (2016) The resilience of family farms: towards a relational approach. *Journal of Rural Studies*, 44, 111-122.

Davidova, S (2014) Small and Semi-subsistence Farms in the EU: Significance and Development Paths. *EuroChoices*, 13(1), 5–9.

Davidova, S and Bailey, A (2014) Roles of Small and Semi-subsistence Farms in the EU. *EuroChoices*, 13(1), 10–14.

Davidova, S and Thomson, K (2013) Family rarming: a Europe and Central Asia perspective, Background Report for the Regional Dialogue on Family Farming: Working towards a strategic approach to promote food security and nutrition [draft], Brussels, 11-12 December.

De Janvry, A and Sadoulet, E (2000) Rural poverty in Latin America: determinants and exit paths. *Food Policy*, 25, 389–409.

De Janvry, A and Sadoulet, E (2001) Income strategies among rural households in Mexico: the role of farm activities. *World Development*, 29, 467-480.

De Schutter, O (2010) Agroecology and the right to food. Report presented to the Human Rights Council 8 A/HRC/16/49, 16th Session. New York: United Nations.

De Schutter, O (2014) The transformative potential of the right to food. Report of the Special Rapporteur on the right to food. Human Rights Council, 25th Session. New York: U.N. General Assembly.

D'Odorico, P, Carr, J, Laio, F, Ridolfi, L and Vandoni, S (2014) Feeding humanity through global food trade. *Earth's Future*, 2, 458-469.Djurfeldt, G. (1996) Defining and operationalizing family farming from a sociological perspective. *Sociologia Ruralis*, 36(3), 340-351.

Ellis, F (1988) *Peasant Economics: Farm Households and Agrarian Development*. Cambridge: Cambridge University Press.

Fanzo, J (2017) From big to small: the significance of smallholder farms in the global food system. *The Lancet Planetary Health*, 1(1), e15-e16.

Fanzo, J (2018). The role of farming and rural development as central to our diets. *Physiology & Behavior*, 193(Pt B), 291-297. doi:10.1016/j.physbeh.2018.05.014.

FAO (2011) *Agricultura familiar: evolución conceptual, desafíos y institucionalidad en América Latina y el Caribe*, II Foro del Frente Parlamentario Contra el Hambre, 7 and 8 June, Bogotá (Colombia).

FAO (2012) Marco estratégico de mediano plazo de la FAO em: agricultura familiar en America Latina y El Caribe: 2012–2015. Documento de consulta con los países miembros. Vol. 14, 1 March.

FAO (2013) International year of family farming 2014. Master plan. Rome. http://www.fao.org/fileadmin/user_upload/iyff/docs/Final_Master_Plan_IYFF_2014_30-05.pdf (accessed 15 March 2020).

FAO (2014a) *The State of Food and Agriculture: Innovation in Family Farming*. Rome: FAO.

FAO (2014b) *Agricultura Familiar em América Latina y El Caribe: recomendaciones de política*. Santiago, Chile: FAO.

FAO (2014c) *Deep Roots*. Rome: FAO and IYFF.

FAO and IFAD (2019). *United Nations Decade of Family Farming 2019-2028*. Global Action Plan. Rome: FAO and IFAD.

FIDA (Fondo Internacional de Politica Agrícola) (2014) La agricultura familiar en América Latina – Un nuevo análisis comparative. Rome: FIDA/RIMISP.

Friedmann, H (1978) World market, state and family farm: social bases of household production in the era of wage labor. *Comparative Studies in Society and History*, 20(4), 545-586.

Friedmann, H (1986) Family enterprises in agriculture: structural limits and political possibilities. In Cox, G, Lowe, P and Winter, M (eds) *Agriculture: People and Policies*. London: Allen, 41-60.

Garner, E and de la O Campos, A (2014) Identifying the 'family farm': an informal discussion of the concepts and definitions. ESA Working Paper No. 14-10. Rome: FAO.

Gasson, R and Errington, A (1993) *The Farm Family Business*. Wallingford, UK: CAB International.

Gasson, R, Crow, G, Errington, A, Hutson, J, Marsden T and Winter, D.M (1988) The farm as a family business: a review. *Journal of Agricultural Economics*, 39(1), 1-41.

Gelli, A, Neeser, K and Drake, L (2010) Home grown school feeding: linking small holder agriculture to school food provision. In PCD Working Paper no. 212: Partnership for Child Development.

Gladek, E, Fraser, M, Roemers, G, Munoz, O.S, Kennedy, E and Hirsch, P (2016) *The Global Food System: An Analysis*. The Netherlands: WWF.

Global Panel (2016) Global Panel on agriculture and food systems for nutrition. Food systems and diets: facing the challenges of the 21st century. London: Global Panel.

Godfray, H.C.J, Beddington, J.R, Crute, I.R, Haddad, L, Lawrence, D, Muir, J.F, Pretty, J, Robinson, S, Thomas, S.M and Toulmin, C. (2010) Food security: the challenge of feeding 9 billion people. *Science*, 327(5967), 812–818.

Graeub, B.E, Chappell, M.J, Wittmand, C.H, Ledermanne, S, Kerrf, R.B and Gemmill-Herren, B. (2016) The state of family farms in the world. *World Development*, 36. http://dx.doi.org/10.1016/j.worlddev.2015.05.012, 87, 1–15.

Grisa, C and Sabourin, E (2019) Agricultura familiar: de los conceptos a las políticas públicas en América Latina y el Caribe. 2030 – Alimentación, agricultura y desarrollo rural en América Latina y el Caribe, No. 15. Santiago de Chile: FAO.

Hayami, Y (2002) Family farms and plantations in tropical development. *Asian Development Bank*, 19(2), 70-89.

Hazell, P and Rahman, A (2014) *New Directions for Smallholder Agriculture*. Oxford: IFAD, Oxford University Press.

Hazell, P, Poulton, C, Wiggins, S and Dorward, A (2010) The future of small farms: trajectories and policy priorities. *World Development*, 38(10), 1349-1361.

Herrero, M, Thornton, P, Power, B, Bogard, J.R, Remans, R, Fritz, S, Gerber, J.S, Nelson, G, See, L, Waha, K, Watson, R.A, West, P.C, Samberg, L.H, van de Steeg, J, Stephenson, E, van Wijk, M, and Havlík, P (2017) Farming and the geography of nutrient production for human use: a transdisciplinary analysis. *Lancet Planet Health*, 1, 33–42.

HLPE (2012) Climate change and food security. A report by the High Level Panel of Experts on Food Security and Nutrition of the Committee on World Food Security. Rome: HLPE.

HLPE (2013) Investing in smallholder agriculture for food security. A report by the High Level Panel of Experts on Food Security and Nutrition of the Committee on World Food Security. Rome: HLPE.

HLPE (2016) Sustainable agricultural development for food security and nutrition: what roles for livestock? A report by the High-Level Panel of Experts on Food Security and Nutrition of the Committee on World Food Security. Rome: HLPE.

HLPE (2017) Sustainable forestry for food security and nutrition. A report by the High-Level Panel of Experts on 45 Food Security and Nutrition of the Committee on World Food Security. Rome: HLPE.

IAASTD (International Assessment of Agricultural Knowledge, Science and Technology for Development) (2009) Agriculture at a crossroads – global report. Ed. McIntyre, B.D, Herren, H.R, Wakhungu, J and Watson, R.T. Washington, DC: IAASTD.

IFAD (2016) Rural development report: fostering inclusive rural transformation. Rome: IFAD.

IFAD/UNEP (2013) Smallholders, food security, and the environment. Rome: IFAD.

IFPRI (International Food Policy Research Institute) (2010) *Food Security, Farming, and Climate Change to 2050: Scenarios, Results, Policy Options*. Washington, DA: IFPRI.

Ikerd, J (2016) Family farms of North America. FAO and UNPD, International Policy Centre for Inclusive Growth (IPC-IG) Working Paper No. 152.

IPES-Food (2016) *From Uniformity to Diversity: a Paradigm Shift from Industrial Agriculture to Diversified Agroecological Systems. International Panel of Experts on Sustainable Food systems*. www.ipes-food.org

IPES-Food (2017) Unravelling the food–health nexus: addressing practices, political economy, and power relations to build healthier food systems. *The Global Alliance for the Future of Food and IPES-Food*.

Jollivet, M (2001) *Pour une science sociale à travers champs: paysannerie, capitalism (France XXe Siècle)*. Paris: Arguments.

Lang, T. (2005) What is food and farming for – the (re)emergence of health as a key policy driver. In Butel, FH andnd McMichale, P (eds) *New Directions in the Sociology of Global Development. Research in Rural Sociology and Development*. Vol. 11. London: Elsevier, 123–144.

Larson, D, Otsuka, K, Matsumoto, T and Kilic, T (2012) Should African rural development strategies depend on smallholder farms? An exploration of the inverse productivity hypothesis. Policy Research Paper No. 6190. Washington, DC: World Bank.

Leporati, M, Salomón Salcedo, S, Jara, B, Boero V, and Muñoz, M. (2014) La agricultura familiar en cifras. In Salcedo, S and Guzmán, L (eds) *Agricultura Familiar em América Latina y El Caribe: recomendaciones de política*. Santiago, Chile: FAO, 35–56.

Lipton, M (2005) The family farm in a globalizing world: the role of crop science in alleviating poverty. 2020 Discussion Paper No. 40. Washington, DC: International Food Policy Research Institute.

Lipton, M. (2006) Can small farmers survive, prosper, or be the key channel to cut mass poverty? *The Electronic Journal of Agricultural and Development Economics*, 3(1), 58–85.

Lowder, S.K, Skoet, J and Singh, S (2014) What do we really know about the number and distribution of farms and family farms worldwide? Background paper for The State of Food and Agriculture 2014. ESA Working Paper No. 14-02. Rome: FAO.

Lowder, S.K, Skoet, J and Singh, S (2016) The number, size, and distribution of farms, smallholder farms, and family farms worldwide. *World Development*, 87, 16–29 http://dx.doi.org/10.1016/j.worlddev.2015.10.041.

Mamdani, M (1996) *Citizens and Subjects: Contemporary Africa and the Legacy of Late Colonialism*. Princeton, NJ: Princeton University Press.

Marsden, T.K (1989) Restructuring rurality: from order to disorder in agrarian political economy. *Sociologia Ruralis*, 29(3/4), 312–317.

Marsden, T.K (1990) Towards the political economy of pluriactivity. *Journal of Rural Studies*, 6(4), 375–382.

Marsden, T.K (1991) Theoretical issues in the continuity of petty commodity production. In Wathmore, S, Lowe, P and Marsden, T.K (eds) *Rural Enterprise. Shifting Perspectives on Small-Scale Production*. London: David Fulton Publishers, 12–34.

Marsden, T.K (2011) Towards a real sustainable agri-food security and food policy: beyond the ecological fallacies. *Political Quarterly*, 83 (1), 139–145. doi:10.1111/j .1467-923X.201.02242.x.

Marsden, T.K and Farioli, F (2015) Natural powers: from the bio-economy to the eco-economy and sustainable place-making. *Sustainability Science*, 10, 331–344. doi: 10.1007/s11625-014-0287-z.

Marsden, T.K, Whatmore, S, Munton, R and Little, J (1986) Towards a political economy of capitalist agriculture: a British perspective. *International Journal of Urban and Regional Research*, 4, 498–521.

Medina, G, Almeida, C, Novaes, E, Godar, J and Pokorny, B (2015) Development conditions for family farming: lessons from Brazil, *World Development*, 74(October), 386–396.

Mendras, H. (1987) *La Fin des Paysans, suivi d'une réflexion sur la fin des pasans: vingt ans aprés*, Paris: Actes Sud, Hubert Nyssen, Editeur.

Moyo, S (2016) Family farming in sub-Saharan Africa: its contribution to agriculture, food security and rural development. FAO and UNPD, International Policy Centre for Inclusive Growth (IPC-IG) Working Paper No. 150.

Moyo, S, and Yeros, P (eds) (2005) *Reclaiming the Land: the Resurgence of Rural Movements in Africa, Asia and Latin America*. London and Cape Town: Zed Books and David Philip.

Moyo, S, Jha, P and Yeros, P (2012) Imperialism and primitive accumulation: notes on the new scramble for Africa. *Agrarian South: Journal of Political Economy*, 1(2), 181–203.

Nagayets, O (2005) Small farms: Current status and key trends. In *The Future of Small Farms*. Proceedings of a Research Workshop, Wye, UK, 26–29 June. Washington, DC: International Food Policy Research Institute.

Oostindie, H (2015) Family farming futures. Agrarian pathways to multifunctionality: flows of resistance, redesign and resilience, PhD thesis, Wageningen University, the Netherlands.

Pegler, L (2015) Peasant inclusion in global value chains: economic upgrading but social downgrading in labour processes? *Journal of Peasant Studies*, 42 (5), 929–956. doi:10.1080/03066150.2014.992885.

Ponisio, L, M'Gonigle, L, Mace, K, Palomino, J, de Valpine, P and Kremen, C (2015) Diversification practices reduce organic to conventional yield gap. *Proceedings of the*

*Royal Society B: Biological Sciences*. 282(20141396). http://dx.doi.org/10.1098/rspb
.2014.1396

Popkin, B.M (2014) Nutrition, agriculture and the global food system in low and
middle income countries. *Food Policy*, 47, 91–96.

Pretty, J et al. (2010) The top 100 questions of importance to the future of global agriculture. *International Journal of Agricultural Sustainability*, 8(4), 219–236;

Pretty, J, Toulmin, C and William, S (2011) Sustainable intensification in African agriculture. *International Journal of Agricultural Sustainability*, 9(1), 3–4.

Ramos, A (2014) Compilation of the definitions and methodologies commonly used
and accepted at a national, regional and international level to define and describe
family farming based on its diversity. Final Report of the International Working
Group on Common Criteria on Family Farming (IWG FF). 29 November 2014.

REAF – Reunião Especializada Da Agricultura Familiar Do Mercosul (2011) Bases para
o reconhecimento e identificação da agricultura familiar no Mercosul. MERCOSUR/
VI REAF/DT N° 03/06. ANEXO IX. 2006a. http://www.mda.gov.br/reaf/ (accessed
25 October 2011).

Reardon, T, Berdegué, J.A and Escobar, G (eds) (2001) Rural nonfarm employment
and incomes in Latin America. Special Issue of *World Development*, 29(3), 395–573.

Reganold, J.P and Wachter, J.M (2016) Organic agriculture in the twenty-first century.
*Nature Plants*. 2 (15221), 1–8.

Sabourin, E, Samper, M and Sotomayor, O (2014) Políticas públicas y agriculturas
familiares en América Latina: balance, desafíos y perspectivas. Santiago de Chile, ed.
CEPAL, Red PPAL, IICA.

Salcedo, S and Guzmán, L (eds) (2014) *Agricultura familiar en América Latina y el
Caribe: Recomendaciones de política*. Santiago, Chile: FAO.

Samberg, L.H, Gerber, J.S, Ramankutty, N, Herrero, M and West, P.C (2016) Subnational
distribution of average farm size and smallholder contributions to global food production. *Environmental Research Letters*, 11, 124010.

Schejtman, A (2008) Alcances sobre agricultura familiar en América Latina. Diálogo
Rural Iberoamericano. Documento de trabajo no. 21. San Salvador, El Salvador,
Programa Dinámicas Territoriales Rurales, RIMISP.

Schneider, S (2003) *A Pluriatividade na Agricultura Familiar*. 1st edn. Porto Alegre,
Brazil: UFRGS.

Schneider, S (2013) A agricultura familiar na América Latina: relatório-síntese a partir
de 6 países. Reporte sobre la agricultura familiar en América Latina. Santiago, Chile,
FIDA, RIMISP.

Schneider, S (2014) Family farming in Latin America and the Caribbean. *Deep Roots*.
Rome: FAO, vol 1, 26–29.

Schneider, S (2016) Family farming in Latin America and the Caribbean: looking for
new paths of rural development and food security. FAO and UNPD, International
Policy Centre for Inclusive Growth (IPC-IG) Working Paper No. 137.

Schneider, S and Niederle, P.A (2010) Resistance strategies and diversification of rural
livelihoods: the construction of autonomy among Brazilian family farmers. *Journal
of Peasant Studies*, 37, 379–405.

Shanin, T (1973) The nature and logic of peasant economy. *Journal of Peasant Studies*,
1(1), 63–80.

Shanin, T (2009) Chayanov's treble death and tenuous resurrection: an essay about
understanding, about roots of plausibility and about rural Russia. *Journal of Peasant
Studies*, 36(1), 83–101.

Sourisseau J.-M (2015) *Family Farming and the Worlds to Come*. Paris: Springer, Quae, Cirad.

Sulemana, N (2016) Under the lens of embeddedness: a socio-cultural perspective on home-grown school feeding in Ghana. Wageningen University, the Netherlands, PhD thesis.

Sumberg, J and Sabates-Wheeler, R (2011) Linking agricultural development to school feeding in sub-Saharan Africa: theoretical perspectives. *Food Policy*, 36(3), 341-349.

*The Economist* (2011) The 9 billion people question: a special report on feeding the world. 26 February.

UNDP (2011). *Towards a Green Economy: Agriculture – Investing in Natural Capital*. New York: UNDP.

USDA (2018) America's diverse family farms. Economic Research Service. Information Bulletin, n° 203, December.

van der Ploeg, J.D (2010) The peasantries of the twenty-first century: the commoditisation debate revisited. *Journal of Peasant Studies*, 37(1), 1–30.

van der Ploeg, J.D (2013a) *Peasants and the Art of Farming – A Chayanovian Manifesto*. Hallifax/Winnipeg/Canada: Fenwood Publishing.

van der Ploeg, J.D (2013b) Ten qualities of family farming. *Farming Matters*, 29(4), 8–11.

van der Ploeg, J.D (2016a) Family farming in Europe and Central Asia: history, characteristics, threats and potentials. International Policy Centre for Inclusive Growth (IPC-IG) Working Paper No. 153

van der Ploeg, J.D (2016b) Theorizing agri-food economies. *Agriculture*, 6(3), 30. doi: 10.3390/agriculture6030030.

van der Ploeg, J.D (2017a) *The Importance of Peasant Agriculture: A Neglected Truth*. Wageningen: Wageningen University & Research.

van der Ploeg, J.D (2017b) Differentiation: old controversies, new insights. *Journal of Peasant Studies*, 45(3), 489–524.

van der Ploeg, J.D.V, Ye, J and Schneider, S (2012) Rural development through the construction of new, nested, markets: comparative perspectives from China, Brazil and the European Union. *Journal of Peasant Studies*, 39(1), 133-173.

van der Ploeg, J.D, Roep, D, Renting, H, Banks, J, Melgo, A.A, Gorman, M, Knickel, K, Schaer, B and Ventura, F (2002) The socio-economic impact of rural development processes within Europe. In van der Ploeg, J.D, Long, A and Banks, J (eds) *Living Countrysides, Rural Development Processes in Europe: The State of Art*. Doetinchem: Elsevier, 179-192.

Visser, O and Steggerda, M (2013) Land acquisitions, labour and the export of farm models: the frictions emerging from Western involvement in Russia agriculture. Paper to the *Research in Progress Seminar*, ISS, The Hague.

Visser, O, Mamonova, N and Spoor, M (2012) Oligarchs, megafarms and land reserves: understanding land grabbing in Russia. *Journal of Peasant Studies*, 39(3-4), 899-931.

Whatmore, S, Munton, R, Litle, J and Marsden, T.K (1987) Towards a typology of farm businesses in contemporary British agriculture. *Sociologia Ruralis*, 27(1), 21-37.

Wiggins, S (2009) Can the smallholder model deliver poverty reduction and food security for rapidly growing population in Africa? FAC, Working Paper N° 08, Overseas Development Department, London.

Wiggins, S, Kirsten, J and Llambí, L (2010) The future of small farms. *World Development*, 38(10), 1341-1348.

Wolf, E (1955) Types of Latin American peasantry: a preliminary discussion. *American Anthropologist*, 57(3), 452-471.

Wolf, E (1966) *Sociedades Camponesas*. Rio de Janeiro, Brazil: Zahar Editores.
Woodhouse, P (2010) Beyond industrial agriculture? Some questions about farm size, productivity and sustainability. *Journal of Agrarian Change*, 10(3), 437–453.
Ye, J and Lu, P (2016) Concepts and realities of family farming in Asia and the Pacific. FAO and UNPD, International Policy Centre for Inclusive Growth (IPC-IG) Working Paper No. 139.

## Chapter 8

Abramovay, R (2004) Entre deus e o diabo: mercados e interação humana nas ciências sociais. *Tempo Social – Revista de Sociologia da USP*. São Paulo, 16(2), 35-64.
Bagnasco, A and Triglia, C (1993) *La construction sociale du marché: le defi de la Troisieme Italie*. Paris: Julillet/Editions de l'ENS-Cachan.
Beckert, J (2002) *Beyond the Market: The Social Foundations of Economic Efficiency*. Princeton, NJ :Princeton University Press.
Beckert, J (2007) The social order of markets. Max Planck Institute for the Study of Societies, Discussion Paper 07/15.
Beckert, J (2009) The social order of markets. *Theory and Society*, 38(3), 245–269.
Bernstein, H (1979) African peasantries: a theoretical framework. *Journal of Peasant Studies*, 6(4), 420–444.
Bernstein, H (1986) Capitalism and petty commodity production. *Social* Analysis: The International Journal of Cultural and Social Practice, (20), 11–28.
Bernstein, H (2010) Rural livelihoods and agrarian change: bringing class back in. In Long, N, Jingzhong, Y and Wang, Y (eds) *Rural Transformations and Development – China in Context: The Everyday Lives of Policies and People*. Cheltenham, UK and Northampton, MA, USA: Edward Elgar Publishing, 79–109.
Bernstein, H (2014) Food sovereignty via the 'peasant way': a sceptical view. *Journal of Peasant Studies*, 41, 1031-1063.
Bernstein, H and Oya, C (2014) Rural futures. How much should markets rule? International Institute for Environment and Development. Working Paper.
Blay-Palmer, A, Santini, G, Dubbeling, M, Renting, H, Taguchi, M and Giordano, T (2018) Validating the city region food system approach: enacting inclusive, transformational city region food system. *Sustainability*, 10(1680), 1–23.
Boen, B and Purcell, M (2006) Avoiding the local trap: scale and food systems in planning research. *Journal of Planning Education and Research*, 26, 195-207.
Bourdieu, P. (2000) *Les structures sociales de l'économie*. Paris: Seuil.
Braudel, F. (1985) *Civilization and Capitalism, Fifteenth–Eighteenth Century*, 3 vols. London: Fontana Press.
Brasil, N.S (2019) Mercados Imersos: uma nova abordagem sobre a construção social dos mercados. Tese (Doutorado em Desenvolvimento Rural), PGDR, UFRGS.
Burawoy, M (2010) From Polanyi to Pollyanna: the false optimism of global labour studies. *Global Labour Journal*, 1(2), 301–313.
Callon, M. (ed) (1998) *The Laws of the Markets*. Oxford: Blackwell.
Carolan, M.S (2012) *The Sociology of Food and Agriculture*. London: Earthscan/ Routledge.

Cassol, A (2018) Instituições sociais e mercados alimentares tradicionais: barganha, preços, variedade, qualidade e consumo em feiras. Thesis (Doctorate in Sociology). Universidade Federal do Rio Grande do Sul.

Darolt, M, Lamine, C and Brandenburg, A (2013) A diversidade dos circuitos curtos de alimentos ecológicos: ensinamentos do caso brasileiro e francês. *Agriculturas*, 10(2), 8–13.

Ellis, F. (1988) *Peasant Economics: Farm Households and Agrarian Development.* Cambridge: Cambridge University Press.

Eriksen, S.N (2013) Defining local food: constructing a new taxonomy and three domains of proximity. *Acta Agriculturae Scandinavica Section B: Soil and Plant Science*, 63, 47–55.

Favereau, O, Biencourt, O and Eymard-Duvernay, F (2002) Where do markets come from? From (quality) conventions! In Favereau, O and Lazega, E (eds) *Conventions and Structures in Economic Organization.* Cheltenham, UK and Northampton, MA, USA: Edward Elgar Publishing, 45–67.

Feenstra, G.W (1997) Local food systems and sustainable communities. *American Journal of Alternative Agriculture*, 12, 28–36.

Fligstein, N. (1996) Markets as politics: a political cultural approach to market institutions. *American Sociological Review*, 61(4), 656‑673.

Fligstein, N (2001) *The Architecture of Markets: An Economic Sociology of Twenty-First-Century Capitalist Societies.* Princeton, NJ: Princeton University Press.

Fourcade, M. (2007) Theories of markets and theories of society. *American Behavioral Scientist*, 50, 1015–1034.

Friedmann, H (1978) Simple commodity production and wage labour in the American plains. *Journal of Peasant Studies*, 6(1), 71–100.

Gazolla, M and Schneider, S (eds) (2017) *Cadeias curtas e redes agroalimentares alternativas: negócios e mercados da agricultura familiar.* Porto Alegre, Brazil: UFRGS.

Getz, A (1991) Urban foodsheds. *Permaculture Activist*, 24, 26–27.

Goodman, D (2002) Rethinking food production-consumption: integrative perspectives. *Sociologia Ruralis*, 42(4, October), 271–277.

Goodman, D (2003) The quality 'turn' and alternative food practices: reflections and agenda. *Journal of Rural Studies*, 19, 1–7.

Goodman, D, Dupuis, M.E and Goodman, M.K (2012) *Alternative Food Networks: Knowledge, Practice, and Politics.* Abingdon: Routledge.

Granovetter, M. (1985) Economic action and social structure: the problem of embeddedness. *America Journal of Sociology*, 91(3), p. 481–510.

Grivins, M. and Tisenkopfs, T (2018) Benefitting from the global, protecting the local: the nested markets of wild product trade. *Journal of Rural Studies*, 61, 335–342. doi: 10.1016/j.jrurstud.2018.01.005.

Guthman, J (2014) *Agrarian Dreams: The Paradox of Organic Farming in California.* Berkeley, CA: University of California Press.

Harriss-White, B (2005) Market romanticism and India's regulative order. In *India's Market Society.* New Delhi: Three Essays Press, 1–67.

Hebinck, P, van der Ploeg, J.D and Schneider, S (eds) (2015a) *Rural Development and the Construction of New Markets.* London: Routledge.

Hebinck, P, Schneider, S and van der Ploeg, J.D (2015b) The construction of new, nested markets and the role of rural development policies: some introduction notes. In Hebinck, P, van der Ploeg, J.D and Schneider, S (eds) *Rural Development and the Construction of New Markets.* London: Routledge, 1–15.

Hinrichs, C (2003) The practice and politics of food system localization. *Journal of Rural Studies*, 19, 33–45.

Jennings, S, Cottee, J, Curtis, T and Miller, S (2015) *Food in an Urbanized World*. London: The International Sustainability Unit, The Prince of Wales Charitable Foundation.

Kneafsey, M, Cox, R, Holloway, L, Dowler, E, Venn, L and Tuomainn, H (2008) *Reconnecting Consumers, Producers and Food: Exploring Alternatives*. Oxford: Berg Publishers.

Kneafsey, M, Venn, L, Schmutz, U, Balázs, B, Trenchard, L, Eyden-Wood, T, Bos, E, Sutton, G and Blackett, M. (2013) *Short Food Supply Chains and Local Food Systems in the EU. A State of Play of their Socio-Economic Characteristics*. Seville, Spain: European Commission.

Kremer, P and Schreuder, Y (2012) The feasibility of regional food systems in metropolitan areas: an investigation of Philadelphia's foodshed. *Journal of Agriculture, Food Systems and Community Development*, 2, 171–191.

Lamine, C (2005) Settling the shared uncertainties: local partnerships between producers and consumers. *Sociologica Ruralis*, 45(4), 324–345. https://doi.org/10.1111/j.1467-9523.2005.00308.x.

Lamine, C (2008) Les Amaps: un nouveau pacte entre producteurs et consommateurs? Gap: Ed. Yves Michel.

Lamine, C (2015) Sustainability and resilience in agrifood systems: reconnecting agriculture, food and the environment. *Sociologica Ruralis*, 55(1), 41–61. https://doi.org/10. 1111/soru.12061.

Lamine, C, Darolt, M and Brandenburg, A (2012a) The civic and social dimensions of food production and distribution in alternative food networks in France and Southern Brazil. *International Journal of Sociology of Agriculture and Food*, 19(3), 383–401.

Lamine, C, Renting, H, Rossi, A, Wiskerke, J.S.C and Brunori, G (2012b) Agri-food systems and territorial development: innovations: new dynamics and changing governance mechanisms. In Darnhofer, I. (ed) *Farming Systems Research into the 21st Century: The New Dynamic*. Dordrecht: Springer, 229–256.

Lie, J (1997) Sociology of markets. *Annual Review of Sociology*, 23, 341–360.

Long, N. (2001) *Development Sociology: Actor Perspectives*. London: Routledge.

Long, N, van der Ploeg, J.D, Curtin, C and Box, L (1986) *The Commoditization Debate: Labour Process, Strategy and Social Network*. Wageningen: WU Press.

Lyson, T, Stevenson, G and Welsh, R (2008) *Food and the Mid-Level Farm*. Cambridge, MA: The MIT Press.

McMichael, P (2014) A comment on Henry Bernstein's way with peasants, and food sovereignty. *Journal of Peasant Studies*, 42, 193–204.

Ménard, C (1995) Markets as institutions versus organizations as markets? Disentangling some fundamental concepts. *Journal of Economic Behaviour and Organization*, 28, 161–182.

Mendras, H (1978) *Sociedades camponesas*. Rio de Janeiro: Zahar.

Niederle, P.A and Wez Jr, W.J (2020) *Agrifood System Transitions in Brazil. New Food Orders*. London: Routledge.

Niederle, P.A, Schubert, M.N and Schneider, S (2014) Agricultura familiar, desenvolvimento rural e um modelo de mercados múltiplos. In Doula, S, Fiúza, A.L, Teixeira, E.C, Reis, J and Lima, A.L (eds) *A agricultura familiar em face das transformações na dinâmica recente dos mercados*. Viçosa/MG: Suprema, 43–68.

Oosterveer, P and Sonnenfeld, D.A (2012) *Food, Globalization and Sustainability*. London/New York: Earthscan.

Ostrom, E (2010) Beyond markets and states: polycentric governance of complex economic systems. *American Economic Review*, 100(3), 1–33.

Polanyi, K (1957/1980) *The Great Transformation: The Political and Economic Origins of Our Time*. Boston: Beacon Press.

Polanyi, K (1977) *The Livelihood of Man*. New York: Academic Press.

Polanyi, K, Arensberg, C.M and Pearson, H.W (eds) (1976) *Comercio y mercado en los imperios antiguos*. Barcelona: Labor Universitaria.

Polman, N, Poppe, K.J, Schans, J.W and van der Ploeg, J.D (2010) Nested markets with common pool resources in multifunctional agriculture. *Rivista de Economia Agraria*, 65, 295–318.

Radomsky, G, Niederle, P and Schneider, S (2015) Participatory systems of certification and alternative marketing networks: the case of Ecovida Agroecology Network in South Brazil. In Hebinck, P, van der Ploeg, J.D and Schneider, S (eds) *Rural Development and the Construction of New Markets*. London: Routledge, 79–98.

Raud, C (2005) A construção social do mercado em Durkheim e Weber: análise do papel das instituições na sociologia econômica clássica. *Revista Brasileira de Ciências Sociais*, 57, 127–142.

Raud, C (2007) Bourdieu e a nova sociologia econômica. *Tempo Social, revista de sociologia da USP*, 19(2), 203–232.

Reardon, T and Timmer, C.P (2007) Transformation of markets for agricultural output in developing countries since 1950: how has thinking changed? In Evenson, R and Pingali, P (eds) *Handbook of Agricultural Economics*, vol. 3. London: Elsevier, 2808–2849.

Renting, H, Marsden, T.K and Banks, J (2003) Understanding alternative food networks: exploring the role of short food supply chains in rural development. *Environmental Planing*, 35, 393–411.

Sabourin, E (2014) Acesso aos mercados para a agricultura familiar: uma leitura pela reciprocidade e a economia solidaria. *Revista Econômica do Nordeste, Fortaleza*, 45, 18–30.

Schneider, S (2016) Mercados e agricultura familiar. In Marques, F.C, Conterato, M.A and Schneider, S (eds) *Construção de Mercados e Agricultura Familiar*. UFRGS: Porto Alegre, Brazil: UFRGS, 21–52.

Schneider, S and Escher, F (2011) A contribuição de Karl Polanyi para sociologia do desenvolvimento rural. *Sociologias*, 13(27), 180–219.

Schneider, S, Salvate, N and Cassol, A (2016) Nested markets, food networks, and new pathways for rural development in Brazil. *Agriculture*, 6(4), 1–19. doi:10.3390/agriculture6040061.

Schneider, S, van der Ploeg, J.D and Hebinck, P (2015) Reconsidering the contribution of nested markets to rural development. In Hebinck, P, van der Ploeg, J.D and Schneider, S (eds) *Rural Development and the Construction of New Markets*. London: Routledge, 190–205.

Scoones, I (2009) Livelihoods perspectives and rural development. *Journal of Peasant Studies*, 36(1), 171–196.

Shanin, T (1973) The nature and logic of peasant economy. *Journal of Peasant Studies*, 1(1), 63–80.

Shanin, T (1988) *Peasants and Peasants Societies*. London: Penguin Books.

Simmel, G. (1978) *The Philosophy of Money*. London, Routledge.

Sonnino, R and Marsden, T.K (2005) Beyond the divide: rethinking relations between alternative and conventional food networks in Europe. *Journal of Economic Geography*, 6, 181–189.
Swedberg, R (1994) Markets as social structures. In Smelser, N.J and Swedberg , R (eds) *The Handbook of Economic Sociology*. Princeton: Oxford University Press, 255–282.
Swedberg, R (2005) Markets in society. In Smelser, N.J and Swedberg , R (eds) *The Handbook of Economic Sociology*. Princeton: Oxford University Press, 233–253.
Tregear, A (2011) Progressing knowledge in alternative and local food networks: critical reflections and a research agenda. *Journal of Rural Studies*, 27, 419–430.
van der Ploeg, J.D (1992) El proceso de trabajo agrícola y la mercantilización. In Guzman, E.S (ed) *Ecologia, campesinato y historia*. Madrid: Las Ediciones de la Piqueta, 153–196.
van der Ploeg, J.D (2008) *The New Peasantries. Struggles for Autonomy and Sustainability in an Era of Empire and Globalization*. London: Routledge.
van der Ploeg, J.D (2015) Newly emerging, nested markets: a theoretical introduction. In Hebinck, P, Ploeg, J.D and Schneider, S (eds) *Rural Development and the Construction of New Markets*. London: Routledge, 16–40.
van der Ploeg, J.D (2016) Mercados aninhados recém criados: uma introdução teórica. In Marques, F.C, Conterato, M.A and Schneider, S (eds) *Construção de Mercados e Agricultura Familiar*. Porto Alegre, Brazil: UFRGS, 21–52.
van der Ploeg, J.D and Ye, J (2016) *China's Peasant Agriculture and Rural Society: Changing Paradigms of Farming*. London: Routledge.
van der Ploeg, J.D, Ye, J and Schneider, S (2010) Rural development reconsidered: building on comparative perspectives from China, Brazil and the European Union. *Rivista de Economia Agraria*, 164–190.
van der Ploeg, J.D, Ye, J and Schneider, S (2012) Rural development through the construction of new, nested, markets: comparative perspectives from China, Brazil and the European Union. *Journal of Peasant Studies*, 39, 133–173.
van der Ploeg, J.D, Ye, J and Schneider, S (2015) Rural development: actors and practices. In Milone, P, Ventura, F and Ye, J (eds) *Constructing a New Framework for Rural Development Research in Rural Sociology and Development*, vol. 22. Bingley, UK: Emerald, 17–30.
Weber, M (2000) *Economia e Sociedade: fundamentos da sociologia compreensiva*. Brasília: Editora Universidade de Brasília.
Wilkinson, J (2010) *Mercados, redes e valores: o novo mundo da agricultura familiar*. Porto Alegre, Brazil: UFRGS.
Wilkinson, J (2019) An overview of German new economic sociology and the contribution of the Max Planck Institute for the Study of Societies. MPIfG Discussion Paper 19/3. Cologne, Germany: Max Planck Institute for the Study of Societies.

# Conclusions

Buraway, M (2020) A tale of two Marxisms. *New Left Review*, 121, January/February, 67–99.
Wright, E.O (2010) *Envisaging Real Utopias*. Chicago, IL: University of Chicago Press.

# Index